REMORSE, PENAL THEORY

This monograph addresses a contested but ___ ___ ___ discussed question in the field of criminal sentencing: should an offender's remorse affect the sentence he or she receives? Answering this question involves tackling a series of others: is it possible to justify mitigation for remorse within a retributive sentencing framework? Precisely how should remorse enter into the sentencing equation? How should the mitigating weight of remorse interact with other aggravating and mitigating factors? Are there some offence or offender characteristics that preclude remorse-based mitigation?

Remorse is recognised as a legitimate mitigating factor in many sentencing regimes around the world, with powerful effects on sentence severity. Although there has been some discussion of whether this practice can be justified within the literature on sentencing and penal theory, this monograph provides the first comprehensive and in-depth study of possible theoretical justifications. Whilst the emphasis here is on theoretical justification, the monograph also offers analysis of how normative conclusions would play out in the broader context of sentencing decisions and the guidance intended to structure them. The conclusions reached have relevance for sentencing systems around the world.

Remorse, Penal Theory and Sentencing

Hannah Maslen

·H A R T·
PUBLISHING
OXFORD AND PORTLAND, OREGON
2017

Hart Publishing
An imprint of Bloomsbury Publishing Plc

Hart Publishing Ltd
Kemp House
Chawley Park
Cumnor Hill
Oxford OX2 9PH
UK

Bloomsbury Publishing Plc
50 Bedford Square
London
WC1B 3DP
UK

www.hartpub.co.uk
www.bloomsbury.com

Published in North America (US and Canada) by
Hart Publishing
c/o International Specialized Book Services
920 NE 58th Avenue, Suite 300
Portland, OR 97213-3786
USA

www.isbs.com

HART PUBLISHING, the Hart/Stag logo, BLOOMSBURY and the
Diana logo are trademarks of Bloomsbury Publishing Plc

First published in hardback, 2015
Paperback edition, 2017

British Library Cataloguing-in-Publication Data
A catalogue record for this book is available from the British Library.

ISBN: PB: 978-1-50991-543-9
HB: 978-1-84946-543-4

Typeset by Compuscript Ltd, Shannon
Printed and bound in Great Britain by
Lightning Source UK Ltd

To find out more about our authors and books visit www.hartpublishing.co.uk. Here you will
find extracts, author information, details of forthcoming events and the option to sign up for our
newsletters.

For my parents

Preface

There is clearly a growing scholarly interest in the role of remorse in criminal justice institutions. Since I began working on remorse and sentencing in 2008, a number of books have been published in which significant space is dedicated to examining the role that remorse plays at sentencing, in parole hearings and at other points of interaction between the state and offender. In *Remorse: Psychological and Jurisprudential Perspectives*, Michael Proeve and Steven Tudor examine how a court is to prove that the offender is remorseful, whether remorse should mitigate the offender's sentence, whether a lack of remorse should aggravate the offender's sentence and the role that remorse can play in restorative justice processes.[1] Richard Weisman's *Showing Remorse: Law and the Social Control of Emotions* examines the role that legal institutions play in establishing the rules about when remorse should be felt and the attendant consequences for the wrongdoer.[2] Most recently, Nick Smith examines apologies in the contexts of both the criminal and civil law in *Justice through Apologies: Remorse, Reform, and Punishment*, dedicating a chapter to 'apology reductions' at sentencing.[3]

It is to this growing body of work that this book contributes. It is heartening that some of the arguments I make appear to be in harmony with arguments put forward in the work of Proeve and Tudor, and Smith. However, there remain finer points of disagreement. For example, whilst Proeve and Tudor weigh up the value of acknowledging the offender's self-conception through mitigation *against* the value of doing justice, my Responsive Censure argument makes remorse-based mitigation integral to correctly delivering censure. Smith's self-labelled 'kitchen sink' approach to remorse-based mitigation precludes identification of whether reductions to the remorseful offender's sentence should be understood as 'forgiveness, mercy, leniency, clemency, pardon, amnesty', or something else.[4] Through arguing for the superiority of the Responsive Censure argument, I suggest that the mitigation of the remorseful offender's punishment is deserved. Indeed, through demonstrating the relative success of the various arguments, and

---

[1] M Proeve and S Tudor, *Remorse: Psychological and Jurisprudential Perspectives* (Farnham, Ashgate Publishing, 2010).

[2] R Weisman, *Showing Remorse: Law and the Social Control of Emotion* (Farnham, Ashgate Publishing, 2014).

[3] N Smith, *Justice through Apologies: Remorse, Reform, and Punishment* (New York, Cambridge University Press, 2014).

[4] ibid, 236.

comparing Responsive Censure with Merciful Compassion in particular, I am able to highlight and emphasise the features of Responsive Censure that make it particularly compelling.

Further, through examining the implications of the normative conclusions for sentencing practice, I extend the discussion to consider the consequences of the arguments for remorseful offenders charged with the most and least serious offences. The conclusions, I suggest, lend support to the Responsive Censure account. I also demonstrate how remorse would interact with previous convictions, again showing that the theoretical position one adopts makes a difference to the approach that would follow in practice.

To the extent that my arguments are in accord with proposals made by other theorists, I hope this can be taken to lend additional credence to the position that remorse-based mitigation can be justified within modern desert theories. Through offering an extended analysis, I hope to strengthen this position and demonstrate its wider implications both to theorists and practitioners. Finally, through contributing to the burgeoning literature on remorse, I hope to inspire further theoretical and practical discussion of remorse and its proper place in our justice systems.

Acknowledgements

I am grateful to Julian Roberts and Andrew Ashworth for their guidance and encouragement during and since the completion of my doctorate. Their generosity with their time is particularly appreciated and I thank them for comments on earlier drafts of this monograph.

I note that parts of the discussion presented in Chapters 8 and 10 draw on and develop ideas originally presented in H Maslen and JV Roberts, 'The Role of Remorse at Sentencing: An Analysis of Guidelines and Empirical Practice' in A Ashworth and JV Roberts (eds), *Sentencing Guidelines: Exploring the English Model* (Oxford, Oxford University Press, 2013). Chapter 9 is a substantially amended version of H Maslen, 'Penitence and Persistence: How Should Sentencing Factors Interact?' in J Roberts (ed), *Exploring Sentencing Practice in England and Wales* (Palgrave McMillan, in press).

Over the course of my research and writing on remorse I have been fortunate to have had many sources of unwavering support, without which my work and my well-being would have been much the poorer. My Mum and Dad, Ben, Tomasz and Jonny have contributed to both these things in ways they might not realise. The completion of this book would simply not have been possible without Jonny's love, patience, and willingness to discuss things over and over.

Contents

1

Remorse and its Relevance to Penal Theory

Northampton County Judge FP Kimberly McFadden sentenced Dennis Francis
Wechsler Jr to 49 to 150 years behind bars for sexually abusing girls ages 15,
8 and 7.... [McFadden] said she believed he was truly remorseful for his actions,
and she accepted the apologies he offered his absent victims. Those words,
however, could not undo the damage he had caused, she said.[1]

REMORSE CANNOT CHANGE the past. No matter how deeply
and genuinely sorry an offender is for the harm he caused, what is
done cannot be undone. How, then, can remorse ever be relevant
to the sentence an offender receives? This question is most challenging
for theories of punishment concerned with the offender's desert. If the
punishment an offender deserves is proportionate to the seriousness of
his offence, remorse seems to have no legitimate role to play. Desert theories are said to be backward looking. They are concerned with the facts
surrounding the offence—the degree of harm caused or risked, and the
offender's culpability for it. Subsequent remorse cannot, it would seem,
be amongst these facts.

But, the prima facie irrelevance of remorse is in great tension with the
societal and, indeed, penal significance often attached to it. The recent
media coverage of the trial of Rolf Harris produced many headlines
focused on his lack of remorse: 'Rolf Harris: Jailed for five years and nine
months but shows no remorse',[2] 'Rolf Harris sentenced to five years and
nine months after showing "no remorse at all" over child sex offences',[3]
'Remorseless Rolf Harris is handed six-year jail term'.[4] His lack of remorse

---

[1] www.lehighvalleylive.com/bethlehem/index.ssf/2014/02/bethlehem_sexual_predator_
sent.html.
[2] www.telegraph.co.uk/news/uknews/crime/10947647/Rolf-Harris-Jailed-for-five-years-
and-nine-months-but-shows-no-remorse.html.
[3] www.metro.co.uk/2014/07/04/rolf-harris-sentenced-to-five-years-and-nine-months-after-
showing-no-remorse-at-all-over-child-sex-offences-4786892/.
[4] www.heraldscotland.com/news/home-news/remorseless-rolf-harris-is-handed-six-year-
jail-term.1404476999.

was perhaps seen as confirming once and for all that he was well and truly lacking in moral fibre. When he later launched a bid to appeal against his conviction, the response of at least one of his victims (and, consequently, the headlines) was to again condemn his lack of remorse: 'It really shook me up and it's really wrong of him. It shows that he's got no remorse in any shape or form'.[5]

In addition to the significant societal interest in the offender's response to his offence, the presence of remorse is considered to be a mitigating factor in many jurisdictions around the world. According to the 2012 Crown Court Sentencing Survey conducted in the courts of England and Wales, remorse was the most common mitigating factor taken into account by judges.[6] Its role is often formalised in guidelines or becomes firmly established through precedent within case law. In capital cases it can often make the difference between life and death.[7]

But, how can this practice be justified if remorse does not alter what was done? For sentencing rooted in consequentialist justification of punishment, the possibilities are clear: if—and the 'if' is contingent on empirical likelihood—remorse were to indicate a reduced need for specific deterrence or particular amenability to rehabilitation, then it would justify imposing a less severe sentence. Pure consequentialist theories of punishment are concerned with preventing future crime at the lowest material and human cost. If the remorseful offender does not require as much punishment as the unremorseful, then it would be more efficient to impose the lesser quantum.

However, the relevance of remorse for desert theories cannot be founded on any effect remorse might have on future behaviour. Remorseful and unremorseful offenders alike are punished in proportion to their past misconduct. Being thus, must sentencers be adopting consequentialist sentencing aims when they reduce an offender's sentencing based on his remorse? Correspondingly, if a sentencing regime were to be based solely on the foundations of desert, must it relinquish remorse as a mitigating factor?

OVERVIEW OF THE BOOK

This book is divided into two parts. The first part examines five potential desert-compatible arguments for the mitigating role of remorse at sentencing. The second part examines implications of the theoretical arguments for

---

[5] www.bbc.co.uk/news/uk-england-28644110.

[6] Sentencing Council, *Crown Court Sentencing Survey*, Annual Publication (Office of the Sentencing Council, 2012), http://sentencingcouncil.judiciary.gov.uk/docs/CCSS_Annual_2012.pdf.

[7] See R Weisman, *Showing Remorse: Law and the Social Control of Emotion* (Farnham, Ashgate Publishing, 2014) chapter 3.

sentencing practice and provides an introduction to the approaches taken in various jurisdictions.

Part I: Retributive Arguments

In the first part of this book I examine various arguments that seek to reconcile desert theories with the mitigating role of remorse. Drawing on judicial sentencing remarks and guidance, I consider five types of argument that could be advanced to explain why the remorseful offender should receive a reduced sentence: the Changed Person argument, the Reduced Harm argument, the Already Punished argument, the Responsive Censure argument and the Merciful Compassion argument.

The first argument relies on the idea that the remorseful offender is a changed person. I consider both the stronger version of this argument—that the remorseful offender is a different person from the person who committed the offence—and weaker versions of the argument, which claim that the remorseful offender has become less responsible or blameworthy for the offence due to his remorse. I conclude that none of these arguments succeed.

Second, I consider the argument that remorse reduces the harm of the offence. If the harm of the offence is reduced, it might be claimed, then the quantum of punishment due is correspondingly reduced. I examine both the argument that remorse can forestall significant psychological harm to the victim and the argument that remorse reduces the overall 'badness' of the offence. I conclude that there are limited circumstances under which the former argument succeeds but that estimations of harm at sentencing require harm to be temporally bounded. The latter argument is shown only to succeed to the extent that remorse provides evidence of lesser culpability. It cannot retroactively alter facts about the offender's state of mind at the time of the offence.

The third argument addressed is founded on the idea that remorse might substitute some of the deserved punishment. Remorse involves a kind of suffering. If the remorseful offender is already suffering, it might be claimed, the state need not inflict as much hard treatment as it otherwise would. Examining this possibility in relation to prominent desert theories, I conclude that where the infliction of punishment is justified by its penitentiary function, self-imposed penances constitute some of the deserved punishment. I demonstrate that other theories are committed to the view that punishment must be delivered by the state and that remorse cannot therefore serve as a substitute.

The fourth argument draws on the emphasis in modern desert theories on the censuring role of punishment. If, to communicate disapproval, punishment appeals to the offender's reflective capacity then it could be claimed that the offender's remorse is of relevance to this function. I argue that optimal communication will be attuned to its recipient and that, where the recipient has already conceded the message, as demonstrated in his remorse, censure should be responsive to this. I suggest that this argument is not only compatible with communicative desert theories but also implied by them.

The final argument I consider is that remorse justifies showing merciful compassion towards the offender. According to this argument, remorse evokes the legitimate sympathy of the judge and, based on this charitable concern for the offender, a degree of leniency can be extended. I suggest that mercy may not be the appropriate response to the remorseful wrong-doer and that, even if it were, the Responsive Censure argument developed in Chapter 5 provides a more principled basis for remorse-based mitigation. Further, in operating more 'internally' to deserved censure, it is preferable to a justification based on merciful compassion.

Part II: Remorse and Sentencing Practice

In the second part of this book I turn to sentencing practice and the role that remorse plays therein. In doing this, I draw on the arguments assessed in the first part of the book to demonstrate the implications they have for different elements of sentencing guidance. Examining the practical implications of a normative argument serves to prompt reflection on its validity. I argue that implications of the Responsive Censure argument lend it support.

In Chapter 7 I examine how the nature and seriousness of different offences might influence the extent to which remorse should mitigate an offender's sentence. I address the claim that remorse can only have a limited role to play for offences of the greatest seriousness. I then consider whether remorse is the appropriate response to certain offences of lesser seriousness and propose an alternative approach to remorse-based mitigation for such offences, drawing on the concept of 'civic duty'. The outcome of this chapter is a series of suggestions that would add more nuance and direction to sentencing guidelines, based on the nature of remorse and its relationship to mitigation.

In Chapter 8 I address the issue of interactions between different—and potentially conflicting—sentencing factors. In particular, I consider how the remorseful offender with previous convictions should be sentenced. Drawing on the principal justifications for the aggravating role of previous convictions, I examine whether and how—if we were to accept their tenets—the mitigating role of remorse would be affected. I demonstrate that the answer differs depending on which model of previous convictions is accepted. I discuss the implications of this for sentencing guidance.

The ninth chapter provides a survey of sentencing guidance on remorse. It presents the guidelines system operating in England and Wales and then introduces contrasting approaches taken to remorse and sentencing in three other jurisdictions. I examine the different approaches in light of the preceding issues addressed throughout the course of the book.

SETTING THE SCENE: REMORSE

Court transcripts, newspaper articles and even victim impact statements demonstrate that there is great emphasis on whether or not an offender has shown remorse. Apologies are anticipated, body language is scrutinised and post-offence conduct is discussed and showcased as evidence of the presence or absence of remorse. But quite what remorse amounts to is not immediately clear. Sometimes an offender claims to feel remorse but his claims are rejected with the suggestion that what is felt is 'not really remorse'. Sometimes other emotions are invoked as well or instead—shame, contrition, guilt—and often what is expected involves more than just emotions or words. Before I begin to assess the different arguments that might justify the mitigating role of remorse, something must be said about what is meant by remorse. In reality, emotional experience is often messy. This is particularly evident in Adam Smith's rich description of the 'sentiment' of remorse. His description—some 450 words long—invokes a number of other emotions including shame, horror, consternation, self-hatred, pity, grief, regret, terror, amazement, distress, fear and dread.[8] Objects of the remorseful agent's attention include the attitudes of others towards him and his crime, his own conduct, the plight of the victim, the consequences of the crime more broadly, his status in society, and the punishment that is likely to be imposed upon him. Whilst the description is convincing and evocative, it involves vacillation between elements thought essential to remorse—for example, 'sympathizing with the hatred and abhorrence which other men must entertain for him'[9]—and other elements that some might suggest were in tension: the desire to 'fly to some inhospitable desert, where he might never more behold the face of a human creature, nor read in the countenance of mankind the condemnation of his crimes'[10] suggests at least a part of the agent that does not want to 'face up' to what he has done—something required of the 'truly remorseful' agent. However, in Smith's complex description, the 'horror of solitude' drives the agent back into society in order to 'supplicate some little protection from the countenance of those very judges, who he knows have already all unanimously condemned him'.[11]

The messiness of emotional experience precludes the consistent application of sharply delineated ascriptions of different emotions. Nonetheless,

---

[8] A Smith, *The Theory of Moral Sentiments* (Cambridge, Cambridge University Press, 2002) 98–99.
[9] ibid.
[10] ibid.
[11] ibid.

there is still value in characterising the paradigmatic instance of remorse and in attempting to discern what is of value therein.

Remorse is not the only emotional response an individual might have to his wrongdoing. Shame, guilt and regret are other possible responses and are sometimes used interchangeably in academic and popular discourse. These emotions are likely to overlap in aspects of their phenomenology and may sometimes be experienced concurrently. Indeed, empirical studies reveal a substantial overlap in aspects of the experiences of remorse, shame, regret and guilt.[12] Below I will demonstrate the ways in which these emotions are conceptually distinguishable, whilst acknowledging that actual experience may often not conform to neat prototypes.

Although remorse might sometimes be experienced alongside other emotions, I will argue for a set of characteristics that are essential to remorse. Being essential, they should therefore be understood as collectively denoting the 'minimal' instance of remorse. Additional characteristics may add to the depth and moral quality of remorse, but the features I set out here are necessary for the moral response to be one of remorse. The characteristics are as follows. First, the agent must painfully perceive himself to have done something that he considers to be morally wrong. Most often this involves having harmed another person in some way. Second, the agent must see himself as blameworthy, occasioning self-condemnation. Third, the focus of the agent's attention must principally be on the individual he has wronged, and secondarily on himself as the one who wronged the other. Fourth, there must be a desire to atone, which is likely to manifest itself in apology and reparative activity. Fifth, there must be at least an intention not to repeat the harmful action (failure to achieve what one sets out to do might count as evidence against a genuine intention, but does not necessarily preclude it). Thus, remorse is complex syndrome involving affect, beliefs, desires, intentions and, often, action.

Gaita's Account of Remorse

Raymond Gaita provides one of the richest descriptions of remorse and its connection to morality. He says little that contradicts, and much that expands on, other analyses of remorse in the literature.[13] Gaita focuses

---

[12] See, eg, JR Davitz, *The Language of Emotion* (New York, Academic Press, 1969); see also P Shaver et al, 'Emotion Knowledge: Further Exploration of a Prototype Approach' (1987) 52 *Journal of Personality and Social Psychology* 1061.

[13] R Gaita, *Good and Evil: An Absolute Conception* (London, Routledge, 2004); R Gaita, *A Common Humanity: Thinking about Love and Truth and Justice* (Melbourne, Text Publishing, 1999); Stephen Tudor also provides a thorough analysis of remorse. His work draws on Gaita and is, for the most part, in agreement with his main tenets: S Tudor, *Compassion and Remorse: Acknowledging the Suffering Other* (Leuven, Peeters, 2001); Nick Smith proposes 13 elements present in the 'highest manifestation' of a 'categorical apology': N Smith, *I Was Wrong: The Meanings of Apologies* (Cambridge, Cambridge University Press, 2008).

in particular on the ways in which the reality and value of other people (the victim(s)) are revealed to the wrongdoer in an experience of remorse. He also emphasises the capacity of remorse to fundamentally isolate the remorseful agent. Gaita explains:

> Our sense of the reality of others is partly conditioned by our vulnerability to them, by the unfathomable grief they may cause us. It is also conditioned by our shocked and bewildered realisation of what it means to wrong them. Remorse is that realisation ... It is the perspective in which the meaning of what one has done, what one has become through doing it, and what one's victims have suffered through doing it, are inseparable.[14]

Remorse, then, is a pained realisation of the reality of others and what it means to wrong them: 'Pained bewilderment is the most natural expression of remorse. "What have I done? How could I have done it?"'[15] These questions, that illustrate the intense anguish of remorse, demonstrate a focus both on the wrongdoing and on the self: a shocked realisation of the harm done to the victim, and horror at the realisation that *I* was capable of doing it. These are inseparable because, as Gaita notes, 'that *we* did it is internal to the character of *what we did* and ... to what the victim suffered'.[16]

Gaita argues that we learn about what is really 'evil'—the harming of other people—through studying remorse. In this way he urges a resistance to Kantian-style conceptions of morality that might depict 'evil' in terms of rule violation and transgression of moral codes. When we consider a remorseful murderer, for example, we find he is not haunted by the principles he betrayed or by the moral law he transgressed; he is haunted by the particular individual he killed. Thus: 'Reflection on remorse takes us closer ... to the nature of morality and of good and evil, than reflection on rules, principles, taboos and transgressions can'.[17] Any moral theories that say that a murderer discovers in her remorse how terrible it is to become someone who broke a certain rule or principle are clearly inadequate. According to Gaita, we learn something about the seriousness of murder through the way the murderer becomes haunted by his victim: 'remorse is an awakening to the terribleness of what was done'.[18]

The second of Gaita's particularly instructive insights into remorse is what he describes as its capacity to render one 'radically singular'. He explains that remorse is the only kind of human suffering that can find no consolation from human fellowship. Those who grieve, for example, can find comfort from others who grieve, knowing that they are not alone in their suffering. In remorse, however, there can only be corrupt consolation in the knowledge that others are as reprehensible as we are. In contrast to

---

[14] Gaita, *A Common Humanity* (n 13) 34.
[15] ibid, 31.
[16] Gaita, *Good and Evil* (n 13) 54.
[17] Gaita, *A Common Humanity* (n 13) 32.
[18] Gaita, *Good and Evil* (n 13) 52.

the consolation that the grieving or fearful or frustrated may find in human fellowship,

> it is different with guilt. It should be no consolation if what we did was also done by the best of people. That is not pride because remorse does not focus on what kind of person we are. Its focus is on what we have become only because we have become wrongdoers.[19]

Gaita explains that, as well as remorse going hand in hand with understanding the wrong one has done, it also goes hand in hand with reparation. He argues that someone who often and tearfully expresses remorse but is never prepared to make reparation has a 'desperately thin moral understanding'.[20] Conversely, he claims that attempts to make good the harm caused, whilst feeling no remorse and seeing no need to apologise, are equally unsatisfactory. In fact, he suggests that relieving material and psychological harm does not count as reparation unless the spirit in which that relief is given is informed by a recognition of the wrongs the victim suffered: 'That is part of what we *mean* by "reparation" and it is why we distinguish reparation from other actions which would bring the same material benefits to those who have been wronged'.[21]

So, on Gaita's account, remorse occurs when one realises that one has harmed another human being, painfully becoming aware of his reality. It renders one radically singular, in the sense that one cannot enter into consoling fellowship over one's remorse. Remorse also inspires reparative efforts, which have a particular quality that is not shared by other kinds of compensation unaccompanied by remorse.

Distinguishing Shame from Remorse

Shame most basically involves the feeling of being exposed, of becoming diminished or dishonourable, or in some sense of being at a disadvantage.[22] When experiencing shame one is focused on oneself and one's negative assessment of one's worth. In remorse, one is focused primarily on the other whom one has wronged, but also on the self as the one who wronged the other. Taylor suggests that the fact that shame is not other-focused renders it selfish and less moral than remorse.[23] However, as Tudor notes, shame need not wholly ignore victims if there are victims, but it does not attend to them in the direct and fundamental way needed for 'adequate acknowledgement of their moral reality'.[24] Remorse, in contrast, does attend to victims in this way.

---

[19] ibid, 50.

[20] Gaita, *A Common Humanity* (n 13) 100.

[21] ibid, 101.

[22] B Williams, *Shame and Necessity* (Berkeley, CA, University of California Press, 1993); Tudor (n 13).

[23] G Taylor, *Pride, Shame and Guilt: Emotions of Self-Assessment* (Oxford, Clarendon Press, 1985).

[24] Tudor (n 13) 185.

Being less victim focused, it might be more appropriate to feel shame than remorse for simple deficiency in virtue, when no harm has been done. Malicious thoughts, for example, might more appropriately precipitate shame, where the focus is on one's own flaws, not harm done to others. However, given that criminal offences often do involve harm to others, it should be noted that remorse responds more thoroughly to most instances of criminal wrongdoing.

The action tendencies precipitated in shame may differ from those precipitated in remorse. Whereas one is disposed to make reparation in remorse, one might hide away in shame.[25] Where some sort of positive activity *is* motivated in shame, this is most likely to be focused on rebuilding the self. This is in contrast to the motivation to apologise and alleviate the harm done to the victim, which characteristically accompanies remorse.

Distinguishing Guilt from Remorse

Although attempts have been made to sharply distinguish remorse from guilt, I suggest that these attempts focus only on one specific (and arguably 'corrupt') form of guilt, which primarily involves anxiety at having broken rules, and fear of punishment. This cynical characterisation, whilst no doubt correctly describing some instances of guilt, should not lead to the conclusion that guilt never involves anything morally praiseworthy. Indeed, guilt has aptly been conceived as sometimes describing the emotional state of an agent who 'grieves the misery of which he has been the cause' and 'apprehends the wrong one has done painfully in one's concern for the person one has wronged and for the values one has violated'.[26]

Notwithstanding less cynical descriptions of instances of guilt, it is possible to conceive of situations where someone might feel guilty but not remorseful, suggesting that they are not simply the same thing. Imagine an animal tester who feels guilty but not remorseful about experimenting on monkeys. His staying in his job speaks to his lack of remorse but is compatible with experiencing some guilt. Also instructive is that whilst 'guilty pleasure' is an intelligible concept, 'remorseful pleasure' is not. I might gain pleasure from the car I have stolen whilst also feeling some guilt. If I were to instead feel remorse, it is impossible that I would at the same time be able to enjoy the car. Whilst anxiety is central to many instances of guilt, remorse seems more naturally to command sorrow as its principal affective component (cf Dilman's discussion of 'depressive guilt', as continuous with remorse).[27]

Thus, guilt is much broader in its ambit than remorse, also incorporating much less desirable responses to wrongdoing. Guilt may sometimes

---

[25] JP Tangney, 'The Self-Conscious Emotions: Shame, Guilt, Embarrassment and Pride' in T Dalgleish and MJ Power (eds), *Handbook of Cognition and Emotion* (New York, NY, John Wiley & Sons Ltd, 1999) 541–68.

[26] I Dilman, 'Shame, Guilt and Remorse' (1999) 22 *Philosophical Investigations* 312, 326.

[27] ibid.

describe the emotional experiences of those who do not think much about the victim, who do not accept responsibility for what they have done, who do not take reparative steps, and who do not wish to undo their actions. However, it is not the case that guilt is always a morally worthless or inferior response. Indeed, guilt seems particularly fitting as a response to minor transgressions, where remorse might be seen as an overreaction. So, whilst anxiety over wrongdoing is the central feature of guilt—which, alone, would constitute a morally thin response to most instances of serious wronging—it can be accompanied by more commendable beliefs and intentions and often suffices as a response to less serious wrongdoing.

Distinguishing Regret from Remorse

The possible objects of regret are wide ranging. Most broadly, regret is felt over an unsatisfactory state of affairs. Regret, unlike remorse, can be felt over morally neutral actions, even morally virtuous actions, and for circumstances that are not a consequence of one's own actions. Regret, unlike remorse, does not characteristically involve judgements about the self and does not have to involve concern for others. In regret there might only be disapproval of one's actions in so far as they have affected one's own personal gratification. Accordingly, regret most often focuses on the prudential disvalue of an act rather than any moral disvalue.

What regret and remorse do share is the presence of an intention not to behave in the same way in the future. However, whilst the motivation for this in regret might be that 'it did not work out well for me last time', the firm resolve not to commit the same act again in remorse is motivated by a concern to avoid causing harm, particularly to other human beings.

Since regret involves a desire for things to be different and, commonly, the desire to undo a particular action, remorse might be said to involve regret, but regret alone does not imply remorse. Indeed, both Tudor and Dilman claim that remorse involves a bitter and deeply painful or acute sense of regret.[28]

Clarifying Remorse

I will now demonstrate that only remorse has all of the characteristics I set out at the beginning of the section. The characteristics were as follows:

1. The agent must painfully perceive himself to have done something that he considers to be morally wrong. Most often this involves having harmed another person in some way.
2. The agent must see himself as blameworthy, occasioning self-condemnation.

---

[28] Tudor (n 13); Dilman (n 26).

3. The focus of the agent's attention must principally be on the individual he has wronged, and secondarily on himself as the one who wronged the other.
4. There must be a desire to atone, which is likely to manifest itself in apology and reparative activity.
5. There must be at least an intention not to repeat the harmful action.

Self-condemnation for having done something one one believes to be morally wrong (characteristics 1 and 2) is uniquely necessary for remorse. An act does not have to be perceived as morally wrong to occasion shame (eg failing a test). Further, an agent might feel shame over something for which he was not responsible (eg the performance of the sports team he supports). Similarly, in guilt the agent perceives that he has at least broken some rule, but not necessarily that he has done something morally wrong; the agent may defensively try to deny culpability. In regret no perception of having done wrong need be present other than the perception of a less-than-optimum action as 'wrong' in a prudential sense. These differences in levels of self-condemnation lead to different dispositions. In remorse the agent humbly accepts blame and punishment without defiance. In contrast, both shame and guilt have been shown to have the potential to lead to hostile dispositions.[29]

Remorse is the only one of the four emotions to focus on the victim of the wrongdoing and the harm suffered (characteristic 3). In shame the agent focuses mainly on himself (although this focus may be honourable in its concern with being a worthy human being). In less moral forms of guilt the agent focuses on himself, as one who is likely to receive punishment or is obliged to pay a debt. If present, the outward-looking aspects of shame and guilt are, respectively, towards the disappointed/disgusted other or the angry other. In regret the agent might only be concerned with his own personal gratification.

Remorse is the only one of the four emotions in which a desire to repair the harm, as an end in itself (characteristic 4), must be present. In shame one might be motivated to improve oneself, although this is not a necessary feature. In guilt one might use reparation as a way of discharging one's debt but, again, this is not essential to guilt. Regret may lead to ameliorative action, but in some cases this is aimed only at making things better for the agent himself.

Of the four emotions, remorse and regret are the only ones that necessarily involve the intention not to repeat the action (characteristic 5). Where there is a sense of resolve in shame, guilt or regret, this may (but not necessarily) be so as to avoid experiencing the emotion and the personal consequences in the future. In remorse, although one may want to avoid having reason to feel remorseful in the future, for remorse to be genuine, the intention must be more outwardly focused on wanting to ensure no one else suffers as a result of one's actions.

---

[29] JP Tangney et al, 'Shamed into Anger? The Relation of Shame and Guilt to Anger and Self-Reported Aggression' (1992) 62 *Journal of Personality and Social Psychology* 669.

It would therefore seem that remorse is at least as morally valuable as shame, guilt and regret, if not more so. Being so, the focus on remorse as the response relevant to sentencing is justified. Even if actual experiences of emotions are not as neat as their presentations in conceptual analysis, the focus on remorse serves to illuminate the feelings, beliefs and intentions of the person whose response to their wrongdoing is the most comprehensive and morally serious.

This being said, there might be some offences for which remorse, as I have characterised it, is not necessarily the response we should anticipate. Fairly trivial offences, such as the theft of a small amount of money, might be more likely to engender a more proportionate sense of guilt. Shame might be the response to expect of the person charged with 'breach of the peace', not remorse. Such responses in these situations still suggest an understanding of what one has done. I expand on the implications of this possibility in Chapter 7.

SETTING THE SCENE: PENAL THEORY

If remorse is to be justified as a mitigating factor at sentencing, this practice must be entailed by (or at least consistent with) the underlying justification of punishment. In this book I examine arguments that might be thought to support remorse-based mitigation on broadly retributive theories of punishment. Establishing whether remorse is of relevance to utilitarian theories—theories concerned with maximising the positive consequences of punishment for society—would require engaging with empirical research into remorse and its relationship with deterrence, rehabilitation and reform. To date, there has not been the empirical research conducted to enable any strong conclusions to be drawn, and the evidence that does exist is itself inconclusive, although some recent studies provide more optimistic results.[30]

Further, 'just deserts' theories (the more contemporary versions of retributivism) and an emphasis on proportionality underlie the sentencing policies of many Western states. In England and Wales, just deserts and the proportionality principle play a major role in sentencing.[31] The jurisdictions of Finland, Sweden and Minnesota have also fully embraced

---

[30] See: M Cox, *Remorse and Reparation* (London, Jessica Kingsley, 1999); I F Dufour & R Brassard. 'The Convert, the remorseful and the Rescued: Three different Processes of Desistance from Crime' (2014) 47 *Australian & New Zealand Journal of Criminology* 313; R R Corrado & A M Peters, 'The Relationship between a Schneider-Based Measure of Remorse and Chronic Offending in a Sample of Incarcerated Young Offenders 1' (2013) 55(1) *Canadian Journal of Criminology and Criminal Justice* 101.

[31] A Ashworth, *Sentencing and Criminal Justice*, 5th edn (Cambridge, Cambridge University Press, 2010) 104–05.

proportionality theory.[32] 'Just deserts' has been adopted in the United States more generally[33] and the US Supreme Court has said that retribution is a legitimate purpose of criminal punishment.[34]

It should be noted that jurisdictions that adopt multiple aims for sentencing are still able to appeal to a desert-based justification if considerations of desert and proportionality are amongst those multiple aims. In reality, proportionality is rarely the sole principle or value pursued by a jurisdiction's sentencing policy.[35]

At their most abstract level, retributive philosophies of punishment view punishment as either valuable per se or as a practice required by justice. Since justice is a good that we should promote, obligations to punish are generated where doing so serves to achieve justice. Traditional retributive theories of punishment are backward looking, focusing on the offence committed, although their modern counterparts sometimes include some forward looking aspects. In addition to justice, desert is a key organising concept within retributivism. Desert implies a 'fittingness' between conduct and repercussions and, consequently, requires considerations of proportionality—if one deserves a certain quantum of punishment, then punishing more or less severely is (at least prima facie) unjust: the punishment must be in proportion to the seriousness of the offence (determined by the degree of harm caused or risked, and the culpability of the offender).

Retributive theories come in different (and sometimes incompatible) forms. The classical view, proposed by Kant, has been modified and developed by contemporary theorists to give rise to accounts that have strong support today. I will briefly outline the tenets of Kant's classical retributive perspective and then introduce three modern forms of desert theory.

Classical Retributivism

Immanuel Kant is seen as one of the fathers of classical retributivism. He laid down the foundations for the idea that punishment should not be a means to an end but an end in itself. This claim is what defines all strong

---

[32] ibid, 89.

[33] MH Tonry, *Sentencing Matters* (New York, NY, Oxford University Press, 1996).

[34] J Finckenauer, 'Public Support for the Death Penalty: Retribution as Just Deserts or Retribution as Revenge?' (1988) 5 *Justice Quarterly* 81. The United States Sentencing Manual, examined in Chapter 9, provides more recent confirmation of the relevance of just deserts to sentencing: United States Sentencing Commission, *Guidelines Manual* 2013.

[35] For example, although proportionality is predominant in sentencing in England and Wales, courts must have regard to the following purposes of sentencing: (a) the punishment of the offenders, (b) the reduction of crime (including its reduction by deterrence), (c) the reform and rehabilitation of offenders, (d) the protection of the public, and (e) the making of reparation by offenders to persons affected by their offences (section 142 of the Criminal Justice Act 2003).

forms of retributivism, implying an outright rejection of any consequentialist notion of imposing punishment to obtain beneficial results:

> Juridical Punishment can never be administered merely as a means for promoting
> another Good, either with regard to the Criminal himself or to Civil Society, but
> must in all cases be imposed only because the individual on whom it is inflicted
> has *committed a Crime*. For one man ought never to be dealt with merely as a
> means subservient to the purpose of another...[36]

Kant invokes what he refers to as the 'principle of equality' in his discussion
of punishment. Allegiance to this principle requires that 'the pointer of the
scale of Justice is made to incline no more to the one side than the other'.[37]
When committing a wrongful act, the wrongdoer upsets the balance of the
scale of justice. He inflicts suffering on another, and therefore renders himself deserving of suffering. So, in order to balance the scale of justice, the
'undeserved evil' that the offender inflicted on the victim must be matched
by the same amount inflicted on the offender: the principle of retaliation.
Kant argues that only the right of retaliation (*jus talionis*)

> can definitely assign both the quality and the quantity of a just penalty. All other
> standards are wavering and uncertain; and on account of other considerations
> involved in them, they contain no principle conformable to the sentence of pure
> and strict Justice.[38]

Again, subscription to such a view entails that one renounce any consequentialist considerations since they are contrary to justice. For Kant,
appropriate punishment is solely a matter of what is required to rebalance
the justice scales.

Importantly, the particulars of Kant's view render an arbitrary choice
of type of punishment impermissible. Kant states that the act that the
person has performed 'is to be regarded as perpetrated on himself'.[39] This
is proportionality in its strongest form. In this context, Kant employs the
phrase 'Gleiches mit Gleichem', which is usually translated as 'like for like'
or 'measure for measure', emphasising both quantitative and qualitative
matching in terms of the amount of suffering and type of punishment.[40]
Illustratively, the most straightforward application of this 'like for like'
principle demands that murderers receive the death penalty: according to
Kant, 'whoever has committed Murder, must *die*'.[41]

---

[36] I Kant, *The Philosophy of Law: An Exposition of the Fundamental Principles of Jurisprudence as the Science of Right* (Edinburgh, T&T Clark, 1887) 195.

[37] ibid, 196.

[38] ibid, 196–97.

[39] ibid, 196.

[40] SM Easton, *Sentencing and Punishment: The Quest for Justice*, 2nd edn (Oxford, Oxford
University Press, 2008) 58.

[41] Kant (n 36) 198.

Whether Kant ultimately provides a successful retributive justification of punishment has been contested.[42] However, there are those who argue that he does[43] and it is indisputable that Kant's arguments concerning the distribution of punishment are clearly retributive.

Modern Retributivism

Modern retributive theories, whilst retaining the basic retributive values (relying on concepts of justice, desert and proportionality), are often less 'thoroughly' retributive. By this I mean that, whilst retributive values are of primary import, 'quasi-retributive' or even consequentialist values also may play a role in the theory. Following Metz it may be helpful to draw a distinction between 'narrow' and 'broad' retributivism.[44] Narrow retributivism can be defined as follows: 'The narrow sense of "retributivism" is the desert or pay-back theory, the view that punishment of a certain degree is justified because offenders deserve to be harmed to a like degree for their wrongdoing'.[45] Kant's retributivism would be narrow according to this definition. The broader notion of retributivism covers *any* backward looking theory of legal punishment. In addition to the basic desert theory, the broad sense of retributivism includes two additional backward looking accounts of the *purpose* of punishment:

> [F]airness theory, the view that the government should impose a proportionate penalty because it thereby corrects the degree of unfair advantage that the criminal has taken, and censure theory (or intrinsic expressivism), the view that the government should punish in a way that fits the crime because it thereby expresses disapproval proportionate to its seriousness.[46]

I will briefly outline three retributive theories that have contemporary proponents. The first of these adopts the above-described 'fairness theory', the second and third adopt the 'censure theory', incorporating some additional, non-retributive elements. I draw to varying extents on all three theories as I assess whether various justifications for remorse-based mitigation succeed on modern desert theories.

---

[42] See, eg, BS Byrd, 'Kant's Theory of Punishment: Deterrence in Its Threat, Retribution in Its Execution' (1989) 8 *Law and Philosophy* 151; JG Murphy, 'Does Kant Have a Theory of Punishment?' (1987) 87 *Columbia Law Review* 509; DE Scheid, 'Kant's Retributivism' (1983) 93 *Ethics* 262; M Tunick, 'Is Kant a Retributivist?' (1996) 17 *History of Political Thought* 60.

[43] See, eg, J Johnson, 'Revisiting Kantian Retributivism to Construct a Justification of Punishment' (2008) 2 *Criminal Law and Philosophy* 291.

[44] T Metz, 'How To Reconcile Liberal Politics with Retributive Punishment' (2007) 27 *Oxford Journal of Legal Studies* 683.

[45] ibid, 687.

[46] ibid, 687–88.

Benefits and Burdens Retributivism

The benefits and burdens (or unfair advantage) justification for punishment was, for a time, considered the most plausible theory of punishment by many philosophers. Although some have subsequently altered their thinking, the original proponents of the benefits and burdens theory include Morris, Finnis and Murphy.[47] The theory is an entirely retributivist account, which seeks to justify punishment as the proper response to past crime. It characterises the institution of the criminal law as a mutually beneficial enterprise. A system of law brings benefits to all its citizens (eg freedom from interference with body or property) by imposing burdens on each of them (ie the burden of self-restraint involved in obeying the law). In committing an offence, an offender refuses to accept the burden of obeying the law, whilst accepting the benefits that flow from the self-restraint of law-abiding others. The offender thus assumes an unfair advantage over those who obey the law. Benefits and burdens theorists justify punishment by arguing that it serves to remove the offender's unfair advantage by imposing a proportionate burden. The offender, due to his illegitimate advantage taking, deserves imposition of this burden. Through his punishment, the antecedent balance of benefits and burdens that his crime disturbed is restored.

The Penance Perspective on Retributivism

Antony Duff has developed a retributive theory of punishment that has at its centre the concept of secular penance. His view expands classical retributivism by understanding the criminal sanction in communicative terms. According to Duff, the sanction imposed on the offender does three things: first, it communicates disapprobation of the criminal conduct to the offender and to the wider community; second, it helps to bring the offender to a repentant understanding of his wrongdoing; third, it serves as a penance through which the offender can express his repentance, thus facilitating reconciliation with his community.

Central to Duff's theory is the tenet that offenders deserve the condemnation or censure that punishment communicates.[48] Further, he suggests that offenders also deserve to 'suffer remorse' for what they have done.[49] The criminal sanction, as secular penance, is not only the appropriate, but in fact the necessary, method for fulfilling these requirements. Duff is keen to emphasise that his claim that punishment serves to persuade offenders to repent of their crimes does not render his account partly consequentialist.

---

[47] H Morris, 'Persons and Punishment' (1968) 52 *The Monist* 475; J Finnis, 'The Restoration of Retribution' (1972) 32 *Analysis* 131; JG Murphy, *Retribution, Justice, and Therapy: Essays in the Philosophy of Law* (Dordrecht, D Reidel, 1979).

[48] A Duff, *Punishment, Communication and Community* (Oxford, Oxford University Press, 2001) 27.

[49] ibid, 97.

Instead, 'the very aim of persuading responsible agents to repent the wrongs they have done makes punishment the appropriate method of pursuing it'.[50] Thus, the relation between punishment and its aim is, according to Duff, not contingent but internal.

Censure and Sanction Retributivism

Andrew von Hirsch has developed a censure-focused theory of punishment.[51] At the core of his theory is the idea that criminal wrongdoing deserves censure. It deserves censure because (1) it takes the agent seriously as the author of his misconduct and (2) the state ought to take breaches of law seriously: this is owed to the citizens, and especially to the victims of crime. In order for the state to mean what it says when it declares that certain kinds of conduct are seriously wrong it must be ready to censure such conduct. Censure is retributive in nature because it is essentially backward looking, addressing the past wrongdoing.

The second core idea is that punishment (the criminal sanction) is not only a suitable medium through which this censure can be communicated, but also has the benefit of providing an additional prudential disincentive to offending, which is necessary as many individuals find it difficult to resist wrongdoing for normative reasons alone. Von Hirsch notes the unpalatable results that would occur if the state response to offending served no deterrent function: without the machinery of deterrence 'it seems likely that victimizing conduct would become so prevalent as to make life nasty and brutish, indeed'.[52]

His 'two-pronged' justification for punishment thus involves a consequentialist element of deterrence. However, von Hirsch makes it clear that the *primary* justification is the need to communicate censure to offenders, thereby respecting their rational moral agency and avoiding an institution of 'beast control', which would be engendered by purely deterrent systems.[53]

CONTRIBUTION OF THE BOOK

Each chapter begins with judicial remarks. Implicit in these remarks is a range of arguments potentially lending support to the mitigating role of

---

[50] ibid, 30.

[51] A von Hirsch, *Censure and Sanctions* (Oxford, Clarendon Press, 1993).

[52] A von Hirsch, *Past or Future Crimes: Deservedness and Dangerousness in the Sentencing of Criminals* (Manchester, Manchester University Press, 1985) 48.

[53] Von Hirsch suggests that an institution utilising only the preventative function of punishment would appear to treat the offender 'like a tiger': von Hirsch (n 51) 12. He thus clarifies how, on his model, the preventative function is related to censure in a way that retains respect for the offender as a moral agent capable of understating the message of censure conveyed through the sanction, ibid, 13.

remorse. Taking each argument in turn, I provide a comprehensive analysis of the theoretical justifications that are implicit in current sentencing practice in various jurisdictions.

My analysis does not, however, engage with the empirical question of how to assess remorse. Whilst I acknowledge that identifying genuine remorse can be a challenging task, the prior theoretical question is whether the court needs to consider an offender's remorse at all and, if so, with what consequences for his punishment. Although my emphasis is on theoretical justification, I also demonstrate how the normative conclusions would play out in the broader context of sentencing decisions and the guidance intended to structure them. Crucially, the consequences vary depending on the justification. Ending the book by examining the sentencing practices of a number of jurisdictions, I identify the theoretical commitments operating in each and the way that these shape the content of the respective guidance documents.

Part I

Retributive Arguments

2

The Changed Person Argument

The point that Mr Bennett makes before us today is that this appellant is a very
much changed person from the person he was when he committed the offence,
much changed for the better, and insufficient regard was taken by the sentencing
judge to his remorse and his efforts and indications that he was bent upon
putting this kind of criminal behaviour behind him.[1]

THIS QUOTATION ENCAPSULATES the view, not uncommon
in sentencing remarks and public discourse, that the remorseful
offender is a changed person and, as such, deserves less punishment.
In renouncing his past behaviour and turning his life around, the attitudes
and values of the remorseful offender are difficult to reconcile with those
exhibited by the person who committed the offence—his 'old self'. Such a
categorical shift, the view suggests, renders punishment gratuitous.

In this chapter I examine the relative success of versions of the Changed
Person argument at providing justification for the mitigating role of
remorse at sentencing. Taking leave from von Hirsch and Ashworth's discussion of quasi-retributive values—which may be seen to support species
of the Changed Person argument—I first address the stronger version of the
argument, according to which the remorseful offender is not identical with
the person who committed the offence. This argument involves the claim
that there is a metaphysical discontinuity between the remorseful offender
and his previous, offence-committing self. I then address the weaker version of the argument, according to which the offender, although the same
person, is no longer as blameworthy for his offence due to the effects that
his remorse has on his responsibility for past acts. I conclude that neither of
these arguments is convincing and that the justification for remorse-based
mitigation is unlikely be provided by a Changed Person argument. I return
to von Hirsch and Ashworth's discussion of quasi-retributive grounds in
Chapter 5.

In their 2005 book *Proportionate Sentencing: Exploring the Principles*,
von Hirsch and Ashworth suggest there are quasi-retributive grounds that
should affect sentencing, even though such grounds may be in tension

---

[1] *R v Jamie David Seed, Dean Spencer Kelly* [2002] EWCA Crim 2850 (AC) 14.

with the proportionality requirement (strictly conceived).[2] Von Hirsch and Ashworth state that these grounds 'relate to the wider underlying conceptions of penal censure as a response to criminal offending'.[3] Their discussion of these grounds arises from a discussion of 'equity mitigation' within Sweden's sentencing provisions. In the Swedish statute, equity factors are understood to be factors that do not affect the offence's penal value, but are nevertheless to be treated as reasons for reducing the severity of the sentence. Von Hirsch and Ashworth argue that quasi-retributive grounds are one possible source of justification for the equity mitigation that is evident in Sweden's sentencing provisions. Such justification arises from the nature and purpose of censure, which is at the heart of their desert theory. They argue that censure for an offence provides the offender with reason and opportunity to reflect on his wrongdoing and on why he committed it. Accordingly, they suggest that quasi-retributive grounds might 'address special situations which relate to this reflective process'.[4]

In order to motivate the Changed Person argument, I shall begin by considering von Hirsch and Ashworth's arguments for the sentence mitigation of an offender who is being sentenced a long time after the commission of his offence. Examining these arguments illuminates the application of quasi-retributive grounds and further demonstrates how blame and censure operate in von Hirsch and Ashworth's retributive theory.

PARALLELS WITH THE TIME DELAY ARGUMENT

Von Hirsch and Ashworth offer two arguments in favour of time delay mitigation. The first is evident in the following statement: 'When the offence for which [the offender] is being sentenced was committed several years earlier, the process of eliciting a reflective response may become more problematic after such a long delay'.[5] Their second argument in favour of time delay mitigation appeals to the fact that offenders may change significantly over a long period of time. They point out that as time passes, 'the possibility increases that the actor may have changed significantly—so that his long-past act does not reflect badly on the person he now is'.[6]

Notice that these two arguments are not the same. The former focuses on the offender's capacity for reflection (regardless of whether the act reflects

---

[2] A von Hirsch and A Ashworth, *Proportionate Sentencing: Exploring the Principles* (Oxford, Oxford University Press, 2005). As introduced in Chapter 1, the principle of proportionality requires that the severity of punishment must be commensurate with the seriousness of the offence, determined by its harm and the offender's culpability for it.

[3] ibid, 174.

[4] ibid.

[5] ibid.

[6] ibid, 178.

badly on the actor now). The latter focuses on what we might call blamewor-thiness. The actor now is not as blameworthy for his actions as he was when he committed them. The reason why this might be so, they suggest, is that he has changed significantly. More succinctly, whilst the former argument considers the function of censure, the latter considers its legitimacy. In what follows, I consider this latter claim—concerned with blameworthiness—and the implications it has for the remorseful offender. The former claim—concerned with the offender's reflective response—is of central importance to Chapter 5 and the account I develop of Responsive Censure.

THE STRONG THESIS: CHANGE AND PERSONAL IDENTITY

Von Hirsch and Ashworth suggest that the time delay offender may have changed so much that his offence no longer reflects badly on the person he now is. This claim permits various readings. The language von Hirsch and Ashworth use invites considerations of personal identity. The strongest version of such an argument would be that the person now being censured is not actually the same person as the person who committed the offence. Call this the 'strong thesis'. If the strong thesis were correct, then to punish an offender at a later time would be as illegitimate as punishing a random person picked from the street for this offence. The offence was committed by a person who no longer exists.

I doubt that von Hirsch and Ashworth have such a strong thesis in mind—they still consider censure and the associated sanction appropri-ate, but to a lesser degree than if the offender had been addressed by the sentencing judge soon after commission of the offence. What they could propose, however, is that the offender sentenced after a long time delay is *somewhat* discontinuous with the person who committed the offence, without being an entirely distinct metaphysical entity.

This is congruous with the thinking of philosophers who endorse 'psy-chological' accounts of personal identity. The basic idea underlying such accounts is that a person's identity over time depends in part on their main-taining certain sorts of psychological continuities over time. Although there are a number of modern versions of this view, they are all heavily influenced by the work of the seventeenth-century philosopher John Locke, and draw on his suggestion that a person can be identified as 'a thinking intelligent being, that has reason and reflection, and can consider itself as itself, the same thinking thing, in different times and places'.[7]

---

[7] J Locke, *An Essay Concerning Human Understanding* (Oxford, Clarendon Press, 1975) 335.

Derek Parfit's account of personal identity is arguably the most influential modern psychological account. According to Parfit, a necessary condition of personal identity is what he calls Relation R, described below. It should be acknowledged that although Relation R is necessary for personal identity on Parfit's account, it is not sufficient. However, the reasons for this are not relevant to the issues that I discuss here.[8] Parfit points out that Relation R is sufficient for what matters about *survival* over time, even if it is not sufficient for identity, all things considered. However, whilst personal identity cannot be maintained in the absence of Relation R, it seems plausible to claim that the importance of Relation R lies mainly in the fact that it is what matters about survival.

According to Parfit, Relation R is determined by how *psychologically connected* one is to one's purported past self, and the *psychological continuity* that endures.[9] Psychological connectedness pertains when psychological connections hold directly between a person at one time and at another time. The sorts of connections Parfit has in mind are between past experiences and present memories of these experiences, between intentions and their being acted on, and between beliefs, desires and personality traits at one time and another. Psychological continuity, the other relation of importance, refers to the holding of overlapping chains of *strong* connectedness. It is this relation, in addition to psychological connectedness, that allows persons to continue to exist over long periods of time.

If one were to invoke a Parfitian psychological account of personal identity and survival, one might defend the claim that an offender can deserve *less* punishment after long periods of time, without being committed to the claim that *any* punishment would be illegitimate (as the strong thesis implies). On the Parfitian account, Relation R is a matter of degree; agents can be more or less psychologically connected to (and psychologically continuous with) themselves at later times. Accordingly, those who invoke a Parfitian account might claim that if the offender has maintained a sufficient degree of psychological continuity and connectedness with the person who committed the offence, then the offender can still deserve some punishment. The fact that Relation R is a matter of degree on such theories means that these views can accommodate the thought that an offender may deserve some punishment even if he has changed significantly over time. Importantly, if one were to invoke these claims in an argument for time delay mitigation, then one would be claiming that the offender's being a

---

[8] Briefly, Relation R is not sufficient for identity, because in thought experiments that involve one agent undergoing fission into two separate agents, that agent might plausibly be understood to hold Relation R to two distinct individuals. Since identity is transitive, this would entail a contradiction; the initial agent cannot be identical to both of the post-fission agents *B* and *C*, if *B* and *C* are not identical to each other. D Parfit, *Reasons and Persons* (Oxford, Clarendon Press, 1984).

[9] ibid, 206.

'different person' (or not fully identical) does not simply mean that the offender seems to think about things and feel towards things in a new way. Rather, on such an argument, the person standing before the court does not share complete one-to-one identity with the person who committed the offence. This person has not fully survived, although he has survived to an extent that is sufficient for the legitimacy of some lesser punishment.

If von Hirsch and Ashworth were to propose such an argument for the sentence mitigation of offenders facing the justice system years after their offence, then, I argue, the same reasoning could support the mitigation of the remorseful offender's sentence. I assume here that by 'changed significantly' they mean that the offender might now be described as something like law-abiding, responsible, empathetic etc—an offence would surely not cease to reflect badly on a person unless he had become somehow 'morally better'. The question then arises: if these sorts of changes (which von Hirsch and Ashworth assume are possible with the passage of time) result in the offence no longer reflecting so badly on the offender, then why would an offender's remorse not function the same way?

It is very likely that the sorts of 'significant changes' von Hirsch and Ashworth envisage are likely to correspond with the changes that remorse represents and facilitates. Unless they consider the passage of time to be *necessary* for significant change, or think that time should pass so that we can be sure about these changes, then it seems plausible to claim that the remorseful offender may have undergone a change that is of such significance that his offence no longer reflects quite so badly on the person he now is. Arguably, we can be *more* certain about the changes to a genuinely remorseful person than those that might have occurred to an offender who is simply distanced in time from his offence. After all, it seems plausible to claim that agents can maintain some psychological continuities over long periods of time. For instance, we often identify other people as having certain core character traits that they maintain throughout their lives. Accordingly, we cannot conclude that an agent will have lost key psychological continuities just because a certain amount of time has passed.

So, if von Hirsch and Ashworth's argument should, as I suggest, also apply to the remorseful offender, we must consider whether remorse might plausibly lead to discontinuity of identity. I shall consider this issue in the next section.

Discontinuity of Identity

How might a Parfitian perspective on persons and the way in which they endure help to frame the argument that remorse makes the offender discontinuous with the person before the court? Reminiscent of von Hirsch and Ashworth, in the context of retributive punishment, Parfit proposes two scenarios that might lead to the psychological connections between the offender and the present person in court being insufficiently psychologically related to support desert-based punishment. He suggests that (a) 'when someone is convicted many years after committing his crime' or (b) 'when there is some great discontinuity', such as a religious conversion, the offender may be insufficiently connected to his past self to justify punishment.[10] Following this line of argument, we could suggest that the beliefs, desires and personality traits of the remorseful person might be so discontinuous with those of the offender that they are inadequately connected, and therefore conclude that punishment of the remorseful person is not justified. Such an argument, Parfit suggests, renders the offender's later self like an accomplice. In the same way that an accomplice's desert corresponds to his degree of complicity with the criminal, so the changed offender's desert for a past crime corresponds 'to the degree of psychological connectedness between himself now and himself when committing the crime'.[11]

So, how might remorse affect Relation R, and with what consequences?[12] It could be argued that a powerful, genuine experience of remorse constitutes a 'great discontinuity' not entirely dissimilar from a religious conversion. Or, more specifically, the things about a religious conversion that we might suppose Parfit deems sufficient to make religious conversion a great discontinuity are likely to be the sorts of things we would offer as evidence of discontinuity between the offender and the remorseful person facing sentencing. In both cases, the agent gains a new perspective on himself and the world, new beliefs about wrongdoing, a re-evaluation of his prior behaviour, the modification of his personality traits (or at least a commitment to try to modify those which are less desirable), and so on. These changes, it might be thought, are sufficient to render the remorseful offender different enough from his previous offending self to constitute discontinuity between these persons. On these grounds, punishment, or at least full punishment, is no longer justified.

There are some initial comments I would like to make about Parfit's arguments before I evaluate the effect of remorse on identity in particular. The first is that Parfit's two scenarios—sentencing after a significant time delay and sentencing after undergoing 'some great discontinuity'—involve neutral or positive changes in the offender. In fact, Parfit's own time delay example involves a drunken assailant becoming a (90-year-old) Nobel Peace Prize holder.[13] Likewise, a religious conversion is assumed to be a positive thing insofar as it demonstrates a new commitment to moral

---

[10]   ibid, 325.

[11]   ibid, 326.

[12]   For an extended treatment of the topic of psychological relatedness and retributive punishment, see R Dresser, 'Personal Identity and Punishment' (1990) 70 *Boston University Law Review* 395, 427.

[13]   Parfit (n 8) 326.

values, peaceful behaviour and so on. I will suggest that it is the positive aspects of Parfit's examples of change that lend any plausibility to his conclusion that less (or no) punishment becomes deserved.

Imagine, for example, that an offender undergoes a great discontinuity, which involves dramatic changes to his beliefs, his desires and his personality traits. These changes, however, are very much for the worse. Twenty-five-year-old Bob is being sentenced for a not-very-serious common assault that occurred six months previously, and had been perceived at the time to be out of character. During those subsequent six months, however, Bob became acquainted with, and influenced by, a particularly malicious group of individuals. His whole attitude towards the world and other people has changed. He now often makes his family members cry and delights in the power he has to do this. He no longer does anything to help them, having developed the belief that people should devote all their time to serving him. He has left his job, and his earlier friends lament that it is as if the Bob they knew no longer exists, claiming that they want nothing to do with this 'new' Bob.

Such a significant change in Bob's character, values and behaviour suggests that he has undergone 'some great discontinuity' and, if we return to Parfit's criteria for psychological connectedness—such as steady beliefs, desires and personality traits—he does indeed seem to be distantly related to the man he was when he committed the offence. Would such a case of great discontinuity render punishment unjustified? It does seem that he is not the same person who committed the offence; however, I suspect that our intuitions about the consequences this should have for punishment are not the same as our intuitions about the offender who became a nun or won a peace prize. If we were to claim that psychological discontinuity should entail lesser punishment, then in Bob's case we would have to conclude that his becoming a terribly nasty person following the offence should lead to a reduction in punishment. This is implausible. If he has somehow been brainwashed by this group, then there may be other mitigating factors to take into consideration; however, the mere fact that he is significantly discontinuous with the man who committed the offence does not seem to be sufficient to justify a lesser punishment. Yet, if we are to allow that significant positive changes should have a bearing on personal identity and, consequently, punishment, then significant negative changes that follow the same structure should too.

In a similar vein, we can imagine a religious conversion that constitutes great discontinuity, but lends no appeal to the prospect of reducing punishment on these grounds. Imagine a burglar who undergoes a genuine religious conversion before sentencing. However, instead of the religious conversion leading the offender to dedicate himself to helping the poor and to practising love and forgiveness, he instead becomes an extreme Christian fundamentalist who is intensely homophobic, and also publicly celebrates the death of cancer sufferers as 'God's will'. That this religious conversion could result in a situation where there is insufficient psychological connectedness to support desert would strike many as unpalatable. Yet, such an example of discontinuity follows Parfit's logic. I suggest, therefore, that it is the positive overtones of the changes he provides in his examples that make his ideas somewhat more persuasive than they might otherwise be.

John Kleinig makes a similar point when he argues that unwillingness to punish a person for a much earlier offence is felt not because the person who committed the offence is no longer present, but more persuasively because a change in character is a morally relevant factor.[14] This claim is closely related to the argument that I will explore below—that the remorseful offender is less blameworthy on the grounds that he is now morally improved.

Even if we were to limit the effect that psychological discontinuity could have on punishment to situations where the offender is somehow 'better' (or, at least, not 'worse') than he was, I am now going to argue that remorse cannot be seen to effect *any* change in personal identity and that the very nature of remorse presupposes an enduring self.[15]

Remorse Presupposes an Enduring Self

Remorse felt over someone else's wrongdoing would be unjustified. I might feel regret over the actions of another, but not remorse. If I, remorsefully standing before the judge, am not identical to the person who committed the offence, then why do I (or should I) experience remorse? As Radden suggests, 'one's remorse and contrition are felt over one's own actions—not those of others and not over states of affairs that have befallen one'.[16] Moreover, remorse possesses moral significance precisely because it is experienced by the same person; to suggest otherwise would be to deprive our moral attitudes of what Madell calls their 'essential ground'.[17]

Joel Feinberg elucidates the intelligibility and moral significance of remorse when he suggests that references to offenders being 'different people', inspiring reluctance to punish, must be taken metaphorically.[18] In reality, he argues, the same person persists in such cases. He claims, 'descriptions of the gentle sensitive person on Death Row presuppose for

---

[14] J Kleinig, *Paternalism* (Totowa, NJ, Rowman & Allanheld, 1983) 46.

[15] For a similar argument see J Radden, 'Shame and Blame: The Self through Time and Change' (1995) 34 *Dialogue* 61.

[16] ibid, 71.

[17] G Madell, *The Identity of the Self* (Edinburgh, Edinburgh University Press, 1981).

[18] J Feinberg, 'Autonomy, Sovereignty, and Privacy: Moral Ideals in the Constitution' (1983) 58 *Notre Dame Law Review*, 480.

their intelligibility an *identity* with the savage beast who earlier committed a murder, and a continuity of development of the same self'.[19] It is only if the offender is the same person that his remorse makes sense and has moral significance.

When we think about what a denial of this claim would mean for remorse, we are left with a very undesirable picture, lacking the rich moral value that was discussed in Chapter 1. One possibility might be that the offender feels remorse rationally, but then at some point the remorse is strong and enduring enough that he becomes discontinuous with his offending self. The remorse then becomes irrational if it continues, as he is now a new person. This would mean that wrongdoers themselves never really feel remorse (perhaps just the beginnings) as it is someone different who experiences remorse for the things that they did. It would also have the consequence that it is illogical for people to *anticipate* feeling remorse for their wrongdoing, as it will be someone else's remorse.[20]

Further, the question would arise whether, on *ceasing* to feel the (now) irrational remorse, the new person might somehow return to being the previous person. Without the identity-changing state of mind and set of beliefs that the remorse consisted in, does he perhaps resume his old identity? Or, has he been irreversibly cut off from the offender, thus enduring as a new person? These scenarios would either make rational remorse very short-lived—on experiencing it one quickly becomes discontinuous with one's offending self—or would make it wax and wane: it tracks the offending identity, which disappears with remorse but re-emerges when remorse fades as it becomes irrational. Neither picture fits the conception of remorse that I explored in Chapter 1, and neither looks morally desirable nor psychologically plausible.

However, one might emphasise that on Parfit's view, remorse might not lead to a complete disjunction of identity. Sufficient psychological connectedness might remain such that remorse is still rational, and yet there may also be enough discontinuity to warrant reduced punishment. Yet, this would also have some peculiar consequences. If remorse leaves the offender only slightly connected to the person being sentenced then this person being sentenced would rationally have to feel remorse to a lesser degree than if he were 100 per cent identical with the offender: it was only 'sort of' him that committed the offence; he is like an accomplice. But, if remorse (as Parfit might suggest) is transformative of identity, then this new instance of moderated remorse would distance him once again from his (new) 'discontinuous self', who would then have to feel even less remorse, ad infinitum.

---

[19] ibid.
[20] See J Perry, *A Dialogue on Personal Identity and Immortality* (Indianapolis, IN, Hackett, 1978) 5–6.

I have argued that remorse requires identity of persons in order to make sense and to be morally valuable. The valuable elements drawn out in Chapter 1 are valuable precisely because it is the *offender* who understands what *he* did wrong, who condemns himself, apologises, and so on. However, it should be pointed out that just because remorse has been seen not to transform identity, this does not provide a total refutation of Parfitian-style reductionism. Whilst it does not make sense to understand the remorseful offender as discontinuous in ways that have consequences for desert, there might be other situations in which matters of personal survival can be illuminated by thinking about the extent to which someone is psychologically connected and continuous with his or her past self. The offender who becomes insane might be a convincing example of the offender not 'surviving', due to great psychological discontinuity. The justification for not punishing this person, however, is probably more conclusively found in the conditions necessary for censure, such as the offender being able to understand.

We cannot, therefore, use an argument based on a psychological account of personal identity or survival to explain why an offender's having changed significantly through his remorse justifies a reduction in punishment. However, even if remorse does not alter identity, it could be argued that this (identical) person is somehow less *blameworthy* as a consequence of his remorse. It is to this argument that I now turn.

THE WEAK THESIS: CHANGE AND BLAMEWORTHINESS

When considering von Hirsch and Ashworth's Time Delay argument—and, by extension, the remorseful offender—we can posit a weaker, and more plausible version of the Changed Person argument to justify mitigation. The thesis is that, despite the offender being metaphysically the same person who committed the offence, he is no longer as *blameworthy* for it. Such a possibility requires appeal to a concept broader than the temporally static notion of culpability employed by many desert theorists and codified in sentencing guidance. An offender's culpability is set at the time of the offence: the offender either intended to commit the offence or did not, he either foresaw the likely consequences of his actions or did not—these facts cannot be changed retrospectively.[21] In contrast, the alternative concept

---

[21] For the purposes of assessing crime seriousness 'the punishment a defendant deserves is, to put it somewhat metaphorically, fully congealed at the time of the crime': SP Garvey, 'As the Gentle Rain from Heaven: Mercy in Capital Sentencing' (1996) 81 *Cornell Law Review* 989, 1030.

of blameworthiness would allow temporal flexibility, allowing a person to become more or less blameworthy over time. The utilisation of such a concept would be necessary if von Hirsch and Ashworth want to argue that past acts can reflect more or less badly on a person over time—the inflexible concept of culpability is not enough to make their argument viable.

We need next to explore the proposed concept of blameworthiness. What might be meant by the assertion that an offence no longer reflects badly (or as badly as it might have otherwise) on a person? I suggest that there are two possible arguments. The first possibility is that the offender is no longer (or as fully) *responsible* for his offence. The second is that the assessment of blameworthiness is made about the moral quality of the *person*, and so the morally improved person is less blameworthy, despite still being responsible for the offence. Thus, the two options for an argument of the sort that von Hirsch and Ashworth make are that blameworthiness is located either in responsibility or in character (constituted by attitudes etc). I will attend to the possibility of remorse reducing the offender's responsibility for his offence first.

Blameworthiness as the Attribution of Responsibility to the Offender

In relation to the remorseful offender, I will first consider the possibility that he is less blameworthy for his offence because he is no longer as responsible for it. Meir Dan-Cohen argues for such a possibility in his paper 'Revising the Past: On the Metaphysics of Repentance, Forgiveness, and Pardon'.[22] I note during my discussion the potential differences between repentance and remorse, and the particular understanding of repentance held by Dan-Cohen. I argue that difficulties—resulting from his concepts of responsibility and repentance—result in Dan-Cohen's argument failing to offer support for the possibility that the remorseful offender is no longer responsible for his offence. It will emerge that no version of this argument could prove successful.

Dan-Cohen's argument attempts to characterise repentance as one of three 'revisionary practices' (the others being forgiveness and official state pardon) that redraw the boundaries of the offender so that his wrongdoing is left outside, eliminating his responsibility for it. The consequence, Dan-Cohen argues, is that negative reactive attitudes towards the offender for his wrong are no longer appropriate. Indeed, they become entirely

---

[22] M Dan-Cohen, 'Revising the Past: On the Metaphysics of Repentance, Forgiveness, and Pardon' in A Sarat and N Hussain (eds), *Forgiveness, Mercy, and Clemency* (Stanford, CA, Stanford University Press, 2007).

misplaced. Thus, if an offender redraws his boundaries in this way, then he would cease to be blameworthy for his offence. In effect he is changed, so that his wrongdoing does not reflect badly on his newly bounded self.

Dan-Cohen uses a political analogy to illustrate how a person's boundaries can change so as to exclude the wrongful act. As a consequence, the person remains the same person (there is no change in identity in any strong sense) but ceases to be responsible for his wrongdoing. He gives an example to illustrate his analogy, as follows:

> Imagine that the state of Arcadia has near its border a pollutant that causes environmental damage to the neighbouring states. As a matter of course, Arcadia bears responsibility for this pollutant: it is required to take measures to reduce the damage, to compensate the affected states, etc. It is equally obvious that this responsibility would expire if, say by treaty or by war, Arcadia's border were redrawn so as to exclude the offensive site.[23]

The wrongdoer's repentance is meant to constitute a redrawing of his boundaries in an analogous way, leaving him no longer responsible for his wrongdoing and rendering negative reactions towards him for his wrongdoing without basis. Dan-Cohen explains further how this is possible in the case of persons, drawing on the notions of 'self-constitution' and 'social construction'. These ideas pertain to the proposition that human beings create themselves: individuals can be the authors of their own identities, and social practices—discursive and otherwise—also serve to shape them. Dan-Cohen suggests that such symbolic interactionism takes place in the medium of meaning, pointing out that 'the self is the product of the web of meanings we spin around various objects and events, most importantly the human body and its career'.[24] So, although we cannot change facts of the past, what can and does change is the significance we attach to past events and our attitudes towards them.

Dan-Cohen states that his account implies that 'the revisionary practices are inconsistent with a continued insistence on punishment, so that they must either occur subsequent to punishment or as a substitute for it'.[25] Thus, the pre-sentence repentant offender eliminates the justification for his punishment through his relinquished responsibility: he is no longer blameworthy for his wrongdoing and thus punishment would be unjust.

I am going to argue that there are significant difficulties with the political analogy that Dan-Cohen uses, making the conclusions he draws from it problematic. Following this, and for additional reasons, I am going to argue that the very notion that the remorseful offender can lessen his blameworthiness through shaking off responsibility is untenable. This will raise the

---

[23] ibid, 122.
[24] ibid, 128.
[25] ibid, 136, n 28.

question of what Dan-Cohen really means by repentance, and whether its practice (so conceived) would be entirely positive.

To begin this argument, reconsider Dan-Cohen's political analogy. It seems that there are some important disanalogies between the state of Arcadia and individual wrongdoers. These disanalogies arise from an understanding of responsibility that may be applicable to states, but is not applicable to individual wrongdoers. This is evident when we consider some of the features of Dan-Cohen's description of the state of Arcadia's altered responsibilities.

First, consider Dan-Cohen's suggestion concerning the reallocation of responsibility that would occur in the political scenario. He writes: '... the political scenario makes vivid the constructive and indispensable role played with regard to the reallocation of responsibility by the process or action by which the boundary is changed'.[26] He also suggests later in the chapter that

> ... the answer to the question what a boundary change is and to the question how it releases Arcadia from responsibility is one and the same: a border change ultimately just is reallocation of responsibility concerning the pollutant.[27]

Such a political scenario may well seem plausible, but problems with drawing an analogy to personal boundary change become apparent when we think about the notion of 'reallocation' upon which the account depends. In the personal scenario there is no one to whom we can reallocate responsibility for a wrong that we have committed; the very idea that we might is absurd. In contrast, the need for some political body to be responsible for the pollutant in the political scenario is solved by the fact that the pollutant will now sit on the other side of the border, in a different state. In the personal scenario, however, if boundaries are redrawn in the way Dan-Cohen suggests, the result is that no one is responsible for the wrongdoing. No one can be held to account.

Perhaps this disanalogy is not fatal to the argument. Indeed, we could conceive of a 'no man's land' into which the pollutant becomes situated. Perhaps then no state is responsible. However, there is a more significant disanalogy between Arcadia and the repentant offender concerning the basis for responsibility. The pollutant just happens to be within Arcadia's borders: it does not make sense to make any attribution of fault with respect to the pollutant. The wrongdoing of the offender, however, did not just happen to fall within his boundaries. To suggest that it did would be to deny his moral agency and his freedom to make choices, even if they are bad ones. Indeed, in the case of the offender it does make sense to make ascriptions of fault. Perhaps we might schematically draw a distinction

---

[26] ibid, 122.
[27] ibid, 125.

between X *generating responsibilities* and *being responsible for* X. The former more accurately describes the Arcadian scenario: the pollutant generates responsibilities for Arcadia, but Arcadia is not responsible for the pollutant in any culpable way. The offender, on the other hand, *is* responsible for his wrongdoing in this sense. It may also generate responsibilities (such as making reparation for the harm caused) but responsibility in the personal scenario runs deeper than in the political scenario.

If we imagine a situation where Arcadia might be said to be responsible in the latter, deeper of the two senses, we can see that the political reallocation of responsibility scenario no longer has intuitive appeal. Imagine Arcadia hides landmines in the fields close to its border in an aggressive attempt to stop non-Arcadians from gaining access to its territory. Whilst the minefields are still active, a border change results in them being outside of Arcadia. In this situation, it seems less easy to accept that the neighbouring state now bears full responsibility for these mines. It would sound unacceptable for Arcadian authorities to claim that this other state is now responsible for the mines within its border. The difference here is that the mines are easily attributable to Arcadian action, whereas the pollutant was probably either naturally occurring or a result of complex environmental impacts and factors which are difficult to trace. Possibly, we would want to say that the minefields generate responsibilities for the authorities of the neighbouring state—they should have the protection of their citizens acutely in mind—but we still would not want to say they are responsible *for* the minefields. Arcadia is still responsible *for* them.

However, Dan-Cohen is careful to spell out exactly the relationship he sees holding between what an entity is responsible for, and the entity's boundaries. He claims that it is not the case that Arcadia is responsible for the pollutant because it is on Arcadia's territory:

> Rather than it being the case that a state is responsible for X because X is within its boundaries, it is the other way round: X is said to be within the state's boundary and counts as part of the state insofar as and in the sense that that state bears responsibility for it.[28]

The pollutant is thus understood to be in Arcadia just because Arcadia is responsible for it. If we work this way from responsibility to territory then the intuition would be that the minefields would always be within Arcadia's borders, politically, regardless of what happens geographically to any boundary line. In fact, it would seem that in cases of deep responsibility, it might never be possible to redraw the political boundaries. Yet, this seems to confirm the intuition that deep responsibility in the personal case cannot just be reallocated.

---

[28] ibid.

Further, if we were to accept Dan-Cohen's responsibility-boundary logic for persons nonetheless, we would be left with the result that anything could be within a person's boundary of responsibility just by virtue of his taking responsibility for it. Perhaps this might be plausible for responsibility in a weak sense. For example, if a person takes responsibility for doing the cooking in their household, this entails obligations and 'being the person who does the cooking' comes to constitute part of the person's identity (albeit a very small part). However, we would not want this to be the case for deeper responsibility. With regard to personal responsibility, Dan-Cohen claims that reactive attitudes such as guilt and resentment play a decisive role in defining such responsibility and that by defining one's responsibilities in this way the person is able to 'participate in the construction of a self'.[29] Although this may be true in the sense that we are to some extent shaped by the way we see ourselves, we would not want ascriptions of deep responsibility to depend entirely on whether we or others thought we were responsible. If we were committed to entirely subjective determination, pathological feelings of guilt and responsibility would generate obligations and justify punishment. However, this is highly implausible.

One potential objection that Dan-Cohen acknowledges against his account is that it might be claimed that revisions in the boundaries of the self, although conceivable, never occur. The evidence the objector could offer, he suggests, is that if any offender were asked point blank whether he had done the wrongful act, he would have to affirm that he had, despite having repented. Whilst this is true, in response Dan-Cohen claims: 'It is inappropriate for the truly repentant to dwell on the past misdeed, and the hypothetical interrogator's bringing up the nasty event would be deemed unfair and obtuse'.[30] The social norms that Dan-Cohen alludes to here—those that prevent us from feeling comfortable bringing up the past event with the repentant offender—do in fact seem to operate. However, what generates these norms is not the absence of the offender's responsibility, but rather the extent to which it becomes right to *blame* the repentant offender.[31] If we reinterpret the norms in this light, the problems that arise for Dan-Cohen disappear and, I will argue, a more realistic picture emerges. Further, the understanding of repentance that Dan-Cohen must be relying on is brought to the fore in these comments, and it becomes possible to contrast this with the conception of remorse outlined in Chapter 1.

[29] ibid, 132.
[30] ibid, 128–29.
[31] This point will become key in developing the Responsive Censure argument in Chapter 5.

Why is it inappropriate for the person to ask the offender about her responsibility for the incident if she has repented? Dan-Cohen argues that it is because multiple versions of the self can co-exist, depending on which revisionary practices have occurred and who is observing the individual. Thus: 'if one insists, cruelly or obtusely, on unearthing the older version and on resorting to it, one is not strictly speaking mistaken but merely cruel or obtuse'.[32] However, the language Dan-Cohen uses here might be masking what really is inappropriate about asking the repentant offender now about his responsibility then. Is referring to the responsibility cruel per se? I think it is not.

To illustrate why, suppose that the mother of a young woman who mugged a passer-by decides to gently start talking to her daughter about the event months later. Inquiring into why she had done it, the mother asks about her motivations and feelings at the time, perhaps asking 'darling, but how could *you* have done something like that?' In this scenario the mother is still very much invoking her daughter's responsibility for her offence but, out of love, tries to understand her daughter. Such a scenario does not strike me as cruel or obtuse. The daughter, even having repented, may actually welcome the chance to explore what happened, and why, with her understanding mother. So, reverting to the previous version of the person and inviting discussion about her is not cruel per se. Rather, it seems that what can make interrogation regarding past wrongdoing cruel in the way that Dan-Cohen suggests, and what is absent in the case of the curious mother, is when there is a high level of *blame* implied in and by the questioning. When the offender has repented, continuing to impart strong messages of blame to the offender does seem to be inappropriate and cruel. It is this intuition in particular that I will focus and expand upon in Chapter 5.

Finally, Dan-Cohen's comments concerning the repentant offender's need to resist dwelling on the past highlight the unusual understanding of repentance on which his argument must rely. Consider the following claim that Dan-Cohen makes:

> A serious wrongdoing invariably casts a long shadow over the offender's life in the form of lasting negative attitudes and other consequences. When, due to the operation of the revisionary practices, the shadow disappears, we ought to conclude that its source in the wrongdoer's life has been removed.[33]

However, lasting negative attitudes and lingering shadows are constitutive of remorse. We would be likely to find an offender's purported remorse suspect if it did not involve such attitudes. As Duff says of repentance: 'it will prevent me from enjoying what I would otherwise enjoy. If I truly recognise

32 Dan-Cohen (n 22) 130.
33 ibid, 129.

and repent what I have done, I will not be able to enjoy, for instance, my usual social pleasures'.[34] The shadow remains.

Moreover, remorse requires that one *accept* responsibility for what one has done. But, of course, this does not entail that remorse must also require that one *condones* one's behaviour. In fact, it seems that part of the discomfort of remorse is one's identification with the deed: knowing that one did it (that one was responsible) yet not recognising it as part of who one is. Duff sums up this idea in the following remarks:

> [R]epentance is anyway not something which is done in a moment. It requires a proper understanding of what I have done, which both owns the wrong as mine and disowns it as something I condemn—a determination to improve myself, and to make such apology and restitution as I can.[35]

Duff's claim that repentance is not simply something that is done in a moment is important. Dan-Cohen says nothing about what he actually means by repentance. It cannot mean something similar to what we are calling remorse, as he envisages repentance assuaging an offender's feelings of guilt. So, on Dan-Cohen's account: through repentance the offender removes his responsibility base by ceasing to understand himself as being responsible and, consequently, he ceases to feel guilty. It is hard to understand what repentance is on this reading, other than that it must be an event of some limited duration, since there is a before and after. But everything Dan-Cohen says of repentance could be attributed to something like self-deception or neutralisation.[36] If I convince myself that I was not responsible then I seem to have repented. But such a conception of remorse would appear to lack any moral value. On the contrary, remorse requires an ongoing painful recognition of responsibility.

It would seem, then, that the first possibility—that a remorseful offender might become less blameworthy due to changes in what he is responsible for—cannot be upheld. One cannot divest oneself of the deep responsibility in the same way as one might divest oneself of weaker, 'X generating responsibility'. It is true in a trivial sense that how we see ourselves is how we see ourselves, so that my 'version' of myself would cease to involve responsibility for X if I deceived myself into believing that I was not responsible for X. But Dan-Cohen's analogies were shown to lend no support to this having any serious consequences for punishment. Further, I argued that a remorseful response of value necessarily involves continued acceptance of responsibility and is logically inconsistent with assuaging itself. I argued

---

[34] A Duff 'Punishment And Penance—A Reply To Harrison' in R Harrison and RA Duff, 'Punishment and Crime' (1988) 62 *Proceedings of the Aristotelian Society, Supplementary Volumes* 139, 164.

[35] ibid, 165.

[36] D Matza, *Delinquency and Drift* (New Brunswick, NJ, Transaction Publishers, 1990).

that continued insistence on bringing up the past wrongs of the remorseful offender can be inappropriate, not because he is no longer responsible, but because it can be a mode of blaming which strikes us as excessive.

So, von Hirsch and Ashworth could not make use of the argument that the 'significant changes' in a person constitute a change in his boundaries: they could not argue that the offence does not reflect badly on the 'person he now is' due to elimination of responsibility. This leads us to consider the second way in which we might want to claim that an offender is less blameworthy: in relation to his character.

Blameworthiness as the Moral Assessment of the Offender

The second way we can interpret von Hirsch and Ashworth's argument that over time the offender can change significantly, so that his offence no longer reflects badly on him, is that there is a sense in which the offence no longer shows the offender to be the bad person (or as bad a person as) he was when he committed the crime. On this view, the crime no longer reflects badly on the offender because the 'image' of the offence-committing offender and the picture of the changed offender are not the same.

As noted, von Hirsch and Ashworth's Time Delay argument suggests that there might be an important disparity between what the offender was like at the time of the offence, and what he is like after a significant passage of time. Having ruled out the possibility of the offender ceasing to be responsible for the offence, we instead must look to what he is like as a person—the attitudes he holds and so on. The argument might be that at the time of the crime, the offender was blameworthy for the complete lack of concern he demonstrated towards another human being and the messages of contempt that his action communicated. Over time, and (or) as a result of remorse, this lack of concern is replaced with compassion, and the derisory messages retracted. He is much less reprehensible as a person now as compared to then.

However, the claim that such an understanding of reduced blameworthiness—as an assessment of the reprehensibility of the person—should justify mitigating the offender's sentence is not convincing. Although this diachronic 'moral assessment' is a coherent idea in itself—we *can* judge a person's changing attitudes to be morally better or worse—it does not give us what we need to fully support an argument for mitigation based on remorse, unless we were to adopt a version of character retributivism. For remorse to reduce punishment on the grounds of an improved score on his general moral assessment, calibrating punishment based on a general moral assessment of the offender would have to be integral to the justifying aim of that punishment, as it is in character retributivism.

Character retributivism is the view that punishment should be delivered in proportion to a person's 'inner viciousness'.[37] On such an account the court would have to assess the whole of the person's being: his hopes, desires, attitudes. However, character retributivism does not have much contemporary support, for both practical and normative reasons. First, it is impossible for the state to know and consider all of the elements of the offender's heart and mind that bear on his degree of viciousness. Further, if character were to be assessed following the offence, the offender's blameworthiness could change daily or even hourly. One day he could be experiencing compassion towards all he encounters and the next he may be full of hate and malice. Viciousness is too capricious a phenomenon to constitute the means by which deserved punishment is determined, unless it were tied tightly to the viciousness displayed in the act. But an assessment of the viciousness displayed in the act is essentially an assessment of culpability, and is accordingly temporally bounded. Finally, from a normative perspective, character retributivism is considered too intrusive for a liberal state required to respect the autonomy of its citizens. As Tasioulas argues: 'After all, how can we be autonomous centres of decision-making if every aspect of our thoughts, motivations and character traits is liable to be held up to public scrutiny with the severity of the sentence hanging in the balance?'[38] So, the claim that remorse affects our general assessment of the offender's moral character would, in order to have any consequences for punishment, need to be coupled with adherence to an unattractive and seldom supported theory of punishment.

One final problem with any suggestion of the offender's reduced blameworthiness, whether due to modified responsibility or improvements in character, is that it invites the suggestion that the person who becomes less blameworthy should therefore feel less bad about what he or she did. This is in tension with what is central to remorse—full acceptance of responsibility for the harm caused.

CONCLUSION

The Changed Person argument does not justify mitigating the remorseful offender's punishment unless character retributivism is accepted. Given that character retributivism is not a desirable view, we must look elsewhere for

---

[37] JG Murphy, 'Remorse, Apology, and Mercy' (2006) 4 *Ohio State Journal of Criminal Law* 423.

[38] J Tasioulas, 'Repentance and the Liberal State' (2006) 4 *Ohio State Journal of Criminal Law* 487, 504.

an argument to justify remorse-based mitigation. Central to much more persuasive retributive theories is the claim that the offender's punishment must be in proportion to the seriousness of the offence. The more serious the offence, the more punishment deserved. In the next chapter I consider one way that remorse might lessen the seriousness of the offence and hence the punishment deserved: if an offender's remorse were to result in reduced harm, then he should accordingly receive less punishment.

3

The Reduced Harm Argument

The judge had before him, as we have, a letter from the victim's mother, asking
that a non-custodial sentence be passed ... The victim's father gave evidence
before the judge, indicating that he had seen the appellant regularly since the
accident and talked through it and how each of them were coping. He believed
that the appellant was full of remorse and felt sorry for what the appellant was
going through. Contact with the appellant had in fact helped himself and his
wife cope with the loss of their son. He felt that the appellant going to jail would
or could have a devastating impact on his wife.[1]

T
HE DEGREE OF harm that an offence causes or risks, in combination with the offender's culpability, determines the seriousness
of the offence. The greater the harm caused or risked, *ceteris pari-
bus*, the more serious the offence and the more severe the commensurate
punishment. The harm created by an offence can come in many forms—
physical, psychological, financial—and different offences cause different
combinations and degrees of harm. The above quotation suggests that
remorse might reduce some of the psychological harm experienced by the
victim or the victim's family. Indeed, in this case, the positive effects of com-
muning with the remorseful offender are apparently so pronounced that
the parents of the victim entreat the judge to pass a non-custodial sentence
so they can continue to alleviate some of their emotional distress through
contact with the remorseful offender.

If it were the case that remorse could reduce the harm of an offence,
then this would have important implications for sentencing, since remorse
could then serve to reduce the seriousness of the offence; in turn, this would
mean that the offender deserved a lesser punishment for the offence. In this
chapter, I draw on von Hirsch and Jareborg's Living Standard analysis of
harm to examine the claim that the Reduced Harm argument could justify
remorse-based mitigation.[2] I first examine what is meant by the harm of

---

[1] *R v Coren Paul Andrew Hardy* [2002] EWCA Crim 188 (AC) 14.
[2] A von Hirsch and N Jareborg, 'Gauging Criminal Harm: A Living-Standard Analysis'
(1991) 11 *Oxford Journal of Legal Studies* 1.

the offence, and assess whether remorse has any impact on this dimension. I then ask whether any such effect is relevant for sentencing purposes. I will construct the strongest argument for the thesis that remorse does reduce the harm of the offence in a way that justifies mitigation. I will then address objections and conclude that, although an offender's remorse can in some cases have a beneficial effect on the victim, any such effects are highly contingent on facts about the precise nature of the harm and the victim's relationship with it. The Reduced Harm argument would therefore not justify remorse-based mitigation as a universal principle. Further, mitigation based on voluntary reparation captures much of what is to be taken into account here.

I finally consider the wider conception of reduced harm as reduced wrongdoing and argue that, although remorse may, under certain circumstances, provide *evidence* of reduced culpability, it cannot retroactively change the offender's state of mind at the time of the offence.

To begin, I bring to the reader's attention the fact that there is disagreement about whether the *harm* of the offence should be used as the principle designator of its seriousness. Whilst many retributivists believe that harm, in addition to culpability, captures everything that is relevant to the gravity of an offence, there are some who argue that such an approach fails to comprehensively take into account the *wrong* that was done in carrying out the offence. Whether this is really a substantive disagreement rather than a merely semantic one is beyond the purpose of this chapter. However, I introduce the debate below to draw the reader's attention to the scope of the account of criminal harm that I discuss and in order to pre-empt the objection that it is too narrow: Von Hirsch and Jareborg's Living Standard analysis of harm captures more than just material and psychological injury. I return to the implications of transferring the emphasis from harm to wrongdoing at the end of the chapter.

CRIMINAL HARM AND WRONGDOING

The 'harm versus wrong' disagreement arises within a more general debate about whether an act's being harmful is necessary and sufficient for criminalisation. The answer to this question would, correspondingly, appear to have consequences for the way in which we should assess the seriousness of an offence—on the features relevant to its gravity.

The claim that an act's being harmful is necessary for criminalisation seems to be intuitively plausible. Indeed, such a view is in harmony with the libertarian tradition according to which agents may only be justifiably restrained from acting if their act is *harmful* to another. This view is enshrined in John Stuart Mill's famous 'harm principle', according to which 'The only purpose for which power can be rightfully exercised over any member of a civilized community, against his will, is to prevent harm to others'.[3] However, closer consideration suggests that we also have intuitions that support the opposing view. Those who claim that harm is not a necessary condition for criminalisation often support their claim by pointing to hypothetical scenarios that involve a wrong that causes no harm, but where we seem to have the intuition that the wrong should be criminalised. I shall introduce such a case below; at this point though, it should be acknowledged that consideration of such cases leads some theorists to supplement or replace considerations of harm with those of wrongs or violations of deontological rights in their accounts of what is centrally at stake when an offence is committed.

The suggestion that harm does not capture everything relevant to seriousness is also hinted at in the sentencing literature. Even those who conceptualise offence seriousness as being determined by the harm of the offence and the culpability of the offender acknowledge that harm is not always a rich enough concept to capture what we should take into account when determining the seriousness of an offence. Summing up this sentiment, Ashworth writes:

> [T]he violation of a protected interest is one key component of offence-seriousness, often expressed as harm or harmfulness but also including the concept of a wrong, since it is not merely the physical or psychological consequences but also the *nature of the wrong* done to the victim that is relevant in assessing seriousness.[4]

Let us conceive of an act that might plausibly seem to be wrong but which involves no harm. Imagine a stranger takes and returns your car without your knowledge or consent, but who does so in order to fill it up with petrol and fit new brake pads. In this scenario, it is hard to see what *harm* is done to you, presuming that you had no need of your car whilst it was in the stranger's possession (suppose that you were on holiday overseas at the time)—at least, your subjective wellbeing has not been impaired and your possessions remain the same in number and value. Whilst some would maintain that the mere appropriation of property—even for benevolent purposes—constitutes a harm of sorts as well as a wrong, expanding the notion of harm to incorporate infringement of rights has the result that all wrongdoing is also harmful.[5] Whether this is conceptually defensible is open for debate and may, in part, depend on the theory of criminalisation that one adopts.

Von Hirsch and Jareborg's account of how harm should be conceptualised for the purposes of sentencing is one example of this extensive use of

---

[3] JS Mill, 'On Liberty' in J Gray and GW Smith (eds), *J.S. Mill, On Liberty, in Focus* (London, Routledge, 1991) 30.

[4] A Ashworth, *Sentencing and Criminal Justice*, 5th edn (Cambridge, Cambridge University Press, 2010) 109, emphasis added.

[5] See generally H Stewart, 'The Limits of the Harm Principle' (2010) 4 *Criminal Law and Philosophy* 17.

the term 'harm'. On von Hirsch and Jareborg's understanding, there was a harm done in the above example of the stranger taking your car, in the form of a violation of your interest domain of privacy/autonomy. In comparison, others might understand this scenario more squarely in terms of a violation of rights, distinguishing such a violation from notions of harm. Again, I am not taking a position on this here.

Von Hirsch and Jareborg provide the most comprehensive treatment of harm in relation to sentencing. It is on their account that I will focus to frame the discussion of whether there is any plausible way in which remorse might reduce the harm of an offence. Even if there is disagreement about the extension of the labels 'harm' and 'wrong', their inclusive interpretation of harm will at least not leave anything relevant out, even if their labels could be contested.

THE LIVING STANDARD ANALYSIS OF HARM

Different offences harm victims in different ways, since they can involve intrusions into various personal resources or interests that people have. Von Hirsch and Jareborg aim to find and articulate guiding principles that can be used to assess the various relevant interests involved. They suggest that the most natural organising concept in this domain pertains to the quality of a person's life. They write: 'The most important interests are those central to personal well-being; and, accordingly, the most grievous harms are those which drastically diminish one's standard of well-being'.[6] They term this guiding concept the 'living standard' and they intend it to include not only material support and amenity, but also other non-economic capabilities that affect the quality of a person's life.

Von Hirsch and Jareborg suggest that harms can be gauged according to the extent to which they affect someone's living standard. To assess this, von Hirsch and Jareborg appeal to a grading scheme that consists of four living standard levels: level one is categorised as 'subsistence', level two as 'minimal well-being', level three as 'adequate well-being' and level four as 'enhanced well-being'.[7] Offences can comprise intrusions into interests required to maintain any of these levels. The most serious offences intrude into interests required for subsistence (level one); an example of such an offence would be murder. Intrusions that only marginally affect the living standard, and do not prevent the victim from maintaining an adequate life would be ranked at level four (enhanced well-being). An example of such an intrusion would be the theft of a small amount of money.

---

[6] von Hirsch and Jareborg (n 2) 7.

[7] ibid, 17. For a description of each living standard level, see ibid, 17. Detailed knowledge of every concept employed by von Hirsch and Jareborg will not be necessary to follow my argument. Where detail is required, it will be elaborated in the discussion.

In these examples—murder and petty theft—the two intrusions involved are of different types (and operate at different living standard levels). The difference in type arises from the fact that the intrusions affect different dimensions of well-being; the former intrusion comprises (fatal) damage to physical well-being, whereas the latter is a (very minor) dent to financial well-being. Von Hirsch and Jareborg suggest four generic-interest dimensions that can be intruded upon, which they believe the state has reason to protect. These are: 'physical integrity', 'material support and amenity', 'freedom from humiliation' and 'privacy/autonomy'.[8] Different offences will intrude upon one or more of these interests, and to different degrees. For example, assault affects the victim's physical integrity and his freedom from humiliation, whereas burglary mainly affects the victim's privacy and his material possessions.[9]

How Might Remorse Repair a Victim's Living Standard?

Only one of the generic-interest dimensions that von Hirsch and Jareborg delineate seems to have any potential for being affected by the victim's awareness of the offender's remorse. Remorse could do nothing to repair a victim's physical integrity—bodily wounds will heal no more quickly. Nor could remorse enhance the material support and amenity the victim enjoys—barring acts of reparation, which go beyond an offender expressing his remorse, the property the victim owns remains unchanged.[10] Privacy and autonomy are also not affected: the offender's remorse does not revoke any intrusion into the victim's personal space; nor does it render any of the criminal activity of the victim's choosing.

However, if a victim is made aware of the offender's remorse, he may no longer feel humiliated by the earlier offence. Von Hirsch and Jareborg explain that freedom from humiliation—or 'degrading treatment'—'refers to those injuries to self-respect that derive from others' mistreatment'.[11] The perception that victimising criminal activity sends a message to the victim that may result in his feeling humiliated or losing self-respect occurs elsewhere in writings on retribution. For instance, Murphy argues that victims often perceive part of the harm of the offence to be the insult or degradation

---

[8] ibid, 19. For a description of each interest dimension, see ibid, 20. Again, detailed knowledge of every concept employed von Hirsch and Jareborg will not be necessary to follow my argument. Where detail is required, it will be elaborated in the discussion.

[9] ibid, 19.

[10] As noted in Chapter 1, genuine remorse will be likely to inspire reparative efforts and apology. However, the focus here must be on the expression of remorse itself as not all offences will be amenable to material redress.

[11] von Hirsch and Jareborg (n 2) 20.

that the offence symbolically communicates.[12] On Murphy's account, the offender is understood to send a message to the victim through the offence, saying that the victim is inferior and exploitable. This causes the victim distress; in some cases, the victim may even feel that he is inferior and exploitable, and come to blame himself for the harm suffered.[13] However, on Murphy's view, if the offender repents, then the message is withdrawn and some of the harm lessened. Hampton espouses a similar conception of the symbolic communication, suggesting that the 'insult' conveyed by the offender can prompt the victim to question his own value, conceiving that the victimising conduct was somehow justified by his lack of worth.[14]

So, if such perceptions do indeed play out in the experiences of victims, it is possible that remorse might reverse, undercut or counterbalance the message that the criminal behaviour communicated. Knowing that the offender is remorseful could serve to reaffirm a victim's sense of worth—perhaps the victim thinks: 'the offender is (justifiably) feeling bad because he wronged *me* ... he sees me as valuable enough to dwell on the harm he caused me and to regret it'. Thus, the victim may no longer feel humiliated as he ceases feeling worthless.

The Living Standard Time Frame

If we grant that remorse may have the effect of reducing or eliminating the humiliation a victim of an offence feels, we still need to consider whether this can be relevant for sentencing. One source of uncertainty with respect to this relates to the temporal perspective of von Hirsch and Jareborg's Living Standard analysis. They consider what sort of temporal perspective should be adopted in order to appropriately judge the impact of an offence on a victim's well-being, concluding that a mid-term perspective is suitable: 'The appropriate perspective is a middle-term one—something approximating "How has your year been?"'[15] This is appropriate given that living standard judgements are intended to relate to the global quality of a person's life.

So, when assessing the intrusion into the physical integrity of an assault victim, for example, their approach requires that we think longer term than

---

[12] JG Murphy, *Getting Even: Forgiveness and Its Limits* (Oxford, Oxford University Press, 2003).

[13] This latter sort of distress is more plausibly associated with some offences than others. For instance, it is commonly reported that victims of rape and domestic abuse engage in this self-reproach. However, if someone burgles my house, it will cause me distress, but I won't normally blame myself.

[14] J Hampton, 'Forgiveness, Resentment and Hatred' in JG Murphy and J Hampton, *Forgiveness and Mercy* (Cambridge, Cambridge University Press, 1988).

[15] von Hirsch and Jareborg (n 2) 22.

just whether the victim was bleeding and in pain on the night of the offence. Perhaps—and I speculate—pain and bruising would have to persist for at least a month or so in order to qualify as significantly affecting one's year in terms of physical well-being. Or, if the pain inflicted was so severe, even though it may not persist much beyond the assault, it may constitute the most excruciating physical experience of the victim's year. Accordingly, von Hirsch and Jareborg point out that 'a physical assault, and its immediate trauma, may soon be over; yet if the experience was painful or humiliating enough, it may still loom large in the evaluation of, say, the quality of a whole year's experience'.[16] Although the experience must be detrimental to the victim's living standard from the perspective of the proposed time frame in order to be significant, it must be remembered that this time frame remains mid-term. If, in four years time, the victim cannot even remember what pain or injury he sustained from the assault, this does not detract from the significance it had within the year that immediately followed.

To return to the freedom from humiliation dimension in view of this discussion, it seems plausible to claim that any humiliation that affects the victim's well-being for many months might be alleviated were he to be made aware of his assailant's remorse. Moreover, the above remarks from von Hirsch and Jareborg attest to their belief that it could, in some cases, principally be the humiliation precipitated by an assault—'painful *or* humiliating enough'—that diminishes the victim's living standard, from the mid-term perspective. The harm that can potentially be forestalled by remorse, therefore, is not insignificant. The victim may in fact (although perhaps not virtuously) feel a sense of power in the face of the offender's remorse: it is now the offender who experiences humiliation.

Thus, from a mid-term perspective, the effect of the offender's remorse on the victim's living standard may be significant. In order to complete the argument that remorse could mitigate the seriousness of the offence, one final step is required: we must establish that, if knowledge of remorse reduces the harm done to the 'freedom from humiliation' interest dimension, then this serves to mitigate the seriousness of the offence. I shall now consider some challenges to this conditional claim. In particular I shall argue that the view that the harm is 'set' at the time of the offence limits the extent to which post-offence conduct can be said to reduce harm. *Pace* arguments that appear to reject what I call the Set Harm view, I show why this view is theoretically and practically necessary for sentencing. I conclude that there may be some limited cases in which remorse might reduce the psychological harm of the offence, but that these will be rare. Further, I demonstrate that the particular concept of humiliation that von Hirsch and Jareborg employ for the purpose of harm assessment at sentencing is even more limiting.

---

[16] ibid.

Distinguishing Between Time Frames

The claim that remorse reduces the harm of the offence can be challenged to some extent by the fact that remorse can emerge long after the harmful act occurred. This fact might tempt us to argue (contrary to the conditional claim introduced above) that whilst subsequent remorse may have some beneficial effects for the victim, the harm of the offence itself is nonetheless set at the time it occurred. According to this view, although the harmful *effects* of the offence may continue to reverberate in the life of the victim, this harm emanates from the day of the offence. The offender can do nothing to alter the fact that a certain amount of harm was set in motion on that day. Call this the Set Harm view.

The first thing to clarify about the Set Harm view is that it is, perhaps despite appearances, compatible with von Hirsch and Jareborg's approach, which assesses harm from the perspective of a whole year. To see this, we must disentangle the two distinct temporal dimensions involved in judgements of harm. On the one hand, there is the duration of the offence itself; on the other, there is the time frame from which we should view the importance of the offence and the effects it has on the living standard of the victim. On the Set Harm view, it cannot be the case that the seriousness of the offence continues to be established throughout the year, and that subsequent actions of the offender can accordingly increase or decrease the harm of the offence. However, even if the extent of the harm has been *set* at the time of the offence—at the time of the punches or appropriation of the victim's property—this is not incompatible with the claim that some harmful effects (and their significance) *only become completely clear* after some time; the passage of time reveals how much harm was set by the offence. To illustrate, if an assault victim becomes distressed weeks after the offence, it is not the case that the offence must therefore still be ongoing, still generating new harms. Rather, the assault set up the conditions such that the victim would come to be distressed. Although this harm did not become evident until weeks later, its aetiology dates back to the punches that were thrown during the assault. But the assault itself is over, the act complete. Even if the full harm becomes known only later it is not the case that the offence is still occurring.

A question remains about how we are to determine the time frame of the offence. To a large degree, this will be more or less intuitive and comes down to how the act is individuated, which may be somewhat arbitrary. To assess how much harm a particular act caused, we must know the boundaries of this act so that we consider all and only its consequences. We can make this clearer if we think about the theft of a sum of money. Imagine that an offender stole £100 from a house. He climbed in through an open window, leaving no damage whatsoever. That evening, for one reason or another, he returns the money to the victim. What is the harm of the offence? The answer depends on how we individuate the offence and the acts it comprises. It could be argued that the acts constituting the offence involved stealing £100 and so this constitutes the degree of harm. On this narrow reading, the act of returning the money is outside the boundaries of the set of acts that constituted the offence. As such, although it may be appropriate to claim that returning the money would *compensate* the victim, it cannot alter the fact that the offence caused a harm of a particular extent (loss of £100), and thus cannot *itself* be reduced. That the money was later returned does not mean that the offender stole less money.

For the harm *of the offence* to be lessened by the returning of the money, this latter act must be within the boundaries of the offence: we must individuate the offence as comprising the acts that involve the taking and the returning of the money. This would make the totality of the relevant acts akin to an aborted attempt. However, such an extended perspective on the boundaries of the offence becomes implausible once the criminal behaviour itself is discontinued. For example, as long as the offender in our example is on the victim's premises, he is arguably still committing the offence; however, as soon as he leaves and pursues alternative activities, it seems clear that he is no longer committing the offence, and thus that its harm has been established.

As noted above, how we individuate acts in these cases is, to a large extent, arbitrary. But, offences often have clear elements described by the *actus reus* and, as such, the time frame of the offence will be set accordingly. One final point to note about the time frame of the (narrowly individuated) offence is that, when we ask how much harm the offence caused, this question does not restrict us to considering only the harm that was *experienced* at the time of its commission. The harmful impact of the offence and the boundaries of the offence do not have to be temporally coextensive. Some offences are only discovered after their commission and the harms are therefore experienced later. Thus, the narrow individuation entailed by the Set Harm view does not prevent us from distinguishing between the harm experienced by the victim *as the offence is being committed* and the harm experienced *as a result of the offence being committed*. However, both will be relevant to determining the seriousness of the offence. The point is simply that the amount of harm that the offence has caused or will cause is set during the narrowly individuated offence.

Challenging the Set Harm View

Having distinguished the two time frames—that of the offence itself and that from which we assess the significance of the consequences of the offence—we can now ask whether remorse might reduce the harm caused by the offence itself, contrary to the Set Harm view outlined above. To do this, I will analyse Smith's Time-Release theory of harm, and argue that, for most types of harm, the Set Harm view must be correct. Whilst remorse might, in limited cases, affect the persistence of some aspects of psychological harm, thus providing a challenge to the Set Harm view in these cases, the scope for mitigation is limited by their rarity and the practical difficulties that arise if an indeterminate concept of harm is employed at sentencing.

Nick Smith has recently argued that categorical apologies can reduce many of the harms associated with an offence.[17] The time frame distinction I drew above is of particular importance in clarifying aspects of his argument. Smith proposes a 'time-release theory of harm', according to which the offending 'unfolds over time along various vectors of harm'.[18] Adopting such a theory (as he argues we should) would have the consequence that apologies can reduce the harm and, correspondingly, the seriousness of the offence. A less serious offence begets reduced punishment, and so apology-based mitigation should be part of the retributive calculation, on Smith's view.

To illustrate the Time-Release theory of harm, Smith invokes cases of sexual violence. In such cases, only some of the harm caused occurs during the physical attack. Other harms, he claims, 'come in waves after the offender has fled and continue crashing against the victim'.[19] As noted above, the harms of some offences, particularly those with enduring effects on the victim's state of mind, may not fully materialise until well after the offender has fled. Certainly, the extent of the harm caused will only be clear after some time in many cases. Indeed, this is precisely why von Hirsch and Jareborg argue for adopting a mid-term perspective on the extent and significance of the harm caused by an offence. Again, just because the harm comes in waves following the offence, this does not change the fact that these waves were generated at the time of the offence. The offending set in motion a causal chain which, if left unattended, delivers harm for months beyond its inception.

However, Smith makes the case that some harms of offending can be stopped in their tracks by an apology and, further, that there are ways in which the offender *continues* to harm the victim if he does not apologise.[20] In the former situation, a harm is set in motion but can be reduced by apology. Without apology, this harm does not get worse as such, but it unfolds and persists. According to the latter possibility, a harm is exacerbated by a lack of apology—it becomes worse and worse until the offender apologises.

---

[17] N Smith, *Justice Through Apologies: Remorse, Reform, and Punishment* (Cambridge, Cambridge University Press, 2014) 17–38. Smith has developed an account of categorical apologies and their necessary and sufficient criteria. The elements I identified as essential to remorse are all captured in Smith's 13 features of the categorical apology but additional elements are also included. I therefore use apologies and remorse interchangeably whilst discussing his view, but note that his apologies involve additional elements.

[18] ibid, 156.
[19] ibid.
[20] ibid.

Of course, some vectors of harms, once set in motion, cannot be altered by remorse or apology. As I pointed out above, even if the full extent of a physical harm does not become clear until months or years after the offence, the harm cannot be stopped in its tracks by apology. Imagine that the victim of a serious assault suffers an aneurism as a direct result years later. Although it is true that the harm in a sense unfolds over time, it is not the case that the victim could reduce this harm (through apology nor any other conceivable means). Furthermore, Smith's claim that the lack of apology 'continues' the harm of the offence is slightly problematic in its application to an assault case, in so far as the term 'continue' might be understood to imply that the lack of apology propagates the same kind of harm. It seems clear that this need not be the case. For instance, in the aneurysm example it seems clear that the offender exerts no continued causal impact on the physical dimension of the victim's well-being, even if the harm of the assault is only being revealed now. The harm caused by a lack of apology, if any, is certainly not the same as the physical harm caused by the assault.

The harms caused by damage or destruction of property of high personal value will also persist regardless of any attempts at compensation. Again, even if the loss of the property becomes significant much further down the line, it is not the case that the offender is still inflicting harm on the victim. Rather, the harm that was caused *at the time of the offence* becomes salient later and nothing can be done to forestall this particular vector of harm.

To see the ways in which Smith thinks apology can reduce harm, we need to identify the various 'vectors of harm' that he thinks can be forestalled by apology or exacerbated by lack of apology. Smith provides many examples, which can broadly be classified as pertaining to psychological vectors of harm, and community vectors of harm. Smith suggests that an apology can reduce the harm of the offence to the extent that an apology can correct the victim's belief that she was at fault (if such a belief is present), assuage her fear of re-victimisation, and put an end to her continued experience of degradation by the offender. He further suggests that apology can reduce the harm done to the wider community in terms of the pain associated with protracted efforts to learn what happened and why, and the 'generalized anxiety'[21] produced by the perception of eroding legal and moral authority.

Smith identifies three main ways in which apology can have these harm-reducing effects. First, he suggests that *corroborating the factual record* goes a long way to reducing the victim's fear of re-victimisation—'Who did this? Why? Will they do it again?'[22]—and the pain associated with the uncertainty involved in protracted court proceedings. Second, he suggests that *accepting blame* can exonerate the victim from thinking she deserves fault for the injury.[23] Finally, he suggests that a failure to apologise

---

[21] ibid, 158.
[22] ibid, 156.
[23] ibid, 156–157.

exacerbates the harm of degradation: 'I harm you because I find you and your dignity subordinate to mine'.[24] Smith claims that the failure to apologise exerts a 'continued affront' to the victim: 'the longer it goes on the worse it becomes'.[25] When the offender accepts blame, he 'puts an end to some aspects of this stream of harm'. Accepting blame, according to Smith, also has the effect of reinforcing the legal and moral authority of the values in question. In apologising, the offender ends the vector of generalised anxiety triggered by the belief that one's world is collapsing.

Even if Smith is correct to claim that these are ways in which apologies can reduce harm, we should acknowledge that his claims here have limited scope. Consider the claim that corroborating the factual record can reduce harm. Notice first that an offender's corroborating the factual record will normally amount to a guilty plea. Yet, in recognition that the offender's guilty plea often prevents the pain associated with a protracted court process, many jurisdictions already grant mitigation for a guilty plea. Crucially, receipt of this mitigation is not dependent on evidence of remorse or apology. Furthermore, the fear of re-victimisation is only likely to be reduced significantly for those who suffered a personal attack by someone they knew. When the offender is unknown to the victim and the victim was not personally targeted, a detailed confession from the offender explaining what he did and why will do little to alleviate a heightened fear of crime. Indeed, it could have the opposite effect: 'if this stranger was able to attack me then perhaps others will too'. This is also true of the harm-reducing powers of *reform*.[26] Believing that the offender will not harm once again will not always allay the worry that someone else might. Indeed, far from alleviating the 'specter of the violent unknown',[27] an explanation of how the offender can come to commit the offence may increase the fear of others, whose possible intentions remain unknown.

Consider now Smith's claim that the acceptance of blame can exonerate the victim from thinking she deserves fault for the injury. Whilst this might be true for offences such as rape, the feeling that one deserved to be victimised is not an experience common to all offences, as Smith acknowledges. Although remorse or apology may reduce this vector of harm where it occurs, it often does not constitute the greatest part of the harm of an offence, if it constitutes any of the harm at all.

Finally, consider Smith's claim that, in apologising, the offender ends the vector of generalised anxiety triggered by the belief that one's world is collapsing. Whilst this again is an empirical claim in need of support, it is not clear to me that the generalised anxiety associated with increases in violent

[24] ibid.
[25] ibid.
[26] See ibid, 158.
[27] ibid, 156.

crime can really be assuaged by the apology of one offender. Further, if many offenders apologise in a context of generalised anxiety, the community may instead be troubled by the apparent frequency with which mostly law-respecting individuals can slip into anxiety-inducing crime.

In addition to the harm reduction that apology can bring about, Smith suggests that '*commensurate redress*' 'stops the clock' on harm.[28] Correspondingly, 'the offender providing redress deserves less punishment than the unapologetic offender because she commits a lesser offence'. Again though, it only seems plausible to claim that redress can 'stop the clock' on certain types of harm. Although the true extent of any harm may only become clearer over the course of time, as I argued above, some harms are set at the time of the offence and are unchangeable; this is most obviously true for physical harms.

That said, the inevitability of other harms is less determined, and remorse and apology might be able to influence these harms to a certain extent. This is most true of psychological harms such as feeling humiliated or degraded. It seems likely that these harms (unlike the harm of increased fear of crime, which may dissipate over time and be unaffected by apology) loom larger as time goes on. Certainly, the longer they persist the longer they will have knock-on effects on other aspects of the victim's life. Accordingly, we might agree with Smith that apology can serve to reduce these particular kinds of harm.

However, if Smith is right to claim that these particular kinds of harm might continue to be exerted until the offender apologises (unlike physical injury, for example, which is set at the time of the offence), then this presents an important practical problem for any sentencing regime that must make an assessment of the harm of the offence at the time of sentencing. The problem sentencers face is that it is not possible to know whether the offender will put a stop to this kind of harm tomorrow, in a year or never. The idea that the harm of the offence is still being determined (and not just continuing to unfold) in the way that Smith implies thus makes the assessment of the harm caused by an offence at the time of sentencing impossible.

In light of the indeterminacy of harm over time, it seems that we need to draw a line.[29] Although the offender's remorse might go some way to assuaging the victim's continued feelings of humiliation and worthlessness, the offence itself nonetheless constructed conditions such that the victim would (in the absence of remorse) have experienced humiliation. Had there been no known remorseful response from the offender, the victim's

---

[28] ibid, 158.

[29] Restorative justice perspectives would be much less concerned with determining the precise level of harm of the offence, and would instead focus on how a remorseful apology might alleviate the victim's ongoing harm. From a retributive perspective, however, we need to make an assessment about the seriousness of the offence so that we know how much censure/punishment is deserved.

humiliation may have loomed large in the evaluation of the quality of his year. Moreover, if the humiliation at the time of the offence was particularly severe, then it may still be maximally significant from the mid-term perspective, despite not persisting. Since the offender's remorse does not occur during the commission of the offence,[30] it cannot eliminate the *potential* that was created by the offence for a reduction to the living standard of the victim.

Harm Reduction and Risked Harms

There remains another possible way of re-estimating the post-remorse harm of an offence in line with accepted practice in criminal law. If the victim's awareness of the offender's remorse forestalls persisting humiliation, then perhaps such circumstances should be seen as akin to aborted attempts or offences where there is greater harm risked than actually transpired.

However, there is a problem with drawing comparisons between post-remorse harm reduction and aborted attempts that render this line of thought unpersuasive. The problem is that the concept of 'attempt' is misapplied in this context, since in the case of post-remorse harm reduction we are considering the harms of an offence that was not merely attempted but in fact successfully *completed* offence. The remorseful offender who committed an assault still assaulted their victim; the offence was not aborted and it did not fail. The subsequent alleviation of some of the effects of the offence does not change the status of the offence itself. All elements of the offence are present, so the offence is complete. To suggest otherwise would again be to confuse the duration of the offence with the importance of the experience from the overall mid-term perspective.

The concepts of endangerment and risk creation may seem to have more purchase. Indeed, von Hirsch and Jareborg explain how their model makes room for discounts for threatened or risked harms. They claim 'Many crimes only create a threat or risk to a given interest. Their harm rating should depend not only on the importance of the interest but the degree to which it was risked'.[31] To illustrate, suppose that an offender creates the risk of substantial humiliation, but then prevents it from materialising by remorsefully revoking the messages of degradation. This scenario might be understood as involving an offender risking or threatening humiliation. However, on such an understanding there are still temporal issues to resolve. It would have to be decided within what time frame a domain of harm could still be modulated by the offender such that it was only risked or threatened. Often

---

[30] But see A Duff, *Punishment, Communication and Community* (Oxford, Oxford University Press, 2001) 120–21. Duff discusses the case of the immediately repentant offender. I examine how remorse might provide evidence of reduced culpability below.

[31] von Hirsch and Jareborg (n 2) 30.

a considerable quantity of the humiliation will be experienced at the time of the offence. The difficulty in placing temporal limits on a post-offence downgrade from actual to risked harm again highlights the distance of the remorseful response from the elements of the offence.

Furthermore, it does not seem plausible to claim that such allowances could be permitted in other domains of harm. If an offender returns the stolen goods this constitutes reparation, not transformation of the offence into a risked threat to the interest dimension of material support. It would, if anything, provide the basis for an argument for mitigation outside the assessment of the offence's seriousness. The beneficial effects of apology might be better seen as a form of emotional reparation rather than as diminishment of the seriousness of the offence itself.

Humiliation on the Living Standard Account

So far, I have employed an intuitive understanding of the psychological elements of harm in order to discuss the scope of Smith's view. However, it should be noted that, in order to promote consistency in sentencing, theorists are often careful to define and delimit the factors that should be taken into account. Indeed, it is for these sorts of reasons that von Hirsch and Jareborg present a conception of humiliation that is less contingent on the victim's subjective experiences. Accordingly, their conception does not lend itself easily to the arguments I have discussed in relation to Smith's Time-Release theory of harm. If their view were to be adopted, the scope for mitigation would be even more limited. Recall the perspective (noted above) employed by Murphy and Hampton. They explain how the commission of an offence sends out an insult or message of degradation to the victim. It was suggested that this leads the victim to feel humiliated and without self-worth. Knowledge of the offender's remorse, it was suggested, can retract the message and enable the offender to regain his self-esteem.

Given their remarks about humiliation, it is questionable whether von Hirsch and Jareborg have in mind such abstract exchanges of messages such as these. The first clue to this is that they seem only to regard *violent* offences as damaging the interest of freedom from humiliation.[32] They state that this interest is 'affected by a variety of criminal acts, from physical assault to verbal harassment'.[33] Moreover, when they apply their living standard analysis to hypothetical cases, it is only in relation to violent offences that they cite the interest of freedom from humiliation as having

---

[32] Although, at odds with features of their examples, they do say that 'the idea of humiliation and the idea of loss of privacy are closely related: if one's privacy is intruded upon, one is almost necessarily somewhat humiliated', ibid, 32.

[33] ibid, 20.

been intruded upon.[34] This is in contrast to the view espoused by Murphy and Hampton, who would consider messages of degradation as also being sent out by the offender who, for example, ransacks a person's house: 'You do not matter enough to me to prevent me from doing what I like with your possessions'.

Looking more closely at some of von Hirsch and Jareborg's examples we can begin to understand why their concept of humiliation is closely tied to violent offences, and in so doing better understand their interpretation of the concept. They say that what makes a beating 'deeply humiliating' is the victim's 'being put at someone else's mercy. The person beaten is literally abased—knocked down, abused—and the beater establishes direct *physical* dominion over him'.[35] This focus on the physical relationship of the victim and the offender is different from, although not incompatible with, the offender assuming an elevated status of worth in relation to the victim.

In von Hirsch and Jareborg's above example, we can imagine the offender sneering at the frightened, bleeding victim, smirking at his situation. This contrasts with the more subtle message that Murphy and Hampton envisage. The burglar may have no thoughts about the victim, but his behaviour suggests that he does not see the victim as being of significance. This is the insulting aspect of the message—'I don't have to think about you, I can just do as I please'—and not necessarily a triumphant display of brute power.

Attention to a second example serves to further reveal the precise concept of humiliation von Hirsch and Jareborg have in mind. In relation to 'petty assault' they write: 'having one's face slapped *is* humiliating. But one is not being made helpless, as in the case of the beating. One can extricate oneself with dignity—remonstrate, move away, call the authorities, etc'.[36] Here we can see again that von Hirsch and Jareborg have in mind a more public-related conception of humiliation as a physical power struggle. One may indeed remain dignified, but this does not change the symbolic communication from the offender. The communication would remain the same whether the offender responded with resentment or indignation.

Of course, I agree that the humiliation and loss of self-respect is much greater in the case of assault and battery than it is in the case of petty theft, but the point remains that von Hirsch and Jareborg seem to have a more objective and public conception of what constitutes humiliation resulting from victimising behaviour. It seems that they are primarily concerned with physical and verbal power relations and the offender's exercise of this power. Indeed, they label the violation of the interest of freedom from humiliation as 'degrading treatment'. This emphasis on the behaviour of

[34] Freedom from humiliation is deemed to be intruded upon in offences of 'assault and battery', 'petty assault', 'forcible rape', and 'date rape'.

[35] von Hirsch and Jareborg (n 2) 25, emphasis added.

[36] ibid. The observation that—in the face of 'insult'—one can choose to protest with dignity instead of fighting back mirrors Hampton's distinction between 'indignation' and 'resentment'. See Hampton (n 14).

the offender, rather than the feelings of the victim, mirrors the distinction between *being* humiliated and *feeling* humiliated. It is not irrational to describe an interaction between two people as humiliating even in full knowledge that no humiliation is felt.

Perhaps it is not surprising that von Hirsch and Jareborg want to utilise this more objective conception of humiliation given their additional comments on 'psychological harm'. They do not deny that feeling humiliated will normally follow from being treated in a degrading manner—it is precisely this that makes degrading treatment psychologically harmful. Nonetheless, they focus more on the behaviour that precipitates these feelings as the violation of one's interests, and not the actual feelings that may or may not result.

Von Hirsch and Jareborg provide an explanation for why they do not want to include the subjective experience of 'psychological harm' as a legitimate interest for the state to protect. Some people respond to harm in a disproportionately fearful manner, for example, and it is undesirable for the harm of the offence to depend so much on the capricious *subjective* experiences of victims. However, they acknowledge that many aversive psychological states justifiably flow from various forms of criminal victimisation. They propose that these typical rational modes of distress constitute part of the intrusion into the interest dimension involved. Thus: 'when examining conduct that affects self-respect ... the sense of humiliation is the injury that reduces the living standard'.[37] However, this sense of humiliation will be characterised as the typical rational response, not the particular victim's level of distress.

In view of its objective nature, the concept of humiliation that von Hirsch and Jareborg employ is not particularly amenable to the claim that remorse can reduce the harmful effects of an offence. In applying their concept, they focus foremost on the physical dimension of humiliation and, if at all, only secondarily on psychological harm, to which they also take a more objective approach, so as to avoid great discrepancy. Thus, even more so than on Smith's Time-Release account, the 'mitigating' role of remorse on von Hirsch and Jareborg's account would be limited to the few cases in which remorse altered the degree to which a violent act was (objectively) humiliating. In order to do so, the remorse would have to have occurred within the time frame of the offence.

THE HARM OF WRONGDOING

According to some theorists, the alleviation of material or psychological harms is not the only way in which the harm of the offence can be reduced. There might, they suggest, be other ways of reducing harm—when

---

[37] von Hirsch and Jareborg (n 2) 23.

conceived as wrongdoing—that do not depend on the responses of the victim, and which would thus have much wider application. Bearing similarity to Murphy's suggestion that repentance retracts the 'moral injury',[38] Smith suggests that apologies and other post-offence behaviour can—as well as reducing psychological vectors of harm—'revise the badness' of past wrongdoing.[39] On this view, past deeds are rendered less awful when the offender subsequently apologises. Conversely, when the offender goes on to commit more or worse offences, his previous wrongdoing looks 'more sinister'.[40] In line with his 'dialectical retributivism'—according to which punishment should be calibrated in accordance with the 'character of the act'—Smith suggests that courts should take a wider temporal view on the wrongfulness of a particular action. An assessment that takes in the prior and subsequent behaviour of the offender, he claims, affords a better understanding of the nature of an offence because it is seen in the context of a broader moral narrative. He claims:

> Just as one's behavior and mental states before and after an offence alter culpability because they tell us relevant information about the nature of the act, so, too, one's mental states and behavior before and after an offense impart significance salient to desert.[41]

Pace Smith, I suggest that post-offence conduct has, at most, the capacity to elucidate past culpability. The reason for this is that post-offence repentance cannot change the offender's state of mind at the time of the offence. Of course, remorse can sometimes provide evidence that allows us to reinterpret the event in light of the offender's remorse. Similarly, if, as in Smith's example, we learn that the offender convicted of illegally possessing a weapon went on to commit an armed robbery, the prior offence appears worse because we are now more certain about his ideas and intentions *then*. However, the subsequent offence does not make the prior offence worse; rather, it shows us that our limited knowledge about the offender's state of mind at the time of the previous offence led to an underestimation of his culpability. Any further unease is perhaps due either to the realisation that we can misperceive and underestimate the bad intentions of others or to the realisation that something bad could have been prevented *if only we had known*.

Smith makes an explicit statement about the culpability-reducing potential of a quick apology, saying 'We have reason to believe that someone quick to apologise is more likely to have committed the crime without strong conviction or careful deliberation, as she quickly realizes her error'.[42]

---

[38] See JG Murphy, *Punishment and the Moral Emotions: Essays in Law, Morality, and Religion* (New York, NY, Oxford University Press, 2014) 118–19.
[39] Smith (n 17) 153.
[40] ibid.
[41] ibid.
[42] ibid, 159.

I have written elsewhere about the evidence that immediate remorse can provide for assessments of culpability and agree that, in these limited cases, it is suggestive of lesser culpability.[43] This, crucially, is not because it changes anything retrospectively, but because it provides evidence relevant to estimating aspects of *mens rea*.

However, this leaves open for discussion the question of how much time can pass before remorse or apology is no longer demonstrative of an offender's weaker commitment to her offence at the time of its commission, and the answer to this is unclear. I suggest that the time frame will not be large. If remorse and apology long after the offence were always demonstrative of lesser culpability, this would mean that it would never be the case that an offender who subsequently feels remorse was fully committed to his offence at the time of its commission. But, this seems psychologically unlikely, and is not borne out by the experience of those offenders who become horrified by their past intentions. Being fully committed to carrying out an offence is compatible with a change of heart much later, and part of the pain of remorse involves recoiling at the things that one wholeheartedly did.

Remorse and apology cannot therefore change the wrongfulness of the act, although they can, under limited circumstances, reveal to us that it was in fact less wrongful than it might otherwise have appeared. Epistemic limitations mean we always use subsequent behaviour to interpret past acts, but we use it to interpret the character of the act as it was *then*. The fact that this evidence comes later does not mean that the actual nature of the act changed. Rather, we have more information that we see as relevant and update our estimation accordingly.

In fact, I suggest that on Smith's own terms, we cannot allow post-offence conduct to precipitate a wide-ranging reassessment of the significance of all aspects of the offender's life to the wrongfulness of his offence. Rather, the offence only takes on new meaning in light of our revised assessment of the offender's culpability. Smith explains

> Repentance both revises the meanings of past wrongs and reduces the wickedness of such conduct with respect to the 'totality' of the offender's life. Dialectical retributivism [Smith's preferred view] narrows this perspective to the badness of the offense: to the *character of the act*.[44]

So, even accounting for the character of the act, estimation of its wrongfulness must be based on an assessment of the agent's character at the time of the offence, even if such assessments are sometimes updated in light of new evidence. Apologies far removed in time may do much for what we think of

---

[43] See: JV Roberts and H Maslen, 'After the Crime: Post-Offence Conduct and Penal Censure' in A Simester, U Neumann and A du Bois-Pedain (eds), *Liberal Criminal Theory: Essays for Andreas von Hirsch* (Oxford, Hart Publishing, 2014).

[44] Smith (n 17) 152.

the agent's character overall, but they do not alter his intentions and commitments at the time of the offence.

SUMMARY AND CONCLUSION

The foregoing discussion of the potential for remorse to modify the wrongfulness of acts reveals something about the difference between the use of the terms 'harms' and 'wrongs'. Whereas a harm can be considered independently of culpability, wrongfulness cannot be estimated apart from the intentions and desires of the offender. Having my arm broken by another is, on one reading, just as harmful whether it was the result of an unforeseeable accident or malicious assault. However, the latter constitutes a serious wrong whilst the former does not. Further, some harms such as degradation involve a culpable attitude. It may be that the discussion about whether offences should be conceived as harms or wrongs to a great extent disappears once the culpable nature of the act is factored in.

In constructing the Reduced Harm argument, von Hirsch and Jareborg's Living Standard analysis of harm provided an instructive framework according to which different harms can be categorised. It introduced the possibility that remorse might be able to influence the interest dimension of freedom from humiliation, a proposal that found support from Smith's use of examples of sexual assault. Reflection on von Hirsch and Jareborg's proposal of the time frame from which the quality of a person's life should be assessed revealed a crucial distinction between identifying the harm set at the time of the offence and observing the unfolding of this harm over time.

The scope for remorse reducing the harm (or wrong) of the offence is limited. The possibility that remorse reduces psychological harm was shown to be highly dependent on subjective features of the offence and victim, providing rare occasion for remorse-based mitigation. It was granted that there are some harms that can be alleviated at a much later date by knowledge of the offender's remorse. However, there are practical problems in knowing how to accommodate this. Sentencers must estimate the harm of the offence at the time of sentencing and a harm that could be exacerbated or reduced ex post poses problems, since the seriousness of the offence could therefore be subject to change. Harms that merely unfold over time (such as some physical injuries) also pose similar problems, but to a lesser degree. This is because their gravity cannot be altered—it is set—it just may not yet be fully visible. Further, in the case of psychological harms sensitive to remorse, it should be remembered that remorse does not undo the psychological harm experienced up to that point, and this may already be considerable, persisting but not increasing in severity.

In contrast to grounding mitigation on the reduction of the victim's humiliation, Smith's further suggestion that apologies can revise the 'qualitative badness' of the harm by overwriting it with revised meanings would, if true, have implications regardless of victims' subjective experiences. However, I argued that this must collapse into a limited consideration of culpability, as badness can only be revised where post-offence conduct provides evidence of reduced culpability at the time of the offence. For his view to imply anything more than this, past mental states would remain continuously indeterminate and would have the curious result that offenders who come to feel remorse were never fully committed to their conduct at the time of its commission. Remorse, it was concluded, cannot have the retroactive power that would be required to reduce the wrongfulness of the past offence, although it can in some cases offer retrospective evidence pertaining to the offender's state of mind at the time of the offence.

Finally, if Smith's Time-Release theory of harm is taken to its furthest conclusion, the harm of the offence increases indefinitely unless the offender apologises. This means that estimations of harm remain indeterminate. But, for practical reasons, sentencers must estimate harm based on the suffering the victim actually endured, even if it has now dissipated. In addition, I suggest that mitigation on the grounds of voluntary reparation and guilty plea discount cover much of what Smith wants to claim for apology reduction. This is not to say that apologies do not have some of the same effects and may often be co-instantiated with reparative efforts and pleading guilty. However, in many jurisdictions, these beneficial effects are already taken into account.

I have argued that the harms that remorse can plausibly reduce are restricted to certain types of offence—those causing humiliation and degradation—and are contingent on victims' experiences of these harms (how much they impact on their well-being) and the offender's remorse (whether it in fact reduces any of the psychological harms, where present). To take such effects into account would undermine consistency in the sentencing of remorseful offenders: two offenders who commit the same offence and feel equally remorseful may receive very different sentences if one of the victims was thoroughly psychologically unburdened as a result of the offender's remorse whilst the other victim remained psychologically scarred. Further, many offences would be unaffected by the offender's remorse if this were the only justification for mitigation.

In the next chapter, I shall consider an argument that changes the focus from the degree of the psychological suffering of the victim (and the potential remorse has to reduce it) to the degree of the psychological suffering of the offender, and asks whether the offender is—to any degree—already punished by his remorse.

4

The Already Punished Argument

The most significant aspect of Mr Joblin's report is his conclusion that he has no
doubt whatsoever that you are suffering great distress as a result of what you
did. He considered that you were contrite and extremely remorseful. He also
offered the opinion that the guilt that you are suffering has led you, to some
degree, to become socially isolated and withdrawn.[1]

It is certainly my view that it is true that you deeply regret the death of
Mr Edgar, and you will have to live with that for the rest of your life.[2]

AS THESE QUOTATIONS suggest, experiencing remorse is inherently painful, long lasting and its effects often reach far into all
domains of the remorseful person's life. Indeed, Adam Smith goes
as far as saying that 'of all the sentiments which can enter the human
breast [remorse is] the most dreadful'.[3] These quotations raise the question
of whether living with one's remorse might be the worst punishment of
all—the remorseful offender has, to some extent, already been punished.
Whether a retributive theory of sentencing could—or should—allow that
an offender's remorse constitutes some of the punishment that he legally
deserves depends on the theory's definition of 'punishment' and what it
takes the aims of this punishment to be. In this chapter I assess this possibility in relation to versions of the 'unfair advantage' theory, Duff's Penance
Perspective and von Hirsch's desert theory. It will emerge that remorse
alone cannot constitute any of the deserved punishment in these accounts,
but for different reasons in each instance.

NATURAL PUNISHMENT

I begin with a brief consideration of the concept of natural punishment,
of which remorse might be thought to constitute an example. Natural
punishment occurs when wrongdoing has bad consequences for the

---

[1] *R v Leatham* [2006] VSC 315.
[2] *R v David Herbert* (1993) 14 Cr App R (S) 792.
[3] A Smith, *The Theory of Moral Sentiments* (Cambridge, Cambridge University Press, 2002) 99.

wrongdoer. For example, reckless driving may result in the driver sustaining serious injuries. Natural punishment differs from what we might call 'punishment proper', which necessarily involves another agent or agents who intentionally inflict the punishment.[4] This is not the case in natural punishment, which can occur unintentionally and without the agency of another. Natural punishment should also be distinguished from simple bad luck. Whereas a burglar who breaks his leg slipping from the roof of the house he is burgling might be said to have received natural punishment, the burglar who later slips and breaks his leg in a supermarket does not seem to have received natural punishment—he is just unlucky in his injury. These examples help illustrate what is central to the concept of natural punishment: the adverse event must be a direct consequence of the illegal, immoral or imprudent behaviour.

Whilst the idea of natural punishment may seem principally metaphorical, it has been implicitly incorporated into the sentencing practices of some jurisdictions. Notably, the Swedish law regards as mitigating factors the fact that the offender suffered injury as a result of the crime, and the fact that the offender's employment prospects have been damaged as a result of conviction.[5] Some theorists have questioned the legitimacy of the exercise of judicial compassion in cases where the offender has brought foreseeable injuries or difficulties upon himself as a consequence of committing the offence.[6] However, it should be remembered that what is at issue in this chapter is not the potential justification of compassion, but whether the full (unmitigated) punishment is still deserved if something adequately substitutes for some of it.[7]

It could be thought that remorse, which is a direct result of wrongdoing, might constitute natural punishment and therefore justify mitigation. What will be of primary issue in this chapter, however, is not whether the label of 'natural punishment' is conceptually applicable to remorse, but whether remorse can adequately satisfy the definition and/or objectives that punishment theorists set out. The possibility that remorse satisfies penal objectives precipitates the corresponding possibility that a reduction in the severity of punishment to which the remorseful offender is sentenced might therefore be justified on these grounds.

---

[4] J Teichman, 'Punishment and Remorse' (1973) 48 *Philosophy* 335.

[5] See: A von Hirsch and A Ashworth, *Proportionate Sentencing: Exploring the Principles* (Oxford, Oxford University Press, 2005) 166–67.

[6] See, eg, ibid, 177.

[7] N Walker, *Aggravation, Mitigation and Mercy in English Criminal Justice* (London, Blackstone, 1999) 132. Walker draws a similar justificatory distinction when he speculates whether 'retributivists are divided about the justice of regarding "natural punishment" as a mitigating factor, perhaps because it is a notion which seems to be based ... on humanity rather than desert'.

PUNISHMENT PROPER

Many penal philosophers have accepted Hart's conditions for punishment as definitive.[8] Hart defines the standard or central case of criminal punishment in terms of five elements:

1.   It must involve pain or other consequences normally considered unpleasant.
2.   It must be for an offence against legal rules.
3.   It must be of an actual or supposed offender for his offence.
4.   It must be intentionally administered by human beings other than the offender.
5.   It must be imposed and administered by an authority constituted by a legal system against which the offence is committed.[9]

This *definition* of punishment is to be distinguished from the *aims* of punishment, which also usually serve to justify it: the 'general justifying aim of punishment' will usually either be retributive—'the application of the pains of punishment to an offender who is morally guilty'—or utilitarian—the fostering of 'beneficial consequences'.[10]

Whilst Hart provides a definition intended to cover central cases of criminal punishment, the definitions used within various retributive theories—if made explicit at all—are coloured by the different objectives that theorists think punishment should promote. Punishment is often conceived not merely as hard treatment imposed by the state on the offender for his offence, and close attention needs to be paid to any additional criteria that theorists identify.

It should also be noted that there is a difference between the possibility of remorse *constituting* punishment and of remorse being a *suitable substitute for* punishment. For the first possibility, remorse would have to satisfy the definition of punishment.[11] For the latter, it would have to be able to achieve the objectives a theorist sets out for punishment. Either possibility could result in justifying mitigation of state punishment. If remorse were to satisfy the definition of punishment, then some mitigation of state punishment for a remorseful offender would be necessary on retributive theories of punishment, otherwise the offender would be over-punished. If remorse

---

[8] HLA Hart, 'The Presidential Address: Prolegomenon to the Principles of Punishment' (1959) 60 *Proceedings of the Aristotelian Society* 1.

[9] ibid, 4.

[10] ibid, 8.

[11] However, Hart warns against the use of the 'definitional stop' in discussions of punishment. Invoking the definition of punishment as the yardstick against which to test any theory of punishment prevents us from adequately investigating the rational and moral status of any proffered system of punishment. This suggests that investigating the justifying aims underlying different theories of punishment will be more illuminating than a simple test of whether remorse satisfies a definition. See ibid, 5–6.

were to achieve all the aims set out for punishment, this would result in there being a case for the mitigation of state punishment. Of course, this argument would fail if theorists required that the aims of punishment must be achieved through state punishment. On such a view it could be claimed that, although remorse might also achieve the aims of punishment, this is irrelevant to the level of state punishment required. Thus, throughout, we must be sensitive to these two ways in which remorse might count as some of an offender's deserved punishment.

SUBJECTIVE VERSUS OBJECTIVE METRICS OF PUNISHMENT

To begin, I will briefly consider a theoretical debate similar to that which I shall address in this chapter in order to distinguish it and set it aside. This debate concerns whether the offender's individual subjective experience of his punishment alters how severe it is and, if so, how retributive theories should deal with this. The central question in this debate is whether the quantum or means of punishment imposed by the sentence should be sensitive to the way in which the offender is likely to experience it. Those who claim that it should (because, on their view, subjective experience is partly determinative of the severity of punishment) take what I will call the Experience Matters view. If the Experience Matters view is taken seriously, it could be argued that the aversive experience of remorse results in the offender suffering in his punishment more than the unremorseful offender. Accordingly, the argument might go, his punishment should be reduced to the extent that will serve to counterbalance the additional suffering he experiences—a possible justification for mitigation.

It might be thought that any claim that remorse substitutes for punishment *must* be committed to the Experience Matters view: for state punishment to be affected by remorse, it has to take the offender's experience into account in determining the proportionate punishment. However, I shall now argue that whilst remorse would be a relevant consideration on the Experience Matters view, it would not consistently serve to justify mitigation in the way suggested. I shall then demonstrate that the claim that remorse constitutes punishment does not commit us to the Experience Matters view: the argument that an offender's experience *of* state punishment influences its severity is not the same as the argument that some extralegal experiences can *be* or *substitute for* punishment.

Advocating the Experience Matters view, Adam Kolber presents us with a scenario in which two offenders—Sensitive and Insensitive—having committed offences of equal gravity, are sentenced to exactly the same length of prison sentence, which they serve in identical physical conditions (their cells are the same size, the guards treat them in the same manner, etc).[12] Sensitive, however, experiences his sentence as more aversive than Insensitive, due to his fragile disposition. Kolber argues that this difference in experience means that their punishments are not identical in severity and, therefore, that at least one is punished disproportionately. The severity of their respective punishments is at least partly a function of how aversive the punishment is to them.[13]

In order to use such an argument to consistently justify remorse as a mitigating factor the following two things would have to be true: first, remorse would have to reliably correlate with (and perhaps be the cause of) more aversive penal experiences. Second, the Experience Matters view would have to be defended—it would have to be true that subjective experience affects, in a way relevant to retributivism, the severity of the punishment the offender endures.

However, both premise one and premise two can be contested. First, it is an empirical question whether remorse makes people's experiences of punishment worse, and the answer to it is not obvious. In fact punishment might in some cases be more bearable for the remorseful, as they feel it is deserved and serves as a way to atone for their wrongdoing. This might not make their remorse any less painful—they are still haunted by what they did—but it may allow them to adopt an attitude of acceptance with respect to their punishment that makes the experience somewhat less gruelling. Certainly, it seems that there could be a multitude of different ways in which remorseful offenders experience their punishments; and in the absence of empirical data, it seems highly presumptuous to claim that all remorseful offenders consistently experience their punishment as more aversive.

Further, even in a case where an individual remorseful offender does have an overall more aversive experience than the non-remorseful offender, the Experience Matters argument would not be able to posit remorse *per se* as a mitigating factor. The reason for this is that it is the offender's overall experience of his punishment that is the potential mitigating factor, within which remorse will play a complex role. In addition, it would be offenders' experience of (and only of) punishment that could be taken into account, not a more general assessment of his overall hedonic state, which will be influenced by all manner of things unrelated to punishment. Even on the Experience Matters view, the aim of punishment is not to bring the offender *to a particular level* of disutility. The aim, rather, is to reduce the offender's utility *by a particular amount*; what will be sufficient for achieving this will depend on contingent facts about the individual offender. Two offenders

---

[12] AJ Kolber, 'The Subjective Experience of Punishment' (2009) 109 *Columbia Law Review* 182–83.
[13] ibid, 215.

could experience their respective punishments as equally severe, yet one emerge happier than the other due to other factors. So, whilst there might in some cases be interaction, I suggest that we can distinguish between an offender's experience of his punishment and his experience of his remorse. Crucially, it is the former that is taken into account on the Experience Matters view.

Turning now to premise two, the argument that subjective metrics of punishment are essential to ensure proportionality is highly contested. Markel et al take issue with the view that the individualisation of punishment—based on how the offender subjectively experiences it—is necessary to getting retributive justice right.[14] They argue that 'punishment on this view is little more than a complicated pain-delivery device'.[15] Coming from a communicative retributive perspective, their main argument against this view is that human understanding is informed by more than just one's experiences. The deprivation of liberty is objectively bad. The fact that we discover it is objectively bad by experiencing it as subjectively bad does not make the subjective experience *constitutive* of what is bad. Social meaning plays a role which is not reducible to subjective experience: £500 in taxes and a £500 fine for committing an offence may 'generate the same hedonic dip', but the meaning is different.[16] Thus, they conclude that

> as long as it is reasonable for people in our society to think that a politically sanctioned constraint of liberty communicates condemnation, and that stiffer sanctions signal yet great condemnation, adaptation among typical offenders need not play a central or even prominent role when setting sentencing policy.[17]

In contrast to theorists such as Kolber, they believe that it is the objective 'badness' of punishment that is most important in determining the quantum that should be inflicted.

I am not here concerned to resolve the subjective versus objective metric of punishment debate, since the claim that I examine in this chapter does not depend on it. The above argument, that remorse makes the experience of punishment worse, differs in important ways from the argument required to support the contention that remorse might adequately substitute for some of an offender's deserved punishment. In an Experience Matters argument, the main idea would be that the remorseful offender experiences his punishment as unusually harsh and therefore should be punished less than the average offender to maintain proportionality. This is not the same as the idea that remorse embodies or delivers something that approximates punishment (and, therefore delivers additional punishment) *in itself*.

---

[14] D Markel, C Flanders and D Gray, 'Beyond Experience: Getting Retributive Justice Right' (2011) 99 *California Law Review* 605.

[15] ibid, 616.

[16] ibid, 615.

[17] ibid.

So, although the themes discussed in this section will re-emerge in this chapter, it does not matter if we do not reach a conclusion on the subjective vs objective metrics debate at this juncture, as it is separate from the question of whether remorse constitutes punishment. Whilst the conclusions reached in this chapter will suggest whether remorse should mitigate on the grounds that the remorseful offender has already been punished, the Experience Matters argument cannot consider remorse as mitigating per se: sometimes the remorseful person will be more sensitive, but perhaps sometimes they will be less so. Additionally, the sentencer would have to consider all the other elements of the offender's overall disposition that might influence his experience of his punishment. Considerations of remorse would dissolve into this broader consideration.

I now return to the central question of this chapter by exploring whether remorse could constitute or substitute for punishment in the first of our retributive theories: the benefits and burdens theory.

THEORY ONE: BENEFITS AND BURDENS

The particulars of the 'benefits and burdens' (or 'unfair advantage') retributive theory of punishment depend on which version is adopted. However, they all share the same basic logic: the wrongdoer's punishment is necessary to address an imbalance created by the offence. Individuals living in a just society enjoy the freedom to pursue their individual projects without unjustified interference from others. In exchange for this benefit, however, such individuals are required to assume the burden of allowing others to enjoy the same freedom—they cannot interfere with another individual's body or property unjustifiably. The offender who fails to exercise such self-restraint gains an unfair advantage over others exercising that restraint. The burden of punishment then negates this unfair advantage. The first example of this way of thinking about the justification of punishment can be found in the writings of Herbert Morris.[18] He writes:

> It is just to punish those who have violated the rules and caused the unfair distribution of benefits and burdens. A person who violates the rules has something others have—the benefits of the system—but by renouncing what others have assumed, the burdens of self-restraint, he has acquired an unfair advantage. Matters are not even until this advantage is in some way erased. Another way of putting it is that he owes something to others, for he has something that does not rightfully belong to him. Justice—that is punishing such individuals—restores the equilibrium of benefits and burdens by taking from the individual what he owes, that is, exacting the debt.[19]

---

[18] H Morris, 'Persons and Punishment' (1968) 52 *The Monist* 475.
[19] ibid, 478.

So, on this theory, the justifying aim of punishment is to redress the imbalance of benefits and burdens. Punishment is the means to redressing the balance: whatever satisfactorily redresses the balance will be defined as adequate punishment on this view. If an offender's remorse were to be understood as a relevant burden (or as otherwise removing some of the benefit attained by the offender) then it would constitute punishment. For instance, it could be argued that the offender's remorse is a relevant burden and thus constitutes punishment, meaning that a less severe state burden is needed in order to restore the balance of benefits and burdens. Alternatively, it might be argued that the remorseful offender has lost, through his remorse, some of the benefit gained from the offence, and this again constitutes punishment, meaning that a less severe burden is needed to restore balance.

In order to see if remorse can function in this way, it seems that we need to look more closely at what is meant by burden and benefit, and by unfair advantage in this context. Burgh sketches the possibilities for what might constitute the unfair benefit of an offence.[20] He sees four candidates:

> (1) the ill-gotten gain, e.g., money in the case of robbery; (2) not bearing the burden of self-restraint, hence having a bit more freedom than others; (3) the satisfaction from committing the crime; and (4) the sphere of noninterference which results from general obedience to the particular law violated; e.g., each person benefits from property laws insofar as he is free from interference with his property.[21]

I will suggest that remorse could potentially serve to counterbalance the satisfaction generated by the offence or the shirking of self-restraint. However, through examining the implications of conceiving of remorse as a counteracting burden, I will demonstrate that the justifying aim of the benefits and burdens theory could not be achieved and, thus, remorse neither substitutes for nor constitutes punishment on this theory.

The Benefit of Satisfaction

Prima facie, it seems plausible to claim that remorse, as a deeply aversive psychological state, can negate any satisfaction drawn from the offence. Satisfaction is an explicitly hedonic benefit. Within the benefit of satisfaction, we can draw a distinction between the satisfaction *of* committing the crime—the rush during the actual act, which will be necessarily temporary— and satisfaction *from* committing the crime—perhaps drawn from a more positive self-image, a sense of achievement, and the memories of the successfully executed offence, all of which may be more sustained. If the crime

---

[20] RW Burgh, 'Do the Guilty Deserve Punishment?' (1982) 79 *The Journal of Philosophy* 193.
[21] ibid, 203.

was acquisitive, one's satisfaction might partially be derived from the additional resources. If violent, one's aggressive impulses will have been satisfied and one might feel a sense of fulfilment.

Hart alludes to an unfair advantage-style conception of the offender's requirement to 'pay the price of some satisfaction obtained by breach of law'.[22] Hart explains

> it is pointed out that in some cases the successful completion of a crime may be a source of gratification, and in the case of theft, of actual gain, and in such cases to punish the successful criminal more severely may be one way of depriving him of these illicit satisfactions which the unsuccessful have never had.[23]

Punishment, on this view, serves the purpose of removing satisfaction.

Remorse as Dissatisfaction

Although it seems plausible to claim that remorse can negate satisfaction, it would be more precise to say that remorse involves a *loss* of the benefit of satisfaction, rather than to say that it acts as a negating counterbalance. Genuine remorse would result in the offender retaining no satisfaction at all from the offence, in his memory, self-image or sense of fulfilment. These satisfactions would instead be replaced by horror at the memory of the offence and a greatly depleted self-image. The offender might also experience horror at the satisfaction or pleasure he originally gained from the offence. This might be particularly true for sexual offenders.

However, even if remorse does quash all the satisfaction gained from the offence, is a psychological burden really what the unfair advantage theorists envisage as serving to adequately restore balance? There is no denying that many of the sanctions imposed upon offenders are psychologically burdensome. Moreover, the idea that we want to stop an offender feeling good about his or her offence is appealing—the smugness or gloating of an offender would repulse us. But offsetting satisfaction does not seem to be at the heart of what balance restoration means to unfair advantage theorists. If we consider the implications that this view would have for the benefits and burdens theory, we can begin to understand why such a model is not appealing.

The overriding problem is that any model of punishment that is concerned only with the subjective experience of the offender would not only be impossible to adequately implement, but would also lack much theoretical appeal. The reason that such a model would be impossible

---

[22] HLA Hart, *Punishment and Responsibility: Essays in the Philosophy of Law* (Oxford, Clarendon Press, 1968) 47.
[23] ibid, 131.

to adequately implement is that an offender's satisfaction would be very difficult and intrusive to measure. Further, even if such a model were practicable, we have a good reason not to allocate punishment according to the offender's level of satisfaction, since levels of satisfaction are likely to vary drastically from person to person. The satisfaction that one offender might get from, for example, an assault could be much greater than that of another offender who committed exactly the same offence. To illustrate, suppose offender A socialises in a subculture that values and praises aggressive, dominant behaviour. As a result of his offence, offender A grows in confidence, is proud of his behaviour, and has a much higher opinion of himself. The offence leaves him greatly satisfied. Compare this with offender B who gains some satisfaction from hurting someone he disliked but, due to being surrounded by disapproval, gains none of the 'status-satisfaction' that offender A does.

Moreover, the satisfaction that any offender acquires is likely to be influenced day to day by myriad factors—from the offender's mood, to what people say to him about his offence, to comparisons with others' successes at criminal activity. On the model we are considering here, the varying levels of an offender's satisfaction would potentially result in a different severity of punishment being deserved every day.

Similar problems would arise when trying to work out how much dissatisfaction a sanction should mete out in order to restore the balance of benefits and burdens.[24] Although retributive theories of punishment can acknowledge the reality that a given severity of punishment will seem more or less severe to different offenders, a benefits and burdens theory that seeks to balance satisfaction with dissatisfaction would have to be completely engaged with these subjective experiences. It would have to work out how this particular person would be dissatisfied to a degree equivalent to the satisfaction he acquired from his offence. Further problems would arise when we consider that a few offenders might actually gain satisfaction from some aspects of serving their sentences. Being in prison can be seen as a status symbol amongst a small minority. For others, despite forfeiting their liberty, quality of life might actually be marginally preferable in prison, and so not entirely dissatisfying on some level. Of course, this would only be true for some offenders, but it is something that an entirely subjective benefits–burdens model would have to contend with.

Given these difficulties, the unfair advantage cannot just be constituted by how happy, content or fulfilled one feels following one's offence. Indeed, Finnis claims that punishment serves to 'negate, cancel out, the advantage

---

[24] Kolber might argue, however, that although criminal justice institutions might refuse to take subjective experience into account on the grounds that it is too difficult to assess, they nonetheless need to accept that the sentences they impose will often be disproportionate, given differences in subjective experience. See Kober (n 12).

the offender gained in the crime—the advantage *not necessarily of loot or psychological satisfaction*, but of having pursued one's own purposes even when the law required that one refrain from doing so'.[25] The importance of the offender pursuing her own forbidden purposes prompts consideration of the benefit being more appropriately conceived, not as satisfaction, but as 'not bearing the burden of self-restraint'.

The Benefit of Freedom

There are two slightly different interpretations of the benefit of shirking self-restraint, both of which involve 'benefits' that are perhaps better understood as the avoidance of taking on a burden. 'Not bearing the burden of self-restraint' can be understood in a purely psychological sense. Restraining oneself—practising self-control—can take much effort. If a wallet has been left unattended with a large sum of money in it, it might take an individual an enormous amount of will power not to reach out and take the visible notes. The individual might have to keep repeating to himself that he should not take the money, and this mental effort will be accompanied by the frustration of denying himself what he wants. The offender, on the other hand, expends none of this mental energy and feels no such frustration. He lets himself do as he pleases. On this reading, having more freedom than others might be better stated as *experiencing* a bit more freedom than others: the offender feels free, where as the resister feels inhibited.

However, there is a more objective interpretation of this possible benefit. On an alternative reading, rather than the offender *experiencing* more freedom than others, the point is simply that he *exercises* more freedom than others. Again, I refrain from using the term 'having' here, because the non-offender does not *have* any less freedom than the offender. It is not that he cannot reach out and take the money from the wallet; rather he refrains from so doing. The offender does not have greater freedom, but he does engage in behaviour from which the majority would refrain. On this reading, the benefit is objective, resulting from engagement in a larger set of desirable (to the offender) behaviours. The benefit is not, then, drawn simply from the subjective pleasure (or avoidance of displeasure) of not practising self-restraint.

The benefit attained by the wrongdoer has been envisaged in a similar way by Finnis.[26] According to him,

> What the criminal gains in the act of committing the crime (whatever the size and nature of the loot, if any, and indeed quite apart from the success or failure

---

[25] J Finnis, 'Retribution: Punishment's Formative Aim' (1999) 44 *American Journal of Jurisprudence* 91, 102, emphasis added.
[26] J Finnis, 'The Restoration of Retribution' (1972) 32 *Analysis* 131.

of his overall purpose) is the advantage of indulging a (wrongful) self-preference, of permitting himself an excessive freedom in choosing—this advantage ... being something that his law abiding fellow-citizens have denied themselves insofar as they have chosen to conform their will (habits and choices) to the law even when they would 'prefer' not to.[27]

Remorse Re-imposes Self-restraint

It could be argued that the remorseful offender re-imposes restraint on himself. If an offender were to be genuinely remorseful, then he would (at least strongly intend to) not commit the same offence again, if he were to find himself in a similar situation. He would now restrain himself. However, a new enthusiasm for resisting a particular temptation does not seem to counterbalance the benefit of previously indulging one's '(wrongful) self-preference'. It does not seem to constitute a burden over and above that which the majority of people take on in obeying the law when they might be tempted not to. However, if we consider what Finnis says about the important aspects of punishment, we gain a clearer understanding of what could constitute the relevant burden, and whether remorse can go any way to being an appropriate substitute. Finnis says that punishment is to be defined:

> ... not, formally speaking, in terms of the infliction of pain (nor as incarceration), but rather in terms of the subjection of will (normally, but not necessarily, effected through the denial of benefits and advantages of social living: compulsory employment on some useful work which the criminal would not of himself have chosen to do would satisfy the definition).[28]

So, according to Finnis, to offset the offender's indulgence of his wrongful self-preference, his will needs to be subjected. Finnis states explicitly that this 'punishment' does not necessarily have to be incarceration, but that in most cases it is achieved through denying the offender the 'benefits and advantages of social living'. If this is what is required to offset the offender's unfair advantage, might remorse go some way to effecting such denial? Remorse certainly should have a profound effect on the offender's capacity for enjoying even the most simple of social pleasures. With the reality of what one has done firmly in the forefront of one's mind, one likely feels incapable of engaging in all the activities one once would have, and would not gain much pleasure from them even if one did engage. Duff portrays remorse as categorically rendering the offender bereft of the benefits and advantages of social living. Of remorse, he argues that:

> [I]t will prevent me from enjoying what I would otherwise enjoy. If I truly recognise and repent what I have done, I will not be able to enjoy, for instance, my usual social pleasures. I do not *decide* to deprive myself of them as a punishment;

---

[27] ibid, 132.
[28] ibid, 133.

but I *cannot* enjoy them, any more than I could enjoy them whilst mourning the death of a friend. I cannot enjoy them because my attention and my concern are dominated by the wrong I have done.[29]

This goes beyond the function of remorse to inspire renewed commitment to self-restraint, which I argued did not constitute a burden. The burden here is that the offender is deprived of enjoyment of life. Importantly, as Duff notes, the remorseful offender does not impose this deprivation on himself; rather, he is incapable of finding pleasure in the things he used to enjoy. As with state punishment, this deprivation is not a choice— something Finnis seems to require in order to achieve 'subjection of the will'. Perhaps, then, remorse does impose a relevant burden.

However, it is not clear that what Finnis requires for subjection of the will is simply that the offender is rendered unable to enjoy life. A closer reading reveals that the issue is more about the offender's freedom. The benefits and advantages of social living are not so much to do with hedonic experiences, but rather to do with the freedoms that we have as citizens in a free society. Thus, Finnis explains that the 'disadvantage' the offender must endure involves 'having his wayward will restricted in its freedom by being subjected to the representative "will of society" (the "will" which the offender disregarded in breaking the law)'.[30] The offender's will is not subjected by his remorse, but is merely modified or stifled by its experience. Something external is required for subjection of the will. The offender, having permitted himself an 'excessive freedom in choosing'[31] through acting according to his tastes, is to have his freedom curtailed—his choices restricted—by society to restore balance.

Is there any way, then, that remorse can be relevant within this scheme of benefits and burdens? Within his writing on the relevance of 'private burdens' to fair-play theories, Bayern argues than it can.[32] Bayern considers the offender who 'no longer believes that the excess freedom associated with a prior crime is worth having'[33]—something integral to a remorseful response. Bayern asks what the point is—within fair-play theories—of imposing punishment if we can establish that the offender is no longer the sort of person who considers the excess freedom from her crime to be a benefit.

The argument here seems to be that the benefit that needs to be offset by punishment is the wrongdoer's positive experience of exercising freedoms that are usually renounced. The remorseful offender no longer enjoys a

---

[29] A Duff 'Punishment and Penance—A Reply to Harrison' in R Harrison and RA Duff, 'Punishment and Crime' (1988) 62 *Proceedings of the Aristotelian Society, Supplementary Volumes* 139, 164.

[30] Finnis (n 26) 133.

[31] ibid, 132.

[32] SJ Bayern, 'The Significance of Private Burdens and Lost Benefits for a Fair-Play Analysis of Punishment' (2009) 12 *New Criminal Law Review* 1.

[33] ibid, 40.

sense of freedom in connection with his offence, as his remorse reframes the past events as objectionable wrongdoing. Since the offender no longer values the excess freedom conferred by his offending, there is no benefit, and hence nothing to offset.

However, this argument is unconvincing. Its primary fault lies in the conception of 'freedom' that it adopts. To see why, we can expand on the distinction I drew above between *experiencing* more freedom than others and *exercising* more freedom than others. To flesh out this distinction in a little more detail, notice again that the former is subjective, whilst the latter, objective. The *experience* of exercising freedom as positive is dependent on the agent's attitudes towards it, whilst the mere fact that one has *exercised* more freedom is not. Bayern hints towards this distinction when he wonders if his argument would be convincing to someone adopting a conception of freedom that was 'so abstract that it is divorced altogether from any practical benefits to offenders'.[34] However he does not develop this line of enquiry. Irrespective of this, it seems that Bayern's argument requires a subjective conception of freedom, which must boil down to the offender's maintenance of positive attitudes regarding the freedom he experienced during the offence. However, the maintenance of such subjective positive attitudes seems no different to the benefit of drawing satisfaction from the crime, and fails to be of central relevance for the same reasons.

'Freedom', then, must be understood objectively: the offender appropriated excess freedom through engaging in prohibited activity, regardless of whether he felt liberated or satisfied by it. Punishment, within Finnis's theory must come from the state as only this can be representative of the 'will of society'. The offender's punishment must be a societal matter because the benefits and burdens at issue arise from a system constructed by, and imposed upon, society. Remorse is not a burden that represents the will of society and therefore cannot be a burden relevant to unfair advantage theories.

THEORY TWO: DUFF AND THE PENANCE PERSPECTIVE

I will now consider whether remorse might constitute, or be a substitute for, deserved punishment in relation to Duff's Penance Perspective. For Duff, the imposition of penances is the justifying aim of the criminal sanction. Serving as a penance is necessary for a sanction to be justified. Since remorse is intrinsically tied to what Duff envisages the ideal penance to be and to what it achieves, it seems likely that an offender's remorse will have

---

[34] ibid.

some relevance to the punishment he receives. I am going to argue that the main tenets of Duff's view result in the possibility of a remorsefully imposed penance constituting some of an offender's deserved punishment. However, I shall also highlight why Duff would disagree with this interpretation, and challenge his likely opposition, as well as discussing vacillation in his work.

State Punishment and Self-punishment

In a 1988 article, we find Duff arguing that an account of criminal punishment should be founded on the idea of self-punishment.[35] His idea of prototypical penance as punishment that is undertaken voluntarily is crucial to this argument. Duff begins his argument with the strong claim that 'criminal punishment ... should ideally aim to become self-punishment'.[36] Given the primary importance Duff places on self-punishment in this work, and its purported supremacy over state punishment, might there be scope to portray remorse as constituting part of this self-punishment on his view? I shall argue that this would be possible within Duff's account but that there would be two necessary conditions that may be difficult (although not logically impossible) to meet. It will emerge that for remorse to constitute some of the deserved punishment in the case of a particular individual, he must (1) be capable of experiencing/achieving complete repentance independently and (2) adequately express his remorse though a self-imposed penance. Duff would see both these conditions as unattainable by any existing individual.

Duff's argument seems to be that state punishment is a less-than-ideal substitute for self-punishment. Despite state punishment not being the ideal, Duff claims that it is justified nonetheless. His argument is that in the majority of cases, where offenders do not impose punishment on themselves, there is the hope that the offender will eventually come to want to have punished himself. This would render it more like self-punishment (since the offender retrospectively accepts the state punishment as what he would have wished for himself if he had felt and thought then as he does now). State punishment can meet the relevant aims since, according to Duff, it serves both to facilitate repentance and to express this repentance to the community. It thus functions like a penance and 'in accepting it as a penance, [the offender] accepts it as a punishment which he should impose on himself'.[37]

However, Duff's position is that the state-penitential model is derivative of more authentic self-imposed penance. If state punishment is to be

[35] Duff (n 29).
[36] ibid, 159.
[37] ibid, 163.

justifiably derived from the self-punishment model, we must start with identifying the value of self-punishment. Duff argues that:

> What is essential to [state] punishment is an outward or manifest suffering which gives symbolic expression to the pain of remorse. This meaning is *most easily seen* in the case of self-punishment; and to justify criminal punishment we must then show how imposed punishments can come to have this meaning...[38]

Here we see one of the valuable features of self-punishment—that it expresses the offender's remorse. The vandal who desists and proceeds voluntarily to clear a whole neighbourhood of gratuitous graffiti would likely be seen to understand and to have been moved by the damage he has caused. This understanding prompts him to express his contempt for his behaviour through giving up all his free time in penitential reparative action.

The purpose of state punishment, for Duff, is not only as a vehicle for expressing repentance, either concurrently or retrospectively. In addition, Duff claims that 'Punishment aims to persuade the criminal to accept the justified condemnation of her past crime, and the understanding of the nature and implications of that crime, which it expresses'.[39] So, state punishment is also a means of eliciting repentance, through focusing the offender's mind on his offence and the harm he has caused. The hard treatment 'aims to make the offender hear the message it expresses—to force his attention onto his crime'.[40]

The relationship between hard treatment and self-punishment seems less obvious in connection to focusing the mind. It would seem that the offender's mind must already be focused repentantly on his offence if he is to impose self-punishment, which then functions to express this (already) repentant understanding. However, Duff suggests that self-punishment is required in order for the offender to reach a fully repentant understanding of what he has done. On his view, full repentance is not possible prior to painful penance. Thus, Duff describes penances (self-imposed or otherwise) as 'various kinds of hair shirt which, being essentially uncomfortable, provide an ever-present reminder of my wrongdoing'.[41] This is what makes the 'separate' or 'extra' pain associated with penance necessary. It needs to involve some 'imposition, or deprivation, or burden, which is painful quite apart from its penitential meaning'.[42]

---

[38] ibid, 160, emphasis added.
[39] ibid, 162.
[40] ibid.
[41] ibid, 165.
[42] ibid, 163.

Given Duff's project—to show how the values of self-punishment transfer to state punishment, rendering the latter justified—we might ask whether self-punishment might constitute part of the punishment an offender deserves, especially if self-punishment is actually the ideal. We must be aware from the outset, however, that repentant self-punishment is much more than just the experience of an aversive psychological state. It is remorse *plus* engagement in the penitential behaviour it often motivates. It is this 'active remorse' that plausibly could constitute some of the deserved punishment, within Duff's theory. We can now explore how it might do so.

Eliciting Repentance

Let us look first at punishment's function to facilitate a fully repentant under-standing of the wrongdoing. It might be argued by Duff that full repentance cannot be achieved passively. Indeed, he is cynical about the success indi-viduals can have with experiencing the emotions and cognitions which would characterise the optimal repentant response: 'repentance is achieved through time and only with difficulty; and the difficulty flows from our unwillingness to confront our wrongdoings'.[43] He imagines (almost) perfect beings that rec-ognise and fully repent their wrongs as soon as they are done. These beings, he says, would not need penances or punishments as distinct from the pain that repentance involves. In contrast, we mere mortals, it would seem, require some kind of 'hair shirt'. But the question then becomes whether a self-imposed hair shirt can suffice. Duff might argue that a self-imposed penance can be effective, but that it still has to be prison, because only prison can sufficiently focus the offender's mind. If this were the case, then Duff's vision of the ideal of self-punishment would require that every novice repentant offender would request to go to prison in order to develop his or her repentance (and to express it).

However, this does not seem to be Duff's position. Duff gives the exam-ple of the offender who, having committed acquisitive offences, embarks on a period of material deprivation: 'this would express and reinforce my condemnation of the excessive concern for material goods which my action manifested'.[44] One could argue that self-imposed penances are actually better suited to focusing one's mind than incarceration, especially if (like in Duff's example and the graffiti example above) they involve an offence-related element. Unlike the pain of being in prison (of which one would of course be acutely aware) the pain of these sorts of self-imposed penance forces the offender to think about the exact nature and consequences of the wrong. Indeed, Duff himself has in mind such 'bespoke' punishments within his ideal scheme. He suggests that punishment should illustrate the character of the offence in order to promote refection on the nature of the wrong done. For example, crimes motivated by greed should receive fines,

[43] ibid, 165.
[44] ibid.

violent crimes should be punished by a period of exclusion from the community (ie imprisonment) because they are destructive of the community's basic values, and so on.[45]

Further, if one chooses to impose something on oneself then one is somehow motivated to do so, and in these cases it is because of what one has done. State punishment, on the other hand, even if not ignorable, does not have this psychological link built in. Indeed, Duff sees the burden of proof on this matter to rest with the justification of state punishment. He argues that in order to justify state punishments as penances we would need to show how '... *just as a self-imposed penance can assist repentance, so punishment which is imposed by others can help bring a wrongdoer to repentance*'.[46]

It would therefore seem that self-imposed penance motivated by partial repentance could be sufficient for an offender's becoming fully repentant. According to Duff, an offender cannot become fully repentant without this assistance. Although this is an empirical matter, if we accept his assumptions then remorse must be accompanied by self-punishment in order to achieve full repentance. However, there seems to be nothing in Duff's argument to suggest that repentant self-punishment cannot match or even exceed state punishment's effectiveness in this regard.

Expressing Repentance

What of the expressive function of punishment? Again, Duff imagines (almost) perfect beings for whom no symbolic penance would be required. He says that 'they would know of each other that their repentance was genuine and their apologies fully sincere'.[47] However, beings such as ourselves need to provide an outward and public expression of our painful remorse in order to assure others of the sincerity of our repentance. That we are incapable of this sort of perfection is more clearly the case than the assumption that we are incapable of achieving full repentance without a mind-focusing punishment. We are not mind-readers and, unless we know someone well, we require a lot of behavioural evidence in order to make confident psychological attributions. Even more prohibitively, we would not even know of this behavioural evidence unless we had seen it first hand or it had been made publicly available. So, it would seem that Duff is right to require *some* sort of penance if the wrongdoer's repentance is to be expressed to the community. The question, as with the discussion of focusing the offender's mind, is whether self-punishment suffices.

---

[45] See A Duff, *Trials and Punishments* (Cambridge, Cambridge University Press, 1986) 244.
[46] Duff (n 29) 166, emphasis added.
[47] ibid.

It could be argued that a self-imposed penance is not public enough and that formal state punishment is the only sort of penance of which the community will be aware. Tasioulas makes this argument, saying that a penance undergone at the offender's own discretion does not '[bear] a public meaning accessible to the victim and the wider community'.[48] Legal punishment, in contrast, is 'something inflicted on the offender irrespective of his choice, and it provides him with a *public* vehicle for manifesting his repentance'.[49] The issue of whether voluntariness per se makes the penance more or less suitable aside, the question really is whether a self-imposed penance can adequately express remorse. It would seem that this will not invite a categorical answer. Obviously, a hair shirt concealed by one's garments will express nothing, as it would not be seen.

Not all penances are so private, though. Imagine a woman who, after significant tax evasion, wishes not only to pay what she owes, but also to serve society, instead of taking from it. She commits herself to doing the sorts of things that council taxes usually pay for. She spends some evenings collecting litter from the streets and others volunteering at her local library. Moreover, when people enquire why she is doing these things she openly tells them about her wrongdoing and that she wants to make it up to her community. Such a self-penance would be very public and it might become widely known about, at least within her local community. If this were not considered public enough, then it could easily be noted at sentencing, allowing anyone who is interested in the case to know of her self-imposed penance. The general public primarily know about prison sentences through the news media and, if self-imposed penances were documented alongside the state-imposed penance, they would be just as 'public'. Indeed, many more people would actually see the tax evader picking up litter than would see her in prison.

Moreover, it strikes me that there is more to penitential expression than its 'loudness' (or, public character). There is also its quality. Even if one were to argue that a state punishment is still more public due to its formality, there is still the important point that the quality of a self-imposed penance is better than that of a state punishment. If Duff's concern is really about expressive efficacy (as a function of *what* reaches *whom*), then the quality (the what) of the self-imposed penance cannot be ignored. Such penances express an offender's repentant understanding with more certainty and nuance than state punishment. The community does not know if the prison 'penance' is accepted as such or not, it can only know that it has been imposed.

---

[48] J Tasioulas, 'Repentance and the Liberal State' (2006) 4 *Ohio State Journal of Criminal Law* 487, 505.
[49] ibid.

An objector might argue that a self-imposed penance can never express as much as a state penance because it is nowhere near as burdensome. This might be true in some cases: a violent assault, even if responded to repentantly, might require years in prison in order for repentance to be expressed sufficiently—there is no number of hours collecting litter or overdue books that could suffice in this case. In addition, even if there were, a judge could not know that the offender would continue to impose this work upon herself for years to come. Moreover, some offenders have very little time to engage in penance prior to being sentenced.

I do not think these objections threaten my argument. The question is not whether remorse—or, rather, a repentantly imposed penance—eliminates the need for state punishment, but merely whether it can constitute part of it. Even if the assailant cannot express his repentance in its entirety, he might express some of it, and convincingly so, to a very wide audience, if his penance were to be noted at sentencing.

Self-punishment can Constitute Some of the Deserved Punishment

It would therefore seem that self-punishment, in its mind-focusing and repentance-expressing capacity, can constitute—*is*—some of the deserved punishment, on Duff's account. Indeed, for Duff, 'self-punishment' is a viable concept, implying a rejection of the third of Hart's criteria (considered above), which states that the punishment must be 'deliberately imposed by an agent authorized by the system of rules against which the presumed offence is committed who is acting within his or her official capacity'. Duff, in fact, specifies only that punishment is imposed 'by someone with (supposedly) the authority to do so'.[50] Stating that punishment should be imposed by someone with the authority to do so is subtly different from claiming that it must be *an* authority that imposes the punishment. Having 'the authority to do something' means that one is entitled to do that thing. Being 'an authority' means that one is recognised as having a particular, formal, standing with relation to another person or group of people. It would make sense that we have *the* authority to impose punishment on ourselves.

Duff's criterion suggests either that hard treatment *is not* punishment if imposed by someone without the authority to do so (perhaps it is torture or simply cruel treatment in such a case), or that punishment *is only justified* when imposed by someone who has the authority to do so. On the second understanding, the unauthorised can still punish, but they do so unjustifiably. Either way, the important point is that one can punish oneself—one

---

[50] A Duff, *Punishment, Communication and Community* (Oxford, Oxford University Press, 2001) xv.

has authority. However, as Duff emphasises, the discussion of the definition of punishment must 'rapidly become a normative discussion of how punishment can be justified, if it is to produce a useful account of what we *should* mean by "punishment"'.[51] Whether Duff wants to formalise his definition of punishment or not, it is clear that within his theory a remorsefully imposed self-penance constitutes punishment; it does not merely achieve punishment's aims.

Indeed, this is not really a surprising outcome for a theory of punishment that claims to model itself on self-punishment. At the outset, Duff tells us that self-punishment should be the model for, and justification of, state punishment. This being the case, self-punishment *must* be effective at the things that Duff requires of state punishment. He highlights the worth of self-imposed penances because he wants to show penance as something valuable, and something to emulate in criminal justice. It would be peculiar if he were then to deny that self-punishment was capable of doing the things that he needs it to do in order for him to use it to justify the institution of state punishment.

Duff sees the redundancy of state punishment as a possibility reserved only for those beings 'more perfect than ourselves'.[52] If he insists on his claim that full repentance or sufficient penance is impossible without it, then this conclusion is inevitable. However, as well as being an empirical generalisation, it also relies upon an overly cynical outlook on the human condition. In addition, the argument that only state punishment is 'public' enough was met with the challenge that penances undertaken voluntarily can be announced by a judge just as loudly as a formal sanction, and that the expressive quality of the former might actually be clearer. So, if self-punishment can fulfil the objectives Duff sets out for punishment—and I have argued that it can, perhaps even rendering it 'punishment'—at least some mitigation seems justified.

It should be reiterated that this argument requires that the offender has done a lot. It is not enough for him to feel the emotion of remorse. He must also have embarked on an expressive, burdensome penance that can be communicated to, and understood by, the community as such. It is this penitential expression that can form part of the dialogue between state and citizen. This notion of acknowledging the offender's response to his offence—his input into the communicative enterprise—will become even more important in Chapter 5. There, however, it will be argued that the offender's moral response should result in mitigation even if no burdensome penance has been self-imposed.

---

[51] ibid, xiv.

[52] There are two exceptions to this. He says that it may be permissible to reduce the punishment of 1) someone who had fully repented and accepted informal, vigilante punishment as her penance, and 2) the immediately repentant offender, whose remorse essentially provides evidence of lower culpability. See ibid, 119–121.

Duff's Vacillation

This most explicit of Duff's work on self-punishment is both consistent and at odds with some of his remarks elsewhere. Indeed, a tension seems to run throughout all his work. On the one hand, Duff repeatedly cites his concept of penance as the justifying aim—the 'constitutive justification'— of punishment. He also proposes that sentencers work with 'negative proportionality', which sets upper and lower limits on sentences, but gives 'sentencers room to attend to the concrete particularities of the crime, without worrying about rendering it commensurable with all other crimes in terms of its seriousness...'.[53] According to such a scheme, and if I am right to be optimistic about the efficacy of self-imposed penances to express repentance and the possibility of reaching full repentance with reduced state intervention, then remorseful self-punishment should have a significant role to play in reducing sentences to their lower limits.[54]

On the other hand, elsewhere, Duff expresses explicit commitment to public communicative aims, despite these being of no consequence to an offender's engagement with penance—the 'constitutive justification'.[55] Indeed, in relation to already repentant offenders, Duff argues that there should be no mitigation of sentence because 'to impose a lighter sentence on a repentant offender is thus to imply that repentance renders the crime less serious. But this is not normally true'.[56] Duff seems here to deviate from his negative proportionality proposal, suggesting that there is only one appropriate level of punishment suitable for any crime of a particular degree of seriousness. In fact, he cites von Hirsch in relation to this point about maintaining proportionality. Later, however, Duff says that von Hirsch's adherence to positive proportionality is wrong because it is too 'strict' a position. He claims:

> [P]roportionality, as a relationship between the seriousness of a crime and the severity of its punishment, is only one dimension of the proper relationship between crime and punishment on a communicative conception of punishment as a penance. A communicatively appropriate punishment should communicate, not just a degree of censure proportionate to the seriousness of the crime, but a more substantive understanding of the nature and implications of the crime as a wrong.[57]

So, Duff's work seems to be at variance on two levels. First, he vacillates between his stated justifying aim of punishment—penance—and adherence

---

[53] ibid, 139.

[54] For a similar point see von Hirsch and Ashworth (n 5) 102–03.

[55] These public communicative aims are in addition to the purpose penance serves to communicate the offender's repentance to the community. In addition, Duff here suggests that punishment communicates the seriousness of the offence to the wider public.

[56] Duff (n 50) 120.

[57] ibid, 142.

to ancillary aims of public evaluation of conduct. Second, he seems unclear as to the strictness that should be afforded to the proportionality requirement. Moreover, the levels intersect: whilst a perspective that relies purely on penance would significantly dilute proportionality requirements,[58] commitment to the public communicative functions of punishment may serve to reinforce these requirements. However, Duff seems to be undecided on this point too, suggesting that communicative punishment has communicative functions that transcend proportionate censure.

Ambiguity aside, I have shown that if remorseful penance is taken as the justifying aim of punishment, given that self-punishment constitutes the ideal penance, then remorseful self-penance does constitute some of the deserved punishment.

THEORY THREE: VON HIRSCH AND ASHWORTH—CENSURE AND SANCTION

For von Hirsch, punishment is constituted by both censure and sanction. He writes: 'punishing someone consists of visiting a deprivation (hard treatment) on him, because he supposedly has committed a wrong, in a manner that expresses disapprobation of the person for his conduct'.[59] This emphasis on the communicative facet of punishment suggests—as would also be the case for Duff's account—that a further criterion must be added to Hart's definition of punishment. Indeed, Joel Feinberg points out that Hart's definition fails to distinguish punishment from mere penalties such as overdue notices, late fees and so on.[60] Punishment, when conceived as Duff and von Hirsch conceive it, includes an *expressive* element. However, on von Hirsch's account, this appears to be the *only* additional criterion. We might render the additional clause thus: it conveys an appropriate degree of censure.

Having clarified what constitutes punishment within von Hirsch's sentencing perspective, I now consider whether remorse might either constitute some degree of punishment, or at least be able to serve the functions that justify punishment according to von Hirsch and Ashworth.

Remorse as a Substitute for Sanction

One potential way of demonstrating a degree of redundancy of punishment when faced with an offender's remorse on this view emerges from the

---

[58] See von Hirsch and Ashworth (n 5) 102–03.
[59] A von Hirsch, *Censure and Sanctions* (Oxford, Clarendon Press, 1993) 9.
[60] J Feinberg, *Doing & Deserving: Essays in the Theory of Responsibility* (Princeton, NJ, Princeton University Press, 1970).

way in which the sanction (the hard treatment element of punishment) is justified. Whereas some method of delivering censure is necessary to communicative retributive theories, von Hirsch argues that the imposition of sanction is justified contingently. The sanction provides an additional penal disincentive that helps agents adhere to the moral norms to which they may already be committed. Thus, a prudential reason for desisting is provided to supplement any normative reasons that already function for the offender.[61] Justifying the hard treatment element contingently means that retributive justice could theoretically still be achieved without it. Indeed, von Hirsch and Ashworth argue that, within their theoretical framework, punishment (or, at least, the harsh sanction, as dissociated from any symbolic censure) loses its justification if it can be achieved by other means:

> If the institution of the criminal sanction were incapable of carrying out these [expressive and preventative] public functions (or if those functions could be performed without having to resort to the intrusive features of punishment) then that institution would lose its raison d'être.[62]

The question can then be raised: can remorse carry out any or some of the expressive and preventative functions, rendering the criminal sanction to any degree redundant?

Remorse as a Deterrent

It could be argued that remorse might serve as some sort of deterrent, preventing offending. The intensely aversive nature of the experience of remorse, as described by Adam Smith,[63] is likely to be something that an offender would wish to avoid. Knowing now how wrongdoing makes him feel, the offender may use this as an additional prudential disincentive. He commits himself to avoiding engagement with the wrongdoing that elicits in him this terrible sentiment.

Moreover, there is something else important about this self-originating deterrent: experiencing remorse is much more certain for the offender than punishment prescribed by the court. If the offender has reacted remorsefully on this occasion, she may believe it likely that she would react this way again, regardless of whether she was caught the next time.

If remorse did turn out to have this deterrent effect, then there would be at least an argument for reducing the additional prudential disincentive, as the remorseful offender would be providing one himself. However, the existence of a deterrent effect of remorse is an empirical matter, and the evidence to date does not provide strong support for this effect. Cox's

---

[61] von Hirsch and Ashworth (n 5) 23.
[62] ibid, 100.
[63] Smith (n 3).

discussion of the evidence leads him to conclude that 'The disturbing fact is that there appears to be no firm evidence that [had the remorseless offender] shown remorse, there is less likelihood of him re-offending'.[64]

However, the intuition still remains that the fear of 'feeling bad' if one engages in some particular activity does serve to inhibit the desire to reoffend. The empirical reality is likely to be that some types of offences are susceptible to being partially deterred by remorse whereas others are not. This may account in part for the inconclusive research outcomes to date. An offender might reoffend despite intense remorse and self-loathing if, for example, the offence is highly emotional or motivated by addiction. Jones suggests that 'deterrent methods are of less value in reducing the incidence of those crimes in which strong passions or deep psychological problems are involved'.[65]

There is a peculiarity, though, to the suggestion that fear of remorse can serve as a deterrent. If remorse were to be genuine, then the offender should resist offending because he believes he should, not because he is scared that he will feel bad if he offends. Fear of feeling bad is more plausible where guilt is the emotional response to the wrongdoing. As discussed in Chapter 1, the concept of guilt developed by some theorists, which I called 'corrupt guilt', principally involves anxiety caused by breaking rules and the fear of the consequences for oneself when one transgresses. This sort of response to wrongdoing would be compatible with resistance to re-offending being motivated by a fear of experiencing guilt again. Following genuine remorse, however, the offender would be more likely to refrain from reoffending due to wanting to and believing that he should, not because of a fear of aversive emotions. Remorse would provide normative reasons to refrain, not prudential ones, and von Hirsch argues that additional prudential disincentives are helpful even to those who have internalised the normative reasons to refrain.[66]

There is, then, no strong argument that remorse could be a viable substitute for the prudential disincentive that the criminal sanction supplies. Furthermore, even if remorse did have some deterrent effect, that would not make it eligible to fill the role of the sanction. This becomes clear when we return again to the justification for the criminal sanction on von Hirsch and Ashworth's account. It is not just that it serves as a deterrent; the sanction is chosen as the means of conveying censure (as opposed to, say, purely symbolic means) *because* it has this additional deterrent function. But it is, first and foremost, a mode of expression: 'the preventitive function operates ... only *within* the framework of a censuring institution'.[67] The sanction, then,

[64] M Cox, *Remorse and Reparation* (London, Jessica Kingsley, 1999) 17.

[65] H Jones, *Crime and the Penal System. A Textbook of Criminology* (London, University Tutorial Press, 1956) 123.

[66] von Hirsch (n 59).

[67] von Hirsch and Ashworth (n 5) 24.

does some of the expressive work—might remorse go any way to fulfilling *this* function?

Remorse as Delivering Censure

It seems natural to think of remorse as constituting self-blame. We talk of people emotionally 'kicking themselves' and being angry with oneself is a familiar concept. It is even possible to imagine individuals who actually reprimand themselves in their heads, saying the same sorts of things that someone in an official capacity might say to them. Perhaps some might even be harder on themselves than others would be. Might such self-blame legitimately be perceived as censure?

The barrier to such a possibility is that censure, particularly for von Hirsch and Ashworth, is characterised by its authoritative nature. In fact, they perceive this to be the crucial difference between blaming and censuring. On this view, the most the remorseful offender might be able to do is blame himself, but he does not have the requisite standing to himself to convey censure. Censure requires that the person or institution delivering it stands in authority to the wrongdoer. Thus, even if remorse did provide some prudential disincentive, it could not express censure in the authoritative manner necessary. The state is required to fulfil this function.

The argument that self-censure cannot substitute for state censure should be carefully distinguished from the argument I make in the next chapter that remorse alters the content of the state censure that must be delivered. If self-censure were to substitute for state censure, it would, to some extent, eliminate part of the role of the state in responding to the offender's conduct. In contrast, where the offender's remorse alters the content of the state censure, the state retains its role but the way in which it responds is modified. The reasons why the state should respond to the offender's remorse are proposed and defended in the next chapter.

There is one further possible way in which self-censure might be seen as relevant to the punishment that is delivered. On von Hirsch and Ashworth's account, censure need not by necessity be communicated through hard treatment. They assert that a condemnatory response to culpably injurious conduct might be expressed *either* in a purely symbolic mode, *or* through the visitation of hard treatment.[68] Thus, although delivering deserved censure is central to their desert perspective, the criminal sanction does not *have* to be the way of achieving this. There is a theoretical possibility, then, if self-censure provided sufficient normative reasons to refrain, the symbolic mode of expression would become adequate. However, I have already noted above that von Hirsch and Ashworth would not accept this,

---

[68] ibid.

due to their pessimism surrounding the ability of the average person to be sufficiently motivated to refrain from reoffending by only normative reasons. This is what leads them to argue that a supplementary prudential disincentive be provided by the threat or experience of hard treatment. I shall now expand on this further.

Remorse as Reattachment to Normative Reasons to Refrain

I anticipate that von Hirsch and Ashworth would argue that, although remorse demonstrates attachment to normative reasons for desistance, this does not make prudential ones redundant. Their theory proposes that the criminal sanction is an *additional* disincentive. They already recognise that many people are motivated to some extent by normative reasons to resist offending. The assumption is that will power and intention alone are not strong enough preventative forces. In some cases it may take wrongdoing and subsequent remorse to wake an individual up to these normative reasons: the reasons become real for him. The point is that von Hirsch and Ashworth see an additional prudential disincentive as necessary even for people who are already attached to their moral convictions. This is what prevents their prudential disincentive from being 'beast control': it aids people in adhering to norms to which they already know they should be committed. Reattachment to normative reasons to refrain does not render the supplementary prudential disincentive any more redundant than does the sustained attachment to normative reasons of the law abiding.

Given their theoretical commitments, von Hirsch and Ashworth would have to accept that if no additional disincentive were needed, and there was an alternative, equally effective way of communicating censure, then the harsh sanction would be redundant. However, since remorse cannot perform either the preventative or expressive function of punishment on their view, and since even the remorseful often need assistance in living up to their moral convictions, mitigation cannot be justified on these grounds.

CONCLUSION

This chapter has considered whether remorse might constitute some of the deserved punishment, or otherwise provide a viable substitute. In relation to the benefits and burdens theory, remorse could do neither. Despite punishment not necessarily requiring incarceration on this account, the appropriate burden required objective restriction of freedom, which necessarily had to be imposed by an external agent.

The case for remorse constituting some of the deserved punishment was strongest in relation to Duff's work. I argued that remorse-motivated penance could actually *be* punishment within his account, especially as penance is argued to be the 'constitutive justification' of punishment. The reasons why Duff would disagree with this interpretation were found in his pessimism about the expressive efficacy of self-imposed penance and about the capacity of human beings to reach full repentance without state intervention. I challenged both of these reservations. Duff would also disagree on the grounds that communicative aims require that there is no deviation from proportional censure. This was shown to be an inconsistent line of thought throughout his work. It was noted that the very most that could be argued is that remorsefully imposed *penance* could constitute punishment. Remorse alone, or half-hearted attempts at expressing one's remorse, cannot suffice as they do not adequately express one's repentance to the community.

In relation to von Hirsch and Ashworth's perspective, it was demonstrated that remorse cannot constitute punishment as, for them, censure must be imposed by an external authority. Further, remorse could not go any way to achieving the aims of punishment since it provides no prudential disincentive additional to normative reasons. Indeed, any disincentive that remorse provides is predominantly in the form of these normative reasons, which alone do not secure restraint. Indeed, the inefficacy of normative reasons is the primary impetus for von Hirsch to advocate hard treatment as the means to communicate censure.

Having found limited justification for mitigation of the grounds of remorse based on the Already Punished argument, I next develop an account of Responsive Censure, which I shall argue succeeds in justifying remorse-based mitigation on communicative theories of punishment.

5

The Responsive Censure Argument

[O]ffenders who *appreciate the wrongfulness of their offending and its impact on its victims,* and express a desire to repair the damage and clear their conscience *deserve to receive a material reduction* in what would otherwise be an appropriate sentence.[1]

THIS DIRECTION, FOUND in Australia's *Victorian Sentencing Manual,* appeals to the remorseful offender's appreciation of the wrongfulness of his offending. This appreciation of wrongfulness, combined with desire to repair and atone, is said to reduce the severity of the deserved sentence. In this chapter I will argue that state censure should be responsive to the offender's appreciation of wrongfulness and, accordingly, that this alters the amount of censure the remorseful offender deserves.

OVERVIEW

The Responsive Censure argument comprises five main stages. First, drawing on the work of Scanlon and Bennett, I argue that we can draw a distinction between a person's blameworthiness and the extent to which we should blame or censure him. Second, I explain how the concept of censure is central to the principal communicative retributive theories. Third, I argue that, within these accounts, a dialogical model of censure is superior to a model in which there is no room for input from, and response to, the offender. The principal communicative accounts are shown to have reason to concede this model. Fourth, I argue that communication of remorse is the most valuable, relevant input that the offender can make to the dialogue: his categorical renunciation of his conduct. Fifth, I argue that the dialogical model requires that the censure visited on the offender needs to respond to his communication of remorse. Mitigation embodies this response. Von Hirsch and Ashworth's arguments relating to quasi-retributive grounds for mitigation are shown to reinforce my

---

[1] *Victorian Sentencing Manual* (Judicial College of Victoria, 2006–2014), section 10.13.3, www.judicialcollege.vic.edu.au/eManuals/VSM/index.htm#13888.htm, emphasis added.

arguments. Sixth, if the censure the offender deserves is mitigated, then, I demonstrate, the punishment that communicates this censure is correspondingly mitigated. Finally, I defend my account against some potential objections. The consequence of this chapter will be to put the burden on potential objectors to show why one-way communication is the superior model for sentencing offenders, or why remorse is irrelevant even in a dialogical context.

BLAMEWORTHINESS AND BLAME

Scanlon explores the idea that the concept of blameworthiness can be distinguished from that of blame.[2] For him, to claim that an agent is *blameworthy* for an action is to claim that this action indicates something about that agent's attitudes towards others that impairs his relations with them.[3] This is similar to the second notion of blameworthiness—as moral assessment of the offender—explored in Chapter 2. To *blame* someone, on the other hand, is to go on to hold and express attitudes towards the agent that differ from the attitudes that would be required if one were to have an unimpaired relationship with this person.

Bennett, whose retributive theory of punishment draws extensively on the practice and symbols of blame and apology, also recognises a similar distinction, claiming that 'we can distinguish ... the conditions that make a person *blameworthy* from the conditions that make it appropriate *overtly* to blame them, or to *express* our blame'.[4]

However, we might further distinguish possible blame-related states of affairs as follows: (1) a person can be blameworthy, in a sense that is comparable with the legal notion of culpability or, as Scanlon suggests, as a result of acting in such a way as to reveal relationship-impairing attitudes; (2) a person can assess another person as being blameworthy; (3) a person might go on to hold an attitude of blame towards a person in virtue of his blameworthiness; (4) a person might behave towards another person in a way informed by his attitude of blame; (5) a person might remonstrate with another person about his blameworthiness; (6) a person might remonstrate with another person about his blameworthiness from a position of relevant authority; (7) a person might cease to do any or all of these things, perhaps resulting in/constituting the forgiving of that for which another person is blameworthy.[5]

---

[2] T Scanlon, *Moral Dimensions: Permissibility, Meaning, Blame* (Cambridge, MA, Belknap, 2008).

[3] ibid, 6.

[4] C Bennett, *The Apology Ritual: A Philosophical Theory of Punishment* (Cambridge, Cambridge University Press, 2008) 167.

[5] Presenting these steps as a sequence is somewhat artificial. Not all of them will be passed through and none are necessary for the one that follows. However, there is a logic to the order I present them in, which I trust will make sense to the reader.

Conditions that justify one or some of these states of affairs do not necessarily justify them all. Further, a person's instantiation of one or some of these states of affairs certainly does not mean he or she is instantiating them all. For example, it might be justifiable for a person to hold an attitude of blame towards a stranger that he hears has cheated on her husband. It is debatable, however, whether he would be justified in behaving towards her (perhaps by glaring at her angrily and refusing to engage in conversation) in a way informed by his attitude of blame. It seems even less likely that he would be justified in remonstrating with her about her infidelity. That blameworthiness and all 'steps' of blaming are distinct is most conclusively shown by the fact that a person can cease to blame—perhaps to forgive—without the subject of the prior blame ceasing to be blameworthy.

It might seem that such a conceptualisation of the operation of blame is only applicable to personal relationships and thus cannot be transferred to a state-citizen model. However, this is not the case. Following Scanlon, we might acknowledge the fact that intentions and expectations about how each party will act towards one another are central to both types of relationship.[6] Scanlon suggests that this is true of moral relationships holding between all human beings, and in what such a relationship might consist. In contrast to personal relationships, Scanlon explains that, in the case of moral relationships, 'the relevant conditions do not concern the parties' existing attitudes toward one another but only certain general facts about them, namely that they are beings of a certain kind that are capable of understanding and responding to reasons'.[7] Moreover, for Scanlon, morality requires that human beings hold certain attitudes towards one another simply in virtue of the fact that they stand in the relation of 'fellow rational beings'. Thus, when an individual does not manifest the mutual concern we should have for other human beings, the moral relationship is impaired, and blame becomes appropriate.

Bennett explicitly argues for the relevance of blame (and apology, to which I shall return below) to the institution of state punishment.[8] On his view, private individuals who are engaged in intrinsically valuable joint enterprises (from friendships, to teaching, to simply being neighbours) must respond with blame to individuals' failures to meet the basic standards expected of 'qualified members' of the enterprise.[9] A corollary of this is that the state must respond with condemnation to any qualified members of

---

[6] Scanlon (n 2).

[7] ibid, 139.

[8] Bennett (n 4).

[9] ibid, 95; here Bennett contrasts 'qualified members' with 'apprentices'. Whereas a qualified practitioner can be expected to 'recognise and comply with the responsibilities of her place in the practice autonomously, without external supervision', apprentices (for example, within the collective project of political community, children) require help and direction to learn.

the political community who fail to meet the basic expectations of being a citizen. He uses a 'right to be punished' strategy to argue for this conclusion within both the spheres of private individuals and the state's interactions with its citizens. The main idea is that failing to blame or censure those who act in ways that demonstrate disrespect for the legitimate norms and expectations of an intrinsically valuable relationship would fail to treat them as fully rational, qualified members who should be held to the demands of the relationship. A failure to condemn and temporarily withdraw goodwill is, Bennett argues, incompatible with maintaining the relationship and infringes the right to be punished.

It should be noted that not all of the 'steps' of blaming I identified above can properly be transferred to the state. The state, for example, does not hold attitudes of blame towards its citizens (step 3) in a way that fully meets the phenomenology on an individual level. Whilst it can make assessments of blameworthiness (step 2) (based on the criminal law and sentencing legislation), it does not make sense to ascribe thoughts and feelings to the state. Furthermore, the mode of remonstrating with, or censuring, the offender can *only* be authoritative (step 6). Whereas a teacher can formally censure an 18-year-old student for bullying from her position of professional authority, it is conceivable that she could censure the student for the same thing informally, person to person, in her authority as a member of the moral community, and in a way that would be qualitatively different from formal censure. In sentencing offenders, the state always operates in a formal capacity. Finally, it could be argued that it would be inappropriate to apply the language of forgiveness (step 7) to the state—it is not the state's place, the argument might go, to forgive the burglar, but the victim's.[10]

Bennett, however, would be unlikely to agree with this latter point. He argues that the reacceptance of the offender into the enterprise (of political community)

> looks a bit as if he has been granted a sort of forgiveness: the offence is not quite forgotten, but put into the past: it no longer conditions the offender's relations with the authority and his official status in the group.[11]

This is one of the main reasons that Bennett argues that the symbolism of apology as well as blame should be incorporated into the criminal sanction—that the state should impose proportionate amends rather than simply hard treatment. The amends, he argues, would represent what the offender would be motivated to make himself, were he to be truly sorry. This is necessary because 'the offender's reacceptance looks like the kind of

---

[10] However, if were to adopt a political model in which all offences are conceived as being offences against the state, it might become more convincing that forgiveness (or, perhaps, official pardon) could be something the state can appropriately grant.

[11] Bennett (n 4) 172.

forgiveness that results from a person's having made a sincere and adequate apology'.[12] Consequently, in order to earn the institutional version of forgiveness, the offender has to be made to do something that is the institutional version of apology.

Thinking about the varying appropriateness of blame and the effects of apology invites the possibility of an offender's remorse repairing the moral relationship (*à la* Scanlon) or facilitating one's reacceptance into the political community (*à la* Bennett). When one communicates one's genuine remorse, the offender's concern is shown to be reinstated, and his recommitment to the demands of the collective enterprise demonstrated.

This possibility of an offender going at least some way to repairing his moral relationship with the community is found in Duff's work. He suggests that:

> The crime created a moral breach between the criminal and her fellow citizens or her community ... That breach can be repaired, thus reconciling her with those from whom her crime threatened to separate her, only if she herself is prepared to heal it by repenting and forswearing her crime, which necessarily also involves a resolve and attempt so to reform herself that she avoids such wrongdoing in the future.[13]

These conditions for reconciliation are similar to Bennett's requirement that an offender must perform the ritual of apology (through serving his amends-equivalent sentence) in order for the offender to have his full status returned to him, and thus cease to be condemned by others. However, whereas Bennett envisages that the ritual of apology *follows* state condemnation (or perhaps is concurrent with state condemnation—the condemnation is meted out by requiring the offender to make proportionate amends), I am going to suggest that remorse can affect the appropriateness of censuring (or, at least, the severity that is appropriate) at *prior* steps. Importantly, my argument will not be that the remorseful offender deserves something like forgiveness, but instead that state censure must be attuned to the offender's prior understanding and acceptance of its message. This is particularly the case, I will argue, when censure is approached in dialogical terms, which I will try to show the state has compelling reason to do.

Affecting the Severity of the Blame Deserved

If, as I have suggested, blameworthiness and deserved blame are related but distinguishable, it would be possible that two offenders could be equally blameworthy for their respective offences, but that they might not deserve blame of equal severity. I will argue that an offender's remorse functions

---

[12] ibid.
[13] RA Duff, 'Penal Communications: Recent Work in the Philosophy of Punishment' (1996) 20 *Crime and Justice* 1, 48–49.

to reduce the severity of the blame that he deserves, and conclude that this translates into the requirement that the state censure him less harshly.

There are two possible bases for such an argument—social convention and principle. An argument from social convention would assert that cultural norms determine when communication of blame is tempered and that these same norms should influence the factors we can allow to mitigate an offender's sentence. Such an argument would draw on norms such as those discussed in relation to Dan-Cohen's work.[14] If it seems cruel to insist on the same intensity of blame for the remorseful wrongdoer—for example, by reiterating the wrongdoer's responsibility for his wrongdoing—then this norm should inform the censure we visit upon offenders through punishment.

Manson proposes an argument from convention, pointing out that retributive theorists already concede that some aspects of sentencing depend on what has become conventional.[15] Citing von Hirsch and Ashworth's claim that the censure expressed through penal deprivation is in part *a matter of convention* when 'judged in absolute rather than comparative terms',[16] Manson argues that 'legitimate sympathy' is amongst the justifications for mitigating factors.[17] He claims that if the factor tends to evoke sympathy and is legitimated by serving sentencing aims (rehabilitation and reparation), then it should mitigate the offender's sentence. Crucially, Manson seems to imply that the truly remorseful offender is worthy of sympathy.[18]

However, in the next chapter I shall argue against the supposition that sympathy is the response that the offender's remorse often evokes in others. However, for now I want to argue that it is more convincing to justify remorse as a mitigating factor by adopting a principled, rather than merely conventional, approach. To do so, I will show that communicative retributive theories have reasons internal to their constitutive arguments that oblige them to accept remorse as a mitigating factor.

THE CENTRALITY OF CENSURE TO COMMUNICATIVE RETRIBUTIVE THEORIES

The idea that the offender must be censured for his or her wrongdoing is central to principal communicative retributive theories. For Duff,

---

[14] M Dan-Cohen, 'Revising the Past: On the Metaphysics of Repentance, Forgiveness, and Pardon' in A Sarat and N Hussain (eds), *Forgiveness, Mercy, and Clemency* (Stanford, CA, Stanford University Press, 2007).

[15] A Manson, 'The Search For Principles of Mitigation: Integrating Cultural Demands' in J Roberts (ed), *Mitigation and Aggravation at Sentencing* (Cambridge, Cambridge University Press, 2011).

[16] ibid, 48.

[17] The others justifications being: (1) drawn from a 'principled approach' and (2) 'systemic rationale'.

[18] Manson (n 15) 45.

'punishment communicates the condemnation or censure that offenders deserve'.[19] It is also integral to von Hirsch's theory that the penal sanction conveys censure or blame.[20] Drawing on the work of PF Strawson, he describes the capacity to respond to wrongdoing with reprobation or censure as 'simply part of a morality that holds people accountable for their conduct'.[21] People judge wrongdoers adversely because their conduct was reprehensible. For von Hirsch, 'censure consists of the expression of that judgement, plus its accompanying sentiment of disapproval'.[22] He also specifies some of the 'positive moral functions of blaming', citing its capacity to address the victim, its capacity to address the offender, its provision of the opportunity for the offender to respond, and its ability to express a normative message to third parties, appealing to their sense of the conduct's wrongfulness as a reason for desistance.

However, despite these 'positive moral functions', it should be emphasised that for both von Hirsch and Duff state censure is *deserved*. This is what makes their theories retributive at their core. For censure to be deserved and not just instrumental, censure must valued as an end. If censure were simply a way of trying to manipulate how people behave, it would not be retributive, as it would be simply a way of achieving crime control. Instead, censure is delivered because it is the appropriate response to wrongdoing, even if it may go on to have other benefits, such as persuading the offender to repent. But, some positive consequences are part and parcel of what censure involves. For instance, Duff argues that it is internal to censure that it seeks a response from the offender, persuading him to see his behaviour for the wrong that it is:

> [I]f a citizen does commit such a wrong, the law should aim to bring him to recognise and to repent that wrongdoing: not just because that is a method of persuading him not to repeat it, but because that is *owed* both to him and his victim ... To take wrongs seriously as wrongs involves responding to them with criticism and censure; and the aim internal to censure is that of persuading the wrongdoer to recognise and repent his wrongdoing.[23]

So, whilst censure may have positive consequences in the effects it can have on the offender's attitude towards his wrongdoing and future behaviour, it is delivered because it is owed. It takes wrongdoing seriously.

---

[19] A Duff, *Punishment, Communication and Community* (Oxford, Oxford University Press, 2001) 27.

[20] A von Hirsch, *Censure and Sanctions* (Oxford, Clarendon Press, 1993); A von Hirsch and A Ashworth, *Proportionate Sentencing: Exploring the Principles* (Oxford, Oxford University Press, 2005) 17–19. In collaboration with Ashworth he says that censure is the authoritative analogue of blame. This authoritative character is the only distinguishing feature that they mention.

[21] von Hirsch (n 20) 9.

[22] ibid.

[23] Duff (n 19) 81–82, emphasis added.

Crucially, both Duff and von Hirsch see the criminal *sanction* as part of the communicative enterprise. Punishment *communicates* censure; it does not simply follow it. Duff takes the strongest view, claiming that a communicative conception of punishment provides its complete justification. That is, hard treatment is necessary just because it can serve the communicative aims of punishment more adequately than can mere convictions or symbolic punishments (the communicative aims being those of 1) 'transparent persuasion',[24] whereby the offender is brought to recognise the wrongs he has done and that he should take steps to avoid such wrongs in the future, and 2) the offender's communication of his remorse though penance). So, for Duff, punishment *is* censure and penance, and neither will be adequately communicated without it.

Von Hirsch takes a weaker view, arguing that the harshness of the sanctions cannot be justified on communicative grounds alone. He does see punishment as serving a communicative function saying that 'through the censure expressed by ... sanctions, the law registers disapprobation and blame'.[25] However, he does not see this function as sustaining the severity of the criminal sanction. He argues that the severity is justified by its capacity to provide an additional prudential disincentive which supplements the normative reasons conveyed by penal censure.[26] He makes it clear that the two functions (and justifications) of punishment are not independent, rather, 'the censure and the hard treatment are intertwined in the way punishment is structured'.[27] He also states that in his justification of punishment, the blaming function has primacy, and it is carried out by visiting criminal sanctions upon offenders as they can also play a supplementary role as a disincentive.

So, crucially for the argument I am going to make, blame or censure is conveyed by punishment on these theories. For von Hirsch, punishment also serves to deter, but it primarily communicates. If it were the case that censure was independent of punishment—that censure could be adequately achieved simply through conviction or the judge verbally imparting blame on the offender—then differences in the level of censure appropriate for a particular offender would not be intrinsically linked to the severity of the punishment he should receive. Since my argument will focus on the effect of remorse on deserved censure, censure must be communicated by the sanction in order for there to be necessary consequences for the severity of this sanction. That this is the case—that censure severity is communicated by sanction severity—is, however, held to be true even for von Hirsch's 'two-pronged' justification of punishment. He claims that by altering the harshness of the onerous consequences of breaking the law—consequences

---

[24] ibid, 101.
[25] von Hirsch (n 20) 12.
[26] ibid, 13.
[27] ibid, 14.

which both constitute hard treatment and express reprobation—the degree of censure conveyed will be altered.[28]

Having established that censure is the central element of the communicative function of punishment, I am now going to argue that a dialogical model of this communicative enterprise is superior to one in which censure is simply an isolated message, inattentive to the content of the would-be communications of the offender. Moreover, I will also argue that principles to which the two theories adhere support adoption of this model.

THE CASE FOR RESPONSIVE CENSURE

As explored above, both the retributive theories developed by Duff and von Hirsch are communicative. Duff proposes a 'communicative conception of punishment as communicating to offenders the censure that their crimes deserve'.[29] He emphasises that punishment should be communicative rather than merely expressive, arguing that

> communication involves, as expression need not, a *reciprocal* and *rational* engagement ... it aims to engage [the person with whom we are trying to communicate] as an active participant in the process who will receive and respond to the communication, and it appeals to the other's reason and understanding—the response it seeks is one that is mediated by the other's rational grasp of its content. Communication thus addresses the other as a rational agent, whereas expression need not.[30]

Von Hirsch's conception of punishment is less explicitly dialogical. Whilst, on his view, punishment communicates censure, he does not envisage an active exchange. Nonetheless, he seems to imply that a response from the offender is both expected and is an appropriate object of evaluation. In collaboration with Ashworth, he writes:

> [P]unishment, we believe, should be conceptualized as an expression of censure. Penal censure has important moral functions that are not reducible to crime prevention. A response to criminal wrongdoing that conveys disapprobation gives the individual the opportunity to respond in ways that are typically those of an agent capable of moral deliberation: to recognise the wrongfulness of the action; to feel remorse; to express regret; to make efforts to desist in future—or else to try to give reasons why the conduct was not actually wrong.[31]

Following similar remarks elsewhere, von Hirsch writes: 'a reaction of indifference would, if the censure is justified, itself be grounds for criticizing him'.[32] So, von Hirsch's conception of the communicative function of

[28] ibid.
[29] Duff (n 19) 79.
[30] ibid, 79–80.
[31] von Hirsch and Ashworth (n 20) 92.
[32] von Hirsch (n 20) 10.

punishment involves an expectation that the offender respond—in a way that 'answers' the censure delivered—and that his answer in turn is something that we can appropriately assess as being morally better or worse.

This emerging picture of an exchange, of a conversation that shapes the appropriate censure, suggests a model of sentencing as a species of dialogue; as something that is two-way, in which both participants seek to better understand the subject matter. However, we need at this juncture to explore what really can be meant by 'dialogue' in this context, and why it is better than a non-interactive model.

The classical model of dialogue would be something like the Socratic Method: an intellectual attack and counter-attack designed to uncover truth or to discover new ways of thinking about things. This cannot be what is meant by dialogue here: a sentencing hearing is not a drawn-out iterative exchange where truths slowly dawn on the offender. It is not a critical reasoning exercise.

When I suggest that censure should be conceived in dialogical terms, I am not imagining a literal conversation that occurs between the offender and the judge. Although the offender may say something to communicate his remorse, this will not be in the context of a drawn-out exchange. Moreover, the sentencing dialogue I have in mind is, in some ways, more inclusive than the classical model, since I understand it to incorporate more diffuse modes of communication. Censuring through sanction already extends the meaning of communication—it is not literal speech. In addition, I suggest that although the offender's remorse can be communicated through speech, it can be communicated in a myriad of other (sometimes more meaningful) ways—perhaps through a letter, through a display of emotion, through significant life changes, through efforts at reparation.[33] Moreover, this communication may occur before the offender meets the sentencing judge and will most likely not be directed at him (at least, not primarily). All these instances of communication can be potential elements of the penal dialogue.

One might ask why I use the term 'dialogue', if I am using it in such a non-standard way. The reason is that the term 'dialogue' involves the essential elements that I want to use in my ideal model of censure: it is *responsive*—what is communicated by participant A is influenced by the prior communication of participant B, with a view to his subsequent response; it involves a *shared topic*—dialogue is incompatible with talking at cross purposes; it necessarily involves *attention to one's interlocutor*—one is not involved in dialogue if one ignores the other

---

[33] Indeed, Weisman shows that, more often than not, 'remorse is communicated through gestures, displays of affects and other paralinguistic devices rather than only through words'. R Weisman, *Showing Remorse: Law and the Social Control of Emotion* (Farnham, Ashgate Publishing, 2014) 10.

participant's input. Mere expression or even simple communication does not have these characteristics. One can communicate something without expecting, nor attending to, a response.

So, whilst dialogue incorporates the characteristics that I will argue should be transferred to the practice of censure, it is not to be thought of as a sequential spoken exchange that occurs in the courtroom. Instead, we can conceive of a broader notion of dialogue, which fits more comfortably with the sentencing context. On this broader notion, it does not matter that there is not a clear sequence of speech acts emerging from and alternating between the judge and the offender. The offender's input into the dialogue might have been made first when he expressed his remorse to the victim and tried to apologise. It need not even be entirely verbal: perhaps the offender's remorse is partly expressed, for example, through his seeking help from anger management programmes. As I argued in Chapter 4, self-imposed penance can be expressive.

The Core Argument

My argument so far, then, is that by engaging dialogically with the offender on the subject of his offence, the quality of the censure will be improved.[34] The offender is better able to understand the wrongful nature of his offence: that it is indeed something in light of which the remorse he feels is

---

[34] Steven Tudor has argued for a similar position, although we arrive at our conclusions via somewhat different routes. Tudor's argument is, in large part, justified by social norms and utilitarian benefits, whereas mine is derived solely from a conception of censure which takes place in a dialogical framework. For Tudor, much of the value of recognising the offender's remorse lies in the psychological effects of, using his language, recognising her self-conception. On his view, recognising the offender's remorse fosters psychological harmony, as it confirms the offender's self-conception, and consequently helps to shape her future conduct in relation to this self-conception. My argument, in contrast, begins with the claim, for which I argued, that a dialogical model of communicative sentencing is superior to a model according to which censure is expressed as an unresponsive statement. The obligation to mitigate the censure delivered—to engage with the offender by responding to his ideal, remorseful contribution to the dialogue—then falls out of commitment to this model. Whereas Tudor weighs up the value of acknowledging the offender's self-conception *against* the value of justice, my argument makes mitigation on the grounds of remorse integral to correctly delivering censure. Less severe censure becomes deserved. If there are further utilitarian benefits in confirming the offender's self-conception then this is a bonus but the justification of mitigation, on my account, does not rest on these benefits. Indeed, Tudor's focus on psychological benefits risks justifying the judicial acknowledgment of any self-conception. The offender who, for example, sees himself as 'above the law' would also be likely to experience psychological harmony, were his self-conception acknowledged through mitigation. On the Responsive Censure view, this self-conception would be irrelevant to the dialogue about the wrongdoing, whereas prior repudiation of the wrongdoing would not. S Tudor, 'Why Should Remorse Be a Mitigating Factor in Sentencing?' (2008) 2 *Criminal Law and Philosophy* 241. Nick Smith has also argued that the tenets of communicative retributivism support the practice of apology reductions at sentencing. N Smith, *Justice through Apologies: Remorse, Reform, and Punishment* (New York, NY, Cambridge University Press, 2014).

appropriate. A modified response to his remorse could communicate this. If censure seeks a response, and this response is already forthcoming, to nonetheless continue to seek this response as if it were absent devalues the censure. If censure is not responsive then it assumes no moral transformation and speaks to the remorseful offender as if he is yet to be convinced of the wrongfulness of his conduct. However, censure that communicates modified disapprobation, in response to the offender's remorse, has greater communicative and moral force. This moral force stems from taking into account the remorseful offender's appreciation of the wrongfulness of his offence, addressing him appropriately to his understanding.

Recall Duff's insistence that communication should be reciprocal, appealing to the other's reason and understanding. Censure that ignored the offender's remorseful communication would fail to be reciprocal. It would also fail to appeal to the offender's reason because it does not address him in his present state of understanding but, rather, deafly seeks the response it should have already heard. Von Hirsch also emphasises that a moral response is sought from the offender. If this ideal 'response' has already been communicated prior to censure, the message of censure that is now appropriate changes. Directing the offender to see the wrongfulness of what he did seems inappropriate. It is as if the agent engaging with the offender had not heard what the offender has already conveyed.

This is not to deny that censure should still condemn the offence and impart blame on the offender. However, it must do this in a way that is *responsive* to the offender's remorse. It addresses him as someone who already understands the wrongfulness of what he did, whilst also confirming that the offender is right in his self-condemnation. This communication has greater moral force as it confronts the offender in his actual level of understanding. Just as the notion of punishment as communication of censure stretches the notion of dialogue, incorporating non-verbal as well as verbal expressions of remorse made before as well as during the sentencing hearing is a comparable extension.

Censure, as we have seen, anticipates a moral response even when it is communicated through punishment. If we accept that the quality of an instance of communication is increased when it pays attention to the beliefs and outlook of the interlocutor—ie when it is dialogical—then, I argue, this has consequences for sentencing. Since censure communicated through a sanction seeks to confront the offender and anticipates a particular response, we should accept that the dialogical model I have presented is superior to unresponsive, unidirectional penal communication.

Support from Communicative Retributive Theories: Rational Agency

As well as making the argument for the superiority of a dialogical model of sentencing independently, I now wish to argue that other values that the principal retributive theories explicitly hold lend support to the acceptance of a dialogical model of censure.

Von Hirsch and Ashworth's retributive theory continually emphasises the need to address the offender as a rational moral agent; that is, someone who is 'capable of moral deliberation' and responsive to reasons.[35] A communicative enterprise that ignores the offender's moral response (where present) would seem to be less respectful of rational moral agency than it could be. Of course, such respect for rational moral agency would preclude coercive attempts to elicit a remorseful response—as von Hirsch and Ashworth note[36]—but it should give the offender an *opportunity* to make such a response and not ignore this response when it is forthcoming.

That communication is at its optimum when it engages with the offender, instead of proceeding indifferently, is also a theme that recurs in Duff's work. He too characterises communication as seeking a response and addressing the other as a rational agent:

> Communication ... is essentially a two-way rational activity. We communicate with another, who figures not simply as a passive recipient, but as a participant with us in this activity; our communication appeals to her understanding, not simply to her unreasoned feelings, and seeks a rational response from her. Communication, that is, addresses the other as a rational agent...[37]

Such engagement most naturally suggests a dialogical attitude: multiple participants engage in the activity of censuring the offender for her wrong, including the offender herself. Moreover, when seeking a response from a rational agent, one consequently puts oneself in a position to respond to the agent's response.

So far I have argued that a dialogical model of sentencing should be the preferred model within communicative retributive theories that focus on the censure an offender deserves. Engaging with the offender enhances the quality of the censure and best serves the aim of addressing the offender as a rational moral agent who is expected to respond. I have also shown how the principal retributive theories are not only compatible with a dialogical model, but also seem to *require* it if communication is to be optimised.

Some Preliminary Concerns

There are two general objections that could be raised to a dialogical model of censure: one arises from the possibility of non-participation, the other from the possibility that some offenders may lack the capacity to understand the meaning of censure, or to engage in dialogue.

---

[35] von Hirsch and Ashworth (n 20) 17.
[36] ibid, 18.
[37] Duff (n 13) 33.

It could be argued that dialogue requires two participants and, if the offender refuses to participate, a dialogical attitude is therefore inappropriate. However, even in the absence of participation, it is still important to give the offender the opportunity to participate if he so chooses, for the reasons explored above. Therefore, a predisposition towards dialogue should be maintained. If dialogue, as I have conceived it in the sentencing context, is an attitude of attention, this does not become redundant if the offender offers no contribution.

The second objection is that since some offenders may not be able to understand the meaning of the censure, or are unable to engage in dialogue (broadly construed) effectively, it is not fair to adopt a model that potentially favours (in terms of outcome) those that can. However, if, as I have argued, a dialogical attitude is generally superior to an unreceptive one, due to the superior quality of the communication achieved by the former, it seems right to commit ourselves to this model across the board, even if we have to adjust our approach in response to the capacities of the offender under consideration. It would be inappropriate to reduce the quality of the censure for all offenders—to cease to engage with them as rational agents— on the basis that some may not be able to grasp entirely the content of the communication. After all, our inability to engage with certain offenders as rational agents (because those offenders lack certain capacities required for such engagement) does not alter our ability to engage with other offenders as rational agents. Accordingly, it could equally be claimed that it would be unfair to deny those who have the relevant capacities the opportunity for engagement.

Remorse is the Offender's Ideal, Relevant Contribution to the Dialogue

If we conceive of the sentencing hearing as dialogical, we can consider what the constituents of the dialogue would be. The subject matter is the offence for which the offender is being sentenced. The sentencer communicates disapproval to the offender—censure is embodied in the sanction that is imposed. Both Duff and von Hirsch expect that the offender will respond to this censure, but he might respond in many ways. He might, for instance, respond with indifference, he might respond defiantly, he might respond remorsefully, or he might offer a complete non sequitur. Importantly, any of these 'responses' might be offered by the offender prior to or during sentencing—as 'responses' to the anticipated censure or simply as reactions to the wrongdoing itself.

Of course, not everything that the offender might communicate is relevant. The communication must be about the offence (not, for example, whether the offender has done good work for charity in the past). This is important because offenders do sometimes communicate things at trial and sentencing that are irrelevant to the topic of the wrongfulness of the offence. I am here reminded of Rolf Harris's impromptu performance of one of his songs during his trial for sex offences.[38] Such communication was clearly irrelevant.

As noted, Duff explains that the response sought is one that 'is mediated by the other's rational grasp of its content'.[39] If an offender were to respond with a list of good things he had done in the past, this would show that he had not really grasped the meaning of the censure. He is being censured for his offence and, correspondingly, his offence is the subject matter of the dialogue. To ignore the subject of the wrongfulness of his actions and instead attempt to draw attention to something non-offence related would not be an appropriate input. The appropriate response from the state would then be to reaffirm the censure and perhaps to explain the reasons for the irrelevance of this particular communication to the offender.

Perhaps another offender might respond indifferently to the message conveyed in censure. In such a situation, it is possible that the offender had fully grasped the content of the censure but simply did not care. Hypothetically: 'I understand that it was wrong but that does not bother me'. Such a defiant response *is* focused on the subject matter at hand; it reveals the offender's attitude both to his wrongdoing and to the censure he is receiving. However, as von Hirsch suggests, such a response might be grounds for further criticism—understating the degree of harm caused and yet being indifferent or even gleeful towards it is arguably worse than not grasping the implications of what one had done.[40] A remorseful response, on the other hand, is both relevant—it focuses on the offence—and desirable: it is the appropriate moral response following the commission of the offence. It demonstrates understanding of the harm caused and concern for those harmed.

However, a lack of remorse should not be grounds for aggravation. The default censure assumes that the offender does not appreciate the wrongfulness of his conduct. Thus, the indifferent or defiant offender should be confronted with full censure, which is sufficient to communicate the appropriate message.

QUASI-RETRIBUTIVE GROUNDS AND VON HIRSCH AND ASHWORTH'S TIME DELAY ARGUMENT

At this juncture, it is illuminating to return to the arguments von Hirsch and Ashworth advance to explain why the person who is sentenced a long

---

[38] See www.independent.co.uk/news/uk/crime/rolf-harris-trial-entertainer-sings-jake-the-peg-to-jurors-in-indecent-assault-case-9439079.html.

[39] Duff (n 19) 79–80.

[40] von Hirsch (n 20) 10.

time after the offence should receive mitigation. In Chapter 2 I examined their claim that, as time passes, 'the possibility increases that the actor may have changed significantly—so that his long-past act does not reflect badly on the person he now is'.[41] This, I suggested, if true for the time delay offender would also be true of the remorseful offender although, ultimately, I argued that such a claim requires one to adopt character retributivism. I now focus on the other claim they make: 'When the offence for which [the offender] is being sentenced was committed several years earlier, the process of eliciting a reflective response may become more problematic after such a long delay'.[42]

Consideration of this second claim serves to emphasise their focus on the reflection-facilitating function of censure and the occasions for mitigation they think this can create. Conceiving of censure as reflection-facilitating shows a commitment to censure being not merely a 'statement', but a communication that is sensitive to the responses for which it provides an opportunity. Recall that von Hirsch and Ashworth express commitment to quasi-retributive grounds that 'may address special situations which relate to this reflective process'.[43] Although the censure communicated by the sentence is not tailored to elicit remorse, they emphasise that 'the rationale underlying the censuring response has something to do with the capacity of an offender, as a moral agent, to engage in certain kinds of moral reflection'.[44] Their Time Delay argument shows that they accept that there are ways in which the offender can change, particularly with regard to his reflective capacity, that are relevant to the censure he receives. As in Chapter 2, I will argue that if this holds for the time delayed offender, then a parallel argument can be made for the remorseful offender.

Von Hirsch and Ashworth claim that the process of eliciting a reflective response may become problematic after such a delay.[45] The assumption made here is that an offender may no longer easily be able to think very deeply or feel very strongly about an event that occurred long ago. I am not sure this is an obvious assumption: on the contrary, sometimes the passage of time can give us a clearer perspective on things. However, this assumption shows that von Hirsch and Ashworth deem the function of eliciting a reflective response important for censure, so much so that incapacity of the function might result in the censure being mitigated.

It is inherent in remorse that it constitutes a reflective response, and one that is deemed to be the optimal response to censure. As von Hirsch and Ashworth themselves write: 'when the offender is thus censured, a moral response on his part would be deemed appropriate—for example, an

[41] von Hirsch and Ashworth (n 20) 178.
[42] ibid, 174.
[43] ibid.
[44] ibid, 175.
[45] ibid, 174.

expression of concern, an acknowledgement of wrongdoing, or an effort at better self restraint'.[46] It would seem peculiar if the remorseful offender—the offender *most* engaged in the reflective process—did not receive mitigation whereas the offender who evaded detection for a long time did receive mitigation, on the grounds that he may not be able to reflect effectively. Indeed, it could be argued that an *increase* of censure might be necessary in order to 'jog his memory' and to reiterate the reality and nature of his past conduct.

Von Hirsch and Ashworth also recommend mitigation for the offender who has offered reparation voluntarily, for reasons that are 'related to the values underlying the desert rationale'.[47] They identify this value as giving the defendant the opportunity to provide recognition of how he has wrongfully injured the victim. Again, they relate this to the reflective process that censure gives the offender reason to engage in. They argue that when an offender offers reparation voluntarily he not only has reflected on and recognised the wrongfulness of his actions himself, but has taken action to convey that recognition to the person wronged, in a manner that is closely linked with the wrongful conduct itself.

The remorseful offender, as I have understood him, has also reflected on and recognised the wrongfulness of his actions, and should be disposed to make attempts to apologise and repair. Prima facie, von Hirsch and Ashworth's arguments here might be thought to support my view. However, they explicitly argue that the case for mitigation may become 'considerably weaker where the offender merely feels or expresses remorse but takes no such action'.[48] I shall now argue that their position here overemphasises reparation and underemphasises remorse.

It is in remorse and not reparation that reflection on actions and recognition of their wrongfulness principally occurs. It may be that voluntary reparation makes us more *convinced* of an offender's remorse, but it is remorse itself that is bound up with the reflective process censure is intended to facilitate.[49] Indeed, voluntary reparation could occur without remorse—perhaps the offender simply wants the victim to 'get off his back'. Further, ease of reparation is independent of moral properties. For example, a rich offender may find it very easy to provide ample compensation but a poor offender may find it difficult to offer even meagre redress. This difference in relative ease alone says nothing about the degree to which remorse is the underlying motivation. So, whilst, I argued in Chapter 1 that remorse that did not motivate any attempts to apologise and repair the harm caused

---

[46] ibid, 18.

[47] ibid, 177.

[48] ibid, note h.

[49] Self-imposed penances, as discussed in Chapter 4, are perhaps also bound up with the reflective process but are an unusual form of voluntary reparation (if, indeed, we want to see them as reparation at all).

would to some degree be suspect, voluntary reparation does not guarantee remorse.

It may be the case, then, that voluntary reparation makes us more certain that an offender's remorse is genuine, but we must be clear that it is the remorse that is tied to the reflective process, and not the reparation per se. Reparation may have other instrumental benefits for the victim, but is not intimately linked to the quasi-retributive values relating to the censuring response. So, I argue, it is remorse that should justify the mitigation, even if voluntary reparation is a fairly robust marker.

In sum: if, as von Hirsch and Ashworth argue, the offender's reflective process is important to the rationale underlying the censuring response, then an offender who independently and readily engages with it should be censured in this context. Adopting a dialogical model of censure achieves this, making room for input from the offender on the subject of his wrongdoing. This of course does not mean that censure is not appropriate in such cases where self-condemnation is already present. The censure needs to be reiterated and confirmed, but the offender's mind does not need to be drawn to it and the quality of the censure required in response is altered.

MITIGATION OF PUNISHMENT IS NECESSITATED BY RESPONSIVE CENSURE

As explained above, communicative retributive theories—including the two under discussion—hold that the sanction, or hard treatment, does the work of communicating the censure. Therefore, if the censure deserved is less harsh, then the punishment required to communicate this censure is mitigated. A softening of the tone of delivery of the sentence by the judge would not be sufficient as the *sanction itself* communicates the censure; the meaning of this censure must change in the face of the offender's remorseful input into the dialogue. Remorse therefore mitigates the punishment deserved.

It might be argued that allowing such mitigation on the grounds of remorse might send out the message to society that the conduct was not as serious as the unmitigated sentence would have suggested. However, in line with treating offenders foremost as moral agents and not as a means to achieve deterrence, von Hirsch and Ashworth point out that in receiving a criminal sanction, the offender is 'being confronted with disapproval in virtue of the wrongfulness of his conduct, and *not solely in order to produce preventive or other societal benefits that such censure might achieve*'.[50] Further, since sentencers should explain when passing sentence how they have reached their particular decision, all mitigating (and aggravating) factors should be explained. In theory, the public can then be made aware

---

[50] von Hirsch and Ashworth (n 20) 17, emphasis added.

that the conduct was not less serious but that the reduction in censure constitutes a response to the offender's communication of remorse. This also sends the message that remorse is the appropriate response to moral wrongdoing. Whilst there might be some truth to the claim that the public usually only hear about the sanction and so may not understand how the sentence had been reached, to suggest that this precludes responding dialogically to the offender's remorse would also lead to the conclusion that all mitigating and aggravating factors functioning outside offence seriousness should be eliminated. However, this is untenable.

AN ARGUMENT AGAINST THE PLAUSIBILITY OF THINKING OF PUNISHMENT IN DIALOGICAL TERMS

Brownlee has raised some serious objections to dialogical conceptions of punishment.[51] Since these objections could be levelled against my account, I must show the reader why it nonetheless remains plausible. I will first outline her concerns. These relate to conceiving of censure and sanction in dialogical terms generally, and also to applying such a dialogical conception to remorseful offenders' interactions with the state in particular. I will then argue that, whilst her concerns raise important points about the appropriateness of dialogue as the correct model for criminal punishment, they do not apply with equal force to *all* communicative theories. In consequence, the dialogical model I have argued for remains an appealing modification of von Hirsch and Ashworth's theory. Further, I will show that within her arguments there is a very important difference between assessing whether current practice *does* satisfy the conditions for dialogue and asking whether practice *could* satisfy these conditions. Drawing the conclusion that dialogue is not the appropriate model because what we have does not currently achieve it is a mistake, and it is one to which Brownlee perhaps seems susceptible. The account I have developed shows both how sentencing could become more dialogical, particularly through responding to remorse, and why this would be a good thing.

Brownlee uses Duff's communicative theory of punishment to test the appropriateness of applying the language and logic of dialogue to criminal conviction and punishment. According to Duff:

> [T]he [criminal] trial seeks to engage the defendant in a rational dialogue about the justice of the charge which she faces, and to persuade her—if that charge is proved against her—to accept and make her own the condemnation which her conviction expresses.[52]

---

[51] KL Brownlee, 'The Offender's Part in the Dialogue' in R Cruft, MH Kramer and MR Reiff (eds), *Crime, Punishment, and Responsibility: The Jurisprudence of Antony Duff* (Oxford, Oxford University Press, 2011).

[52] A Duff, *Trials and Punishments* (Cambridge, Cambridge University Press, 1986) 233.

Brownlee emphasises that in Duff's view, punishment not only communicates both condemnation and a desire for repentance and reformation by the offender, but also gives the offender an opportunity to communicate her repentance by accepting the punishment, apologising and making reparation where possible.

Conditions for Dialogue

In order to assess whether accounts of punishment as a communicative practice can be conceived as analogous to interpersonal moral dialogue, Brownlee outlines the following conditions for what constitutes a dialogue. In general:

> [A] *dialogue* is a sustained, purposive conversation or verbal exchange of thought carried out by two or more persons. A *moral* dialogue is such an exchange that has as its subject either a moral issue or an issue that has moral implications. Often a moral dialogue will involve or address some moral disagreement.[53]

First, in claiming that a dialogue is a type of 'exchange', Brownlee states that dialogue involves a degree of *reciprocity between the parties*. She suggests that, for a dialogue to occur, the agents must actively participate such that each participant both communicates and receives.[54]

The second condition is *sustained and extensive interaction*: the sustained and extensive nature of dialogue is contrasted with other kinds of limited reciprocal exchanges such as a simple call and response or an exchange of threats, or a 'wordless meeting of minds'.[55]

The third condition for dialogue requires *purposive conversation marked by mutual recognition of each party's rights and duties*. Brownlee describes dialogue as 'reason-giving, argument-based, progress-oriented interaction'.[56] Crucially, the parties must attend to each other's contributions and modify their responses in light of those contributions; there is a shared goal towards progress in common understanding.

The fourth condition is *fairness and equality*: participants in a dialogue must be equal in activity and empowerment. Such equality means that each participant has an equal right not only to speak when he wishes (provided that he respects the equal rights of the other), but also to be heard and to be understood.[57]

Finally, dialogue requires *willing participants*. In order to ensure that each participant communicates only what they wish to communicate, participants in a dialogue must—to a certain degree—want to be active in

[53] Brownlee (n 51) 57.
[54] ibid, 58.
[55] ibid.
[56] ibid.
[57] ibid.

the exchange, such that they are not subject to duress or manipulation. As Brownlee points out 'non-subjugation is necessary for their exchange to be genuinely and truly reciprocal, and for them to be and to be seen to be equal in the relevant sense'.[58]

Brownlee believes the fourth and fifth conditions to be the most problematic when attempting to construe trial and punishment in dialogical terms. These are presented as problems whether the offender is remorseful or not, applying to dialogical accounts in general. I shall attend to these first, before proceeding to Brownlee's remorse-specific concerns.

The Problem of Offender Unwillingness

Brownlee states that the parties to a dialogue must be broadly willing participants to the exchange in the sense that they are not subject to duress or manipulation. As above, such non-subjugation is necessary for their exchange to be genuinely and truly reciprocal. Unwillingness could occur on either side of the would-be exchange.

In terms of the offender, Brownlee argues that 'willingness ... cannot be presumed to apply to the offender confronting punishment', thus precluding dialogue.[59] However, this is not a problem for the dialogical model. Failure, on occasion, to achieve an aim does not invalidate the aim itself. It is true that if the offender refuses to engage then no dialogue occurs, but the state should not then fail to engage if an offender does invite such dialogical interaction. The dialogical scenario is an ideal towards which the state should strive even if it is not always—or, indeed, often—possible to achieve because of a lack of willingness on the offender's part. As I have argued, this makes the state's communicative aims and mode of imparting censure as legitimate as possible. If offenders are to be respected as agents capable of moral deliberation, it is the state's duty to be ready to heed and to interpret correctly the offender's would-be communications so that dialogue can occur if it turns out the offender is willing to engage. Indeed, as Brownlee notes, Duff himself makes a similar point:

> The moral possibility of trials and punishments does not, of course, depend on their actual success in bringing wrongdoers to engage in the communicative enterprise, or to answer for, to repent, or to make amends for their crimes: we must address the wrongdoer as someone who *could* respond appropriately, else there is no sense in seeking a response from him; but the value and importance of the attempt to engage him in a penal dialogue does not depend on its actual or likely success.[60]

[58] ibid.
[59] ibid, 58–59.
[60] A Duff, 'Can We Punish the Perpetrators of Atrocities?' in T Brudholm and T Cushman (eds), *The Religious in Responses to Mass Atrocity: Interdisciplinary Perspectives* (Cambridge, Cambridge University Press, 2009) 91.

In fact, I suggest that the fact that offenders can choose not to engage in the sort of dialogue that I have discussed is a point in favour of a liberal theory of punishment, since such a theory is thereby able to respect the offender's autonomy. But, again, this does not mean that the state should not be ready and willing to engage when the offender does make an attempt to communicate.

Thus, Brownlee's concern that the unwillingness of the offender to engage poses a problem for a dialogical model is allayed. Dialogue should be aimed for as the ideal, and this is unaffected by the fact that sometimes—maybe even most of the time—it is not attained. The dialogical attitude of the court should be maintained so that if the offender does communicate his remorse, the censure is not inattentive to it. Brownlee is right that this means that sometimes a particular trial and punishment fails to be dialogical, but this does not pose a problem for dialogical models generally. In fact, it was argued, room for non-compliance may be a strength of the model.

The Problem of the Performative Nature of Condemnation

The second of the two general concerns relates to the fourth condition set out by Brownlee: fairness and equality.[61] The crux of her objection is that the state's act of condemning an offender disrupts the conditions of rough communicative equality and reciprocity necessary for genuine moral dialogue. Brownlee maintains that condemnation in legal (and religious) contexts operates differently from the way in which it does in ordinary interpersonal dialogue.

The conditions for ordinary interpersonal dialogue do not rule out the communication of condemnation by one person to another because, in interpersonal interactions, condemnation is relatively innocuous. Brownlee argues that an ordinary person's condemnation of another does not alter the latter's status as a participant in their shared dialogue, unless the condemnation signals a termination of relations rather than an invitation to discuss the charge.[62] When the condemnation does signal a termination of relations, then the condemnation is a *performative act* because any subsequent attempts at communication by the condemned party become mere acts of expression.[63] When, by contrast, condemnation signals an invitation to discuss the roots of the condemnation, the condemned party is still able to engage in dialogue on 'a footing of rough communicative equality and

---

[61] Brownlee (n 51).
[62] ibid, 62.
[63] ibid.

reciprocity because her interlocutor has not exercised his limited power to alter her moral standing in relation to him'.[64]

Whilst there seem to be two options for the ordinary condemner—to invite discussion or to terminate relations—Brownlee argues that only the latter, performative mode is available to the state in the process of criminal justice. She seems to think that this is particularly true on Duff's account, where the quasi-religious language of condemnation is employed, with its connotations of being doomed to punishment and even damned to hell. With respect to the institution of criminal justice, Brownlee suggests that although the notion of *condemnation* is most apt in capital punishment cases, where the sentence really does doom the convicted person, condemnation and hard treatment, even in much milder contexts, 'radically demotes the offender's legal standing, social standing, rights, and duties, in a way that undermines the present possibility for dialogue about the offending conduct'.[65]

However, it is the focus on Duff's communicative theory that gives this objection such force. I shall argue that the quasi-religious language is peculiar to Duff and that other communicative theorists, such as von Hirsch and Ashworth, would be more inclined to substitute the word condemnation for censure. The connotations of 'censure', as Brownlee notes, are not as heavily loaded as those of condemnation. Further, I shall argue that even if censure does have an effect on the ability of the offender to engage in dialogue, this does not threaten my account, as I envisage the offender's remorseful input occurring pre-censure. The censure then *responds to* this input.

Duff's communicative theory is infused with quasi-religious language and metaphor: 'penance', 'atonement', 'condemnation'. His use of examples involving monks in religious communities demonstrates that the borrowing of this language is intentional and meaningful. He wishes to draw instructive comparisons between religious penance and secular penance. This makes a particularly strong reading of 'condemnation' understandable, with its connotations of negating a member's standing within his religious community. Such a reading informs Brownlee's perspective that condemnation has the effect of cutting a person off from all interaction, including dialogical interaction. However, even within Duff's penalogical theory, we must be careful not to take this to an unintended extreme. The so-called three 'R's of punishment are central to Duff's theory, one of which is reconciliation with the offender's community. Duff argues that reconciliation is what those whom the offender has wronged 'must seek if they are still to see her as a fellow citizen'.[66] A complete exiling of the offender is irreconcilable with this objective.

---

[64] ibid.
[65] ibid, 63.
[66] Duff (n 19) 109.

Bennett also endorses condemnation expressed through ostracising treatment of the wrongdoer.[67] In his non-criminal examples he envisages a man appropriately condemning his carousing, noisy neighbour by shunning him on the street and 'cutting him dead'.[68] Similarly, he endorses a university communicating condemnation to a extremely slipshod teacher by temporarily suspending her status as well as requiring her to give her own time to help the students she let down. This, however, is somewhat in tension with Bennett's overall theory. Whilst arguing for an obligation to withdraw recognition and respect from the offender, he also seeks to retain as much from restorative justice as is possible within an overall retributive framework. For Bennett, the ideal censure and sanction scenario is that the victim and offender agree to mediation where, although the severity of the sanction will be determined by a desert-based consideration of proportionality, the precise form this will take will be a product of the conference. Such a scenario seems to maintain a level of respect for and recognition of the offender, rather than subjecting him to exile.

It does seem to be something of a paradox in Bennett's work that the way to respect and recognise the qualified status of the member of the enterprise is to withdraw respect and recognition.[69] He argues that it is because all qualified members deserve respect as such that they must be adequately condemned for what they do. For the focus of this condemnation to be withdrawal of respect seems somewhat puzzling. When he begins to outline how state punishment should work on his theory, however, the emphasis on withdrawal of respect and recognition diminishes in favour of putting as much restorative practice in as possible. Even before this stage, ostracism does not always seem to be his preferred mode of condemnation: 'we respect someone's identity by engaging them in dialogue, not by making them suffer'.[70] Censure, in comparison with condemnation, more decisively seeks a response from the censured, which is incompatible with cutting him off. Whilst censure is not a technique for *evoking* specified sentiments, 'some kind of moral response is expected'.[71]

The dialogical model I have developed envisages offenders communicating their remorse *pre-censure*. This would render any change in the offender's status post-censure unproblematic for my account. Brownlee does acknowledge that the specific nature of Duff's theory fuels the worry that, being condemned, the offender suffers a demotion in status, which affects his present capacity to enter into a dialogue with society about his conduct. She writes: 'in [Duff's] view, the aims and purposes of the

---

[67] Bennett (n 4).
[68] ibid, 104.
[69] There are, however, degrees of respect and recognition. The respect lost could pertain to just this particular relationship or to a particular element of it.
[70] Bennett (n 4) 74.
[71] von Hirsch (n 20) 10.

trial are continuous with those of punishment, and hence the process as a whole is intended to be viewed in the reciprocal terms of moral dialogue'.[72] For Duff, the offender's input into the dialogue is his apology, expressed through his secular penance. Such input *is* post-censure. However, the suggestion that the remorseful offender's input occurs at an earlier stage is also compatible with communicative penal theory. This being so, the offender's standing is actually *maintained* through responding to him with moderated censure. Through engaging in a dialogical approach to censure, the state demonstrates respect.

Despite her overall conclusion that 'it is implausible to think of lawful punishment in dialogic terms', Brownlee does accept that 'such a forum, which precedes condemnation, does seem broadly acceptable as an analogue of interpersonal dialogue, if we put aside cases of unwillingness to plead'.[73] It was previously argued, however, that the refusal of some offenders to engage in dialogue does not undermine its value as the correct aim.

Remorse and the 'Generic-script' Problem

Brownlee presents a remorse-related objection, which she believes further undermines the plausibility of thinking of punishment in dialogic terms. The objection is a specific instance of the more general 'generic-script' problem. The 'generic-script' problem is generated by the formulaic nature of the state-offender 'dialogue' which pays no regard to the offender's actual attitudes and would-be communicative efforts. The state proceeds to tell the offender how he should communicate to society and victims via penance and reparation, and then makes him go through the motions of taking those communicative steps.

This problem is salient in the case of a remorseful offender. Brownlee argues that:

> [I]n particular cases—such as full repentance prior to punishment or suitably constrained conscientious disobedience—the convicted person should not wish to recite the formal script of apology and commitment to self-reformation; and to require her to do so through the ritual of punishment and apology not only disrespects her, but makes a mockery of the ideal of genuine moral dialogue undertaken voluntarily and reciprocally on a plane of roughly equal footing by parties who are responsive to the communicative contributions of others.[74]

There are two responses to this. First, it should be pointed out that this is Duff's script and as such is not essential to communicative theories generally. Whilst, on Duff's theory, the offender (whether he wants to or not)

---

[72] Brownlee (n 51) 65.
[73] ibid, 65–66.
[74] ibid, 60.

'communicates' repentance and apology to his victim and community through his penance, the sanction in von Hirsch and Ashworth's theory is not conceived as communicating anything *from* the offender. Thus there is no generic script, and the offender can input whatever he likes, or remain silent.

Further, even within Duff's theory, there can be departure from the generic script. Brownlee highlights this in relation to conscientious disobedience. Duff demonstrates a departure from the generic script in the case of an offender who believes she did the right thing in going through with a mercy-killing. Duff explains that her punishment must embody the more complex message that even if, for respect-worthy reasons, she dissents from the content of the law, she ought to obey it out of respect for the law and as a matter of her duty as a citizen. He concludes that her punishment 'will probably be lighter than that imposed on someone whose crime did not flow from respect worthy values'.[75]

This shows that even within Duff's theory, departure from his script is possible and stems from dialogical concerns. Whilst Brownlee raises concerns over Duff's solution to the conscientious offender, these concerns actually *support* mitigation on the grounds of remorse. She questions whether the message communicated to the conscientious offender should be censure at all (albeit reduced censure). Further, she argues that the punishment of a conscientious offender might misrepresent a person who wishes to engage in dialogue of about the merits of her cause as *remorseful*.[76] This objection does not apply to a departure that responds to a remorseful offender with mitigation—on the contrary, the implication of Brownlee's argument is that this is the correct response to remorse and that responding in a similar fashion to other types of offenders might misrepresent them as remorseful. Although this is plausible, and shows how genuine dialogue can be established, it should be remembered that Duff himself does not advocate departure on the grounds of remorse.

So, it would seem that even within Duff's theory, remorse does not pose a problem for satisfying the conditions of dialogue. Genuine remorse, if communicated prior to sentencing, can be attended and responded to uniquely through censure, thereby paying attention to the particular offender's attitudes and communicative attempts.

Current Practice is Insensitive to Offenders' Attitudes

Notwithstanding the potential for dialogue outlined above, Brownlee concludes that condemnation just *is* insensitive to offenders' remorse, and that dialogue is therefore not achieved. In her conclusion, she says that, for

[75] Duff (n 19) 122.
[76] Brownlee (n 51) 61.

wholly repentant offenders, 'condemnation that is insensitive to their efforts to engage in genuinely reciprocal interaction fails to respect the moral ... significance of their attitudes'.[77] This objection, in addition to concerns about the performative quality of condemnation (discussed earlier), is taken by Brownlee to speak to her general conclusion that it may be impossible in criminal justice processes for the state and offenders to engage in dialogue.

However, I do not think the fact that condemnation *can* be insensitive to the would-be communications of remorseful offenders rules out the possibility that it could become sensitive. Indeed, it was argued above that moderation of censure could constitute such sensitivity to the offender's input. But, Brownlee simply takes it as axiomatic that the state is unresponsive. She argues that the generic script misrepresents the repentant offender

> by presenting her as being of a similar mind and attitude as unrepentant offenders who need to be brought to appreciate the wrongness of their acts and the reasons for reparation and repentance. As such, her punishment, when comparable in harshness to that of an unrepentant offender, is indefensibly dismissive of her sincere emotions of remorse, regret, and repentance, and her fervent desires to remedy relations.[78]

The simple response to Brownlee's argument here seems to be that the state should moderate the censure of the repentant offender so that it ceases to be dismissive. Indeed, this would be entailed by her third condition for dialogue, requiring that the parties *attend* to each other's contributions and *modify* their responses in light of those contributions:

> If the state, through its criminal justice system, does nothing to alter its communications to such an offender in light of her attempted responses, then the offender's communicative efforts seem to be, in the eyes of the state, mere acts of expression and not communication.[79]

Brownlee's argument seems to be that (within Duff's theory) the state does not heed the offender's attempts to communicate and thus the conditions for dialogue are not met. But Brownlee does not offer a principled argument against changing this practice. Accordingly, we can accept Brownlee's charge against Duff's view, but maintain the claim that we should change our practices, if given good reason. My account provides one such reason, and renders plausible a dialogic model of censuring.

SUMMARY

I began this chapter by drawing a distinction between blameworthiness and the extent to which an agent should be blamed, arguing that this was a

---

[77] ibid, 66.
[78] ibid, 60.
[79] ibid.

distinction that might have relevance to official censure. Having established the centrality of censure to communicative retributive accounts, I then argued that the practice of censuring is best situated within a dialogical model, as it anticipates and hopes for particular responses, and thus should be attentive to any input the offender wishes to make. After demonstrating compatibility with the principal theories (with their emphasis on addressing the offender as a rational moral agent, on seeking a response from the offender, and on his participation in the activity) I explained why remorse would be the relevant input an offender could make to the dialogue. Since remorse indicates that the offender already appreciates the wrongfulness of the offence, censure that would otherwise solicit the offender's understanding should respond in a way that is attuned to his prior insight. I then returned to von Hirsch and Ashworth's quasi-retributive grounds for mitigation to highlight their commitment to censure being sensitive to the offender's capacity for reflection, and the consequences this has for the severity of censure. Having established that this commitment served to support mitigated censure for the remorseful offender, I explained why mitigation of censure results in mitigation of punishment. Finally, I defended my account against a challenging argument that held that dialogue was an inappropriate model for sentencing and that remorse in particular could not be incorporated into such a model.

CONCLUSION

In light of my arguments, it would seem that communicative retributive theories such as von Hirsch's and Duff's should adopt a dialogical model of censure, receptive to communications of remorse, where forthcoming. In order to deny this, they would have to argue that remorse was not relevant to the sentencing dialogue or that the communication should be only one way—from the state to the offender. I have argued that both these contentions would make for a less preferable state of affairs.

Within von Hirsch and Ashworth's work, their claims relating to the significance of the offender's capacity to engage in moral reflection were argued to make this requirement even more pressing. I therefore suggest that mitigation on the grounds of remorse is not only compatible with von Hirsch and Ashworth's theory, but required by it.

The compatibility of my account with Duff's theory was seen to be less obvious. The complexity stems from the idea that, on Duff's theory, punishment not only communicates censure to the offender, but also communicates his repentance by serving as a penance: punishment is a 'communicative, penitential system'.[80] From a censure perspective, my arguments for the

---

[80] Duff (n 19) xix.

superiority of a dialogical model—and the consequences for the remorseful offender that fall out of it—should apply. However, even if the offender deserves less censure, what he has to do to make up for his offence—to be reconciled with the community—may not be affected by remorse. Since remorse does not reduce the seriousness of the offence, the burdensomeness of the penance needed to express the appropriate repentance remains the same, despite remorse. Although I argued in Chapter 4 that a sufficiently burdensome self-imposed penance might go some way to reducing what the state needs to impose, remorse *alone* does not have the expressive quality that Duff requires of penance. Therefore, Duff's vacillation between emphasising the censuring and penitential functions of punishment results in a corresponding vacillation with regard to the mitigating potential of remorse. If punishment communicates both censure and the offender's ideal apology, but only the severity of the censure deserved is reduced by remorse, it is unclear which communicative function takes primacy.

Regardless of the answer to this question, my arguments that explain why the remorseful offender deserves less censure hold just as forcefully for Duff's account as for that of von Hirsch and Ashworth. In the next chapter I contrast my account with the Merciful Compassion argument, arguing that Responsive Censure provides a superior justification for the mitigating role of remorse at sentencing.

6

The Merciful Compassion Argument

> [T]here was no doubt that she had shown genuine and substantial remorse. It was possible to extend a degree of mercy to her, so that her sentence would be reduced to one of 12 months' imprisonment.[1]

THIS QUOTATION IS representative of the view that the remorseful offender is a proper object of judicial mercy. Although references to mercy are common within judicial discourse, there is disagreement amongst penal theorists about whether demonstrations of mercy are ever appropriate and, if they are, under what (presumably limited) circumstances.[2] Mercy appears to at best be in tension with, and at worst to undermine, the principles of justice. On such views, imposing a more lenient sentence on the grounds of mercy will mean that just deserts have not been meted out. Further, there is a common worry that demonstrations of mercy will undermine consistency in sentencing: some judges may be more inclined to show mercy than others. Indeed, it is telling that the judge quoted above says that it was 'possible' to extend mercy to the remorseful offender. The language suggests that, in this case, mercy is not deserved or required, merely permitted.

However, there are theorists who defended the view that there is a role for mercy in criminal justice,[3] with some claiming that this role extends to mitigating the punishment of the remorseful offender. In this chapter, I examine one of the most developed accounts of why mercy should be shown to the remorseful offender.[4]

I contrast this account with the Responsive Censure argument put forward in the preceding chapter, showing why the latter is preferable, and note how it avoids some of the most serious challenges that the Merciful Compassion argument faces.

---

[1] *R v Susan Tagg* [2011] EWCA Crim 3315.

[2] For an overview of the different theoretical positions on mercy, see SP Garvey, 'Questions of Mercy' (2006) 4 *Ohio State Journal of Criminal Law* 321.

[3] D Dolinko, 'Some Naive Thoughts About Justice and Mercy' (2006) 4 *Ohio State Journal of Criminal Law* 349; S Bibas, 'Forgiveness in Criminal Procedure' (2006) 4 *Ohio State Journal of Criminal Law* 329.

[4] J Tasioulas, 'Punishment and Repentance' (2006) 81 *Philosophy* 279.

RESPONSIVE CENSURE AND THE EXERCISE OF MERCY

A prominent example of the Merciful Compassion argument has been developed by John Tasioulas. His central claim is that there is room within communicative theories of punishment for the exercise of mercy to be a justified judicial response to an offender's remorse. According to Tasioulas:

> [M]ercy ... embraces reasons for leniency that arise out of a charitable concern with the well-being of the offender, in particular, the compassion we rightly feel towards him as a potential recipient of deserved punishment given various other facts about his life and circumstances whose salience is not captured by the retributive norm.[5]

Notably, Tasioulas considers remorse to be one such relevant fact about the offender's life. He writes: 'a decent concern with the latter's welfare can justify us in tempering the punishment deserved in order to take account of charitable reasons furnished by his repentance'.[6] In line with the Responsive Censure account, Tasioulas sees repentance as relevant to the communicative process,[7] yet he departs from my arguments in his claim that this justifies a merciful response which functions outside the domain of retributive justice. I am going to argue that my account is preferable.

Showing an offender mercy and engaging dialogically with his remorse are two different scenarios. As the quotation from Tasioulas above suggests, mercy stems from a charitable concern with the well-being of the offender. This involves feeling compassion towards him on the basis of his prospective punishment—compassion evoked by some relevant fact (his repentance). The first thing to acknowledge here is that it is not obvious that a concern for the well-being of the remorseful offender is even intuitively the driving force of the impulse to mitigate his punishment. The concern for the offender's well-being cannot simply be a response to the offender's impending sanction, otherwise all offenders would be candidates for mercy, since the well-being of all offenders is diminished by their punishment. There might therefore be something about the *remorseful* offender's situation that makes his experience particularly burdensome. It could be argued that an offender's punishment *plus* his painful experience of remorse diminishes his well-being to a greater extent compared to that of the unremorseful offender and consequently we are more concerned for him and therefore feel that mercy becomes justified. However, I do not think this is Tasioulas's argument. Rather, it seems that we do not have a charitable concern for the offender's well-being at all *unless* he repents, not that we have a greater charitable concern for the remorseful than the unremorseful.

---

[5] ibid, 312.
[6] ibid, 318.
[7] ibid, 317.

I am going to argue that compassion and charitable concern for well-being do not adequately capture the justification for mitigating the punishment of a remorseful offender. Feeling compassion for an offender as a recipient of punishment, given facts about his life and circumstances, has strong overtones of pitying the offender. Such a conceptualisation of mercy is shared by Murphy, who claims that mercy is 'often regarded as found where a judge, out of *compassion for the plight of a particular offender*, imposes upon that offender a hardship less than his just deserts'.[8] A parallel perspective was present in Manson's argument for mitigation justified by 'cultural demands', where *sympathy* justified leniency.[9]

Whilst such responses might be appropriate for an offender who is, say, terminally ill or very old, they are not appropriate attitudes towards the remorseful offender. We do not (or should not) pity an offender his remorse (although we might recognise that it can be emotionally very painful), rather, we expect (or at least hope for) his remorseful response as we engage with him in communication.[10] Mitigating on the basis of mercy might send the message that we, to an extent, feel sorry for the remorseful offender, not that we want to be receptive to the offender's input into the dialogue—his appropriate moral response to his wrongdoing.

In fact, we may go further and claim that certain responses such as compassion, concern, and sympathy in the face of remorse may actually devalue the offender's response if they were the driving force for mitigation—as if remorse was simply suffering. It is true that we probably do feel more compassion towards the remorseful, in virtue of their appropriate response, which renders them more 'likable'. However, mitigation is justified because we engage with their response per se, not because the response inspires compassion and an accompanying impulse to want to see them suffer less.

My argument is strengthened if we compare how well the contrasting accounts fit within retributive theories founded on communication and censure. Within my account, the offender's remorseful input into the dialogue about his wrongdoing results in the mitigation of the censure he receives. I argued that the remorseful offender should be censured less severely, as the dialogical model requires engaging with his relevant input. Thus, mitigation on these grounds functions within the realms of deserved censure and retributive justice. Engaging with the offender's remorse is internal to the enterprise of delivering censure. Mercy, on the other hand, is external

---

[8] JG Murphy, 'Mercy and Legal Justice' in JG Murphy and J Hampton, *Forgiveness and Mercy* (Cambridge, Cambridge University Press, 1988) 166, emphasis added.

[9] A Manson, 'The Search for Principles of Mitigation: Integrating Cultural Demands' in JV Roberts (ed), *Mitigation and Aggravation at Sentencing* (Cambridge, Cambridge University Press, 2011).

[10] We might pity an offender who experiences an excessive, pathological, amount of remorse since he suffers to a degree far greater than we would consider appropriate.

to the censure the offender receives—it has nothing to do with blaming. On my account remorse mitigates censure, on the mercy account remorse justifies leniency.

Based on concern for the offender's well-being, mercy was said to temper the punishment the offender could justifiably receive. Exercising mercy does not form part of the censuring dialogue, rather, it distorts it in the direction of leniency. Whereas remorse alters the censure due from the state, mercy has no influence on the content of the deserved censure. Mitigation on the grounds of mercy might communicate that compassion is felt towards the offender, evoked by his remorse. However, this is not a substantive response on the part of the state within the dialogue (following the offender's communication of his remorse), but is an emotional, humane reaction to his upcoming suffering, given his moral distress. On my account a substantive response *is* given through mitigation: 'we hear your communication and accept that you have responded in the appropriate way to your wrongdoing. You already fully appreciate the wrongfulness of your conduct'. On the mercy account, what the offender could infer from mitigation is that his remorse has evoked the charitable concern of the judge.

The Role of Mercy

The above argument does not imply that I think there is no room at all for mercy within sentencing. Rather, I hope to have shown how it is not required within communicative theories as a justification for mitigating the remorseful offender's punishment. Mercy may be much more plausibly justified in cases where an offender is, for example, terminally ill. In such cases, the language of compassion, concern for welfare and sympathy are entirely fitting. Moreover, the message that the offender's circumstances invoke such a response *is* the appropriate message. It would be absurd for the offender's illness to influence the substance of the censure, as it is not relevant to the dialogue about the wrongdoing. In contrast, I argued that remorse, as the offender's response to his wrongdoing, is the ideal relevant contribution the offender can make. Remorse is censure-relevant; illness is not. Mercy is not the most appropriate response to remorse, but it might be to terminal illness.

However, an objector might remain adamant that remorse is a legitimate source of reasons for merciful leniency, suggesting that we might still be merciful to the remorseful offender who has independent (censure-based) reasons for mitigation. This would then have an additive effect when it came to reducing the severity of the offender's sentence. In response to this I would emphasise that receipt of mercy is not a right, and the fact that remorse already serves to mitigate the censure (and hence punishment) that the offender deserves might remove the (compassion-based) obligation to exercise mercy (if there is one)[11] that would otherwise be present. If a judge were to nonetheless exercise mercy and reduce the remorseful offender's sentence further, he would still be acting within the justifications mercy provides, but without obligation. So, I would argue that my account, having justified remorse-based mitigation before a sentencer reaches external considerations of mercy, removes the obligation to further mitigate on independent merciful grounds. Whether mercy is an appropriate response to remorse is not, then, of consequence for my overall argument as, if my justification is accepted, it effectively pre-empts the need for mercy, rendering it unnecessary and without obligation.

This argument requires that my justification is indeed internal to calculations of deserved censure, and that mercy is external, so that the mitigation justified on my account is theoretically prior to that which mercy theorists propose. In what follows, I will further defend this claim to strengthen the argument that an internal account is preferable.

A CLOSER LOOK AT THE INTERNAL–EXTERNAL DISTINCTION

In a more recent paper, Tasioulas examines the boundaries of the internal–external distinction that I have employed when making a case for my account over a mercy-based account.[12] His argument is that, seemingly contrary to my claims, mercy operates *internally* to the logic of punishment. The truth or falsity of this would seem to be crucial to the success of my account. This is because I argued that one of the key strengths of my account is that it is superior to a mercy account as it provides a justification for the mitigating role of remorse that is intimately connected with the operation of censure-based desert. If mercy were to also operate thus, then my account would fail to have this advantage. However, Tasioulas is careful to explain what he means by 'internal', defining the domain to which it relates in broader terms than I do.

After carefully outlining his position, I will explain why my account provides a justification that is more intimately 'internal' than is Tasioulas's mercy account. I will also take issue with a couple of features of his account, questioning whether mercy is even as internal to his concept of penal justice as he believes, showing how his focus on remorse as a ground for mercy makes his case seem stronger than it perhaps is. Instead, the

---

[11] See Tasioulas (n 4).
[12] J Tasioulas, 'Where Is the Love? The Topography of Mercy' in R Cruft, MH Kramer and MR Reiff (eds), *Crime, Punishment, and Responsibility: The Jurisprudence of Antony Duff* (Oxford, Oxford University Press, 2011).

intimate connection with punishment that he establishes for remorse demonstrates its unique status within the set of potential grounds for mercy. It will be argued that the reasons for its uniqueness actually lend support to the contention that it operates differently from other potential grounds for mercy, in a way consistent with my account.

In his paper Tasioulas takes issue with Duff's positioning of mercy as operating externally to the concerns of justice. He seeks to show why Duff is mistaken, pointing to a conflation of two meanings of 'justice'—'retributive' and 'penal'. Whilst mercy *is* at odds with the former, Tasioulas argues that it is compatible with, indeed, internal to, the latter.[13] We must be very clear about the distinction he draws between retributive justice and penal justice here. In defining *retributive* justice, Tasioulas explains that the content of the retributive norm is that 'it requires punishment when it is deserved as a way of communicating censure for wrongdoing'.[14] The quantum of punishment deserved as censure is proportionate to the gravity of the wrongdoing in question, where the latter is a complex function of the harm that has been caused or risked and the degree of culpability manifested. This is the conception of retributive justice shared by most communicative theorists, including Duff, von Hirsch and Ashworth. Tasioulas then contrasts this conception of justice with a broader one, which he calls '*penal* justice' saying:

> [S]ometimes 'justice' refers to the whole of morality, or the whole of inter-personal morality, or (in a more authentically Aristotelian vein), that part of interpersonal-morality that may be aptly legalised. Let us, following in the precedent set by translators of Aristotle, call this the concept of 'universal justice', focussing on the third specification just given.[15]

He argues that it is this 'universal' sense of justice, rather than retributive justice that is alluded to in expressions such as 'criminal justice' and 'penal justice'. Penal justice extends beyond retributive desert to additional considerations that are thought to have a legitimate bearing on punishment. Thus, if mercy is apt for legal embodiment, then it falls within—is internal to—penal justice: 'for on the understanding of "justice" as interpersonal morality, mercy (like charity generally) *is* part of justice'.[16]

Accordingly, whilst Tasioulas agrees with Duff that mercy does not operate inside retributive justice, he wants to show that there is still an important sense in which mercy does operate internally to 'justice'—or, the

---

[13] ibid.
[14] ibid, 39.
[15] ibid, 40–41.
[16] ibid, 41.

'logic of punishment'—when justice is understood in the sense that is more naturally implied when people speak of criminal or penal justice.[17]

Mercy and its Relationship to Retributive Justice

In explaining his conception of mercy, Tasioulas emphasises that mercy is concerned only with the treatment of those who deserve punishment. As in his previous work (see above), he describes mercy as 'a source of genuine but defeasible reasons, grounded in proper concern for the welfare of the offender, for leniency towards him, i.e. for punishing him less severely than he deserves to be punished according to retributive justice'.[18] Crucially, in relation to retributive justice, mercy's reasons do not affect the assessment of the punishment the offender deserves, nor do they confer on the offender a right to more lenient treatment. But, he argues, they influence our judgement of how much punishment, if any, is all-things-considered *justified*.

In order to understand mercy's relationship to penal justice, we need to establish what it is that makes a particular value count as *internal* to the institution of criminal punishment (penal justice), and thus able to influence the judgement of how much punishment is *justified* (cf deserved).

What Makes a Value Internal to a Conception of Justice?

Tasioulas claims that we should 'relate the idea of values internal to the institution of punishment to our best account of the justification of that institution'.[19] Although retributive justice is at the core of Duff's communicative theory, and defines its logic, Tasioulas argues that this does not preclude other considerations from playing a role within this logic (being internal to it), but only on the condition that they are appropriately related to the overarching norm of retributive justice. For Duff, this involves two dimensions: first, the other considerations must bear an 'appropriate

---

[17] See also A von Hirsch and A Ashworth, *Proportionate Sentencing: Exploring the Principles* (Oxford, Oxford University Press, 2005) 168. Von Hirsch and Ashworth also point out a similar distinction between a narrow understanding of justice and a broader all-relevant-things-considered understanding: 'When one speaks of the "just" sentence, this may denote either the sentence that is just according to all the normal criteria (but which may subsequently be altered to take account of exceptional considerations, such as mercy or equity factors); or else it may refer to the sentence that is just, taking account of every factor with a good claim to affect sentencing (which would include mercy or equity factors). The former is a defeasible concept of justice, whereas the latter is a conclusory concept'.

[18] Tasioulas (n 12) 40.

[19] ibid, 43.

constitutive relationship to retributive justice'.[20] The second dimension is that the other considerations 'do not, insofar as they pertain to the inner logic of punishment, licence punishing offenders either more or less severely than is required by retributive justice'.[21] However, Tasioulas believes that these criteria are only true for what is internal to *retributive justice*, and sets out to show how only the former is required for a value to be internal to his broader concept of *penal justice*.

What Makes Mercy Internal to Penal Justice?

With reference to Duff's conditions for internality, presented above, Tasioulas argues that mercy satisfies the former but not the latter. It satisfies the former because mercy is a source of reasons that are dependent on retributive justice: he claims that 'mercy is not a self-standing value, but constitutively parasitic on retributive justice ... and can play a significant role *within* the boundaries set by retributive justice'.[22] He argues that the reason for this is that mercy is a dependent value: it can only generate (derivative) reasons of its own when independent reasons of retributive justice to inflict a punishment already exist. If no punishment is deserved, there is nothing to be merciful over.[23]

However, the possibility that mercy might justify a less severe punishment than that required by retributive justice means that mercy does not meet Duff's second condition. Tasioulas explains that this interpretation makes sense of why Duff believes that mercy is an 'intrusion' into the inherent logic of criminal punishment, and hence external to it. Such a conclusion would be valid if *retributive* justice were the domain of relevance. However, within the broader notion of *penal* justice, Tasioulas argues that only the former condition needs to be met.

Tasioulas expands on this first condition. Again, this is that considerations can play a role within penal logic (if they bear an appropriate constitutive relationship to retributive justice). He suggests that other facts can be taken into account when determining the level of punishment justified as censure provided these further facts 'display a requisite connection to the wrongful act to make them bear on the question of what is justified *as*

---

[20] ibid, 44.

[21] ibid.

[22] ibid, 46.

[23] I am not sure this is entirely true. I think it is not a mistake to describe the villain who spares his victim, at the last minute, in response to his pleas, as having shown mercy despite his victim deserving none of what has and could have befallen him. However, if we *specify* the context of retributive justice, then mercy only makes sense when an offender receives less punishment than he deserves, necessitating that a particular quantum was indeed deserved. I will therefore concede Tasioulas this relationship of mercy to retributive justice.

censure for wrongdoing'.[24] He shows how this is true for repentance as a ground for mercy, explaining that the connection is forged by the fact that repentance is precisely the appropriate personal response to the offender's wrongdoing *qua* wrongdoing. He emphasises:

> Indeed, it is precisely the response that the institution of punishment should ideally elicit from criminal offenders. The upshot is that repentance has place *within* the two-way communicative process that is punishment, rather than something that intrudes upon that process from the outside.[25]

Accordingly, for Tasioulas, the derivative relationship that mercy has to desert—one cannot show mercy unless there is deserved punishment to waive—and the role that the grounds of mercy (such as repentance) play within penal logic, both serve to make mercy internal to penal justice. He justifies the exercise of mercy more generally by emphasising its status as a virtue. According to Tasioulas, mercy is a 'manifestation of a more general value that may be called charity, compassion or impersonal love, a value that characteristically issues in reasons to advance the well-being of others, especially by ministering to their needs or relieving their suffering'.[26]

Contrasting Mercy with Leniency

Tasioulas further demarcates mercy's internal position by contrasting it with the operation of simple leniency, which he argues occurs externally to the logic of punishment. He says that there are certain grounds for leniency—for punishing people less severely than they deserve according to retributive justice—that are not aptly regarded as forming part of the logic of punishment. Rather than being integral to the 'tailored justification for punishment', they belong to the 'diffuse class of other "all-things-considered" factors that might defeat, in whole or in part, a *pro tanto* case for punishment'.[27] He gives examples of possible grounds for leniency citing, amongst others, the offender's having saved thousands of innocent lives; the offer of leniency in exchange for a plea of guilty in order to avoid an expensive and protracted trial; gratitude, as when an offender's punishment is moderated in recognition of their outstanding record of community service; and even perhaps if the offender's medical research were to be on the cusp of finding a cure for cancer.

Tasioulas argues that the intuition that motivates the internalist view of mercy is that the standard grounds for mercy in criminal punishment

---

[24] Tasioulas (n 12) 48.
[25] ibid.
[26] ibid, 40.
[27] ibid, 45.

(which he lists as repentance, grief, disadvantaged upbringing and illness) are categorically distinct, not only from the considerations that bear on the level of punishment deserved under the retributive norm, but also from the paradigmatically extraneous considerations cited above. The reason he gives for this is that, although the grounds for mercy do not affect the punishment deserved by the wrongdoer (which on retributive theories should be proportioned to the gravity of their wrongdoing), they nonetheless appear to have an intimate connection with the logic of punishment, unlike such considerations as gratitude, avoidance of protracted trials or non-forestallment of medical breakthroughs.

DOES TASIOULAS SUCCEED IN POSITIONING MERCY INTERNALLY?

Having mapped Tasioulas's internal–external topography, I will now show that my account still positions the justification for remorse-based mitigation more internally than does Tasioulas's. Further, I will argue that Tasioulas's account does not even achieve what it claims. I will question whether mercy is as especially internal to the logic of punishment as he believes, and show how his focus on remorse as a ground for mercy makes his case seem stronger than it perhaps is. I will argue that the intimate connection with punishment that he establishes for remorse demonstrates its unique status within potential grounds for mercy. The reasons for its uniqueness actually lend support to the contention that it operates differently from other potential grounds for mercy, in a way consistent with my account.

Whilst Tasioulas argues for the operation of mercy as being internal to penal justice but not retributive justice, I argued that remorse-based mitigation operates internally to deserved censure. A dialogical approach to censure, which I argued maximises the legitimacy of the censure, must moderate the censure delivered if an offender has communicated his remorse. Since it is *censure* that is deserved and not punishment per se (although punishment is the preferred means of communicating the censure), remorse operates within retributive justice on communicative retributive theories. Crucially, Tasioulas is not working with a different conception of retributive justice. According to him, the content of the retributive norm is that 'it *requires punishment when it is deserved as a way of communicating censure* (or, as I would rather say, more specifically, blame) for wrongdoing'.[28] So we are not talking at cross-purposes: for Tasioulas, too, it is actually the *censure* that is deserved and which must be proportioned to the wrongdoing, communicated through the medium of punishment.

[28] ibid, 39, emphasis added.

Problems with Tasioulas's Account

There are problems with Tasioulas's account. Let us recall the key elements of his argument:

1. Mercy is 'internal to the logic of punishment' as it is necessarily parasitic on the concept of desert.
2. Mercy on the grounds of an offender's repentance is particularly justified as repentance is precisely the appropriate personal response to the offender's wrongdoing qua wrongdoing. Thus, it displays the requisite connection to the wrongful act as it bears on the question of what is justified as censure.

Is mercy's parasitic relationship to desert the foundation of its special internal status? Whilst Tasioulas is correct to point out that mercy does bear this relationship—the exercise of mercy to benefit an individual necessarily requires that the individual in question deserves a certain amount of punishment—I do not see that this is different from the way in which leniency in general is related to desert. After all, it seems that *any* species of leniency is parasitic on the notion of desert, since you need to know what the default severity of punishment ought to be before you can amend it in the direction of moderation. Take, for example, the guilty plea *discount*; it can only function as a discount if there is a full price.

The other option is that it is not mercy's relationship to desert that is special. Instead, it could be the relationship that the *grounds for* mercy have to retributive punishment that confer mercy's special internal status. Tasioulas makes a compelling case for the intimate relationship that repentance has with deserved censure as an example of how these grounds operate. However, on closer inspection it seems that, of all the grounds Tasioulas lists, it is only remorse that bears this intimate relationship. Whilst repentance does, as he argues, bear an appropriate constitutive relationship to retributive justice, grief, disadvantaged upbringing and illness do not.

Repentance displays the requisite connection to the wrongful act to make it bear on the question of what is justified *as* censure for wrongdoing. Grief, disadvantaged upbringing and illness, however, do not display any such connection. Perhaps arguments could be advanced in the case of disadvantaged upbringing, such that the offender is somehow less culpable or less tied to the social contract, but this is not the connection that Tasioulas has in mind. The relationship that repentance has with the wrongful act places it '*within* the two-way communicative process that is punishment, rather than something that intrudes upon that process from the outside'.[29] Grief and illness have no connection to retributive justice. Tasioulas provides no

---

[29] ibid, 48.

arguments as to how they might. He simply states that they have 'an intimate connection with the logic of punishment'.[30]

Further, Tasioulas generally seems unprincipled in his approach to what the legitimate grounds for mercy even are. He cites Card's proposition of giving 'a bit of compensatory good fortune' to offenders who have suffered 'extraordinary severe undeserved misfortunes' in their lives.[31] In relation to this consideration he states that it does not fall under mercy, explaining that 'unlike the classic grounds of mercy, it is not a consideration integral to the logic of punishment'.[32] But, it is not clear how undeserved misfortune, as a ground for leniency, is less intimately related to the logic of punishment than is disadvantaged upbringing. Indeed, the latter appears to be a species of the former.

The 'internal' group certainly is not homogeneous. Even though Tasioulas goes some way to accepting this,[33] it is still not clear what is special about the grounds for mercy, except, perhaps, that they tend to elicit sympathy, which corresponds with Tasioulas's conception of mercy as concern for the offender's welfare, born out of charity, compassion or impersonal love.

Tasioulas's vacillation between citing *mercy* as being integral to the logic of punishment and citing the *grounds for mercy* as bearing this relationship compounds this confusion. I suggest that he makes a kind of category mistake when he relates both repentance and mercy to the first condition for internality (that the consideration must bear an appropriate constitutive relationship to retributive justice). As argued above, none of the other 'classic grounds' that he lists (grief, disadvantaged upbringing and illness) bear the same constitutive relationship as remorse does. So, if he wants to rely on his argument, it is the merciful response to the grounds, and not the grounds themselves that must bear this relationship to punishment. It was also argued, however, that mercy has no closer relationship to the logic of punishment than does leniency more generally.

The Unique Nature of Remorse

As argued above, remorse is the *only* one of the grounds for mercy that has an intimate connection with the logic of punishment. However, I will argue that this connection is to do with deserved censure, not reasons for mercy. Remorse might be a legitimate ground for mercy for other reasons, but it

---

[30] ibid, 45.

[31] C Card, *The Atrocity Paradigm: A Theory of Evil* (New York, Oxford University Press, 2002) 192.

[32] Tasioulas (n 12) 47.

[33] ibid, 48, n 15. In a footnote he states: 'in an additional layer of complexity, one should allow that some grounds for mercy (e.g. repentance) might be situated closer to the core than others (e.g. disadvantageous upbringing)'.

cannot be its connection to censure that is necessary for this; if so, no other grounds for mercy would qualify.

For Tasioulas, repentance is 'a reason for tempering the deserved punishment not on the basis of what the offender deserves or has a right to, but out of a due regard for their welfare'.[34] Indeed, he says that since repentance 'does not come within retributive justice, it seems highly unlikely that it can be anything else [than a merciful consideration]'.[35] *Pace* Tasioulas, I have argued that repentance does come within retributive justice, within communicative theories. In fact, the unique way in which Tasioulas argues that repentance is connected to censure—being within the two-way communicative process that is punishment—supports this view. The fact that it is only repentance that operates thus—singling it out from other grounds for mercy—lends support to the idea that it might play a different, unique mitigating role.

Contra Tasioulas, my account shows that repentance is a reason for tempering deserved punishment on the basis of what an offender deserves; Tasioulas's account seems prima facie plausible because of his focus on repentance. This focus on repentance makes his account seem plausible because repentance *does* have an intimate relationship with censure (and hence deserved punishment), which he wrongly extends to the grounds for mercy in general. However, I have shown that repentance is anomalous amongst Tasioulas's grounds for mercy, and that the reasons for this also render my account particularly plausible.

Summary

I have argued that one of the key strengths of my account in comparison with mercy accounts of remorse-based mitigation is that remorse operates internally to censure-based desert. Mercy, I argued, operates externally to this domain. Tasioulas's arguments seemed to challenge this, threatening the preferability of my account. However, I have shown that the domain to which Tasioulas argues mercy is internal (penal justice) is more extensive than that within which I situated the mitigating role of remorse (retributive justice).

Further, I have argued that his account is not as persuasive as it first seems, as he focuses on an anomalous ground for mercy and extends its unique characteristics erroneously to all the other grounds for mercy. To save his argument, he would need to show that it is mercy, and not the grounds for mercy, that bears the important relationship to the logic of punishment. I have shown, however, that this relationship is not any truer for mercy than it is for leniency in general, and that recourse to demonstrating mercy's special relationship to the logic of punishment based on the

---

[34] ibid, 50.
[35] ibid.

relationship of the grounds for mercy to punishment was circular, as neither relationship was established independently. Finally, it was argued that the anomalous nature of remorse instead invites the possibility of a Responsive Censure account such as mine, which I conclude remains preferable to arguments based on merciful compassion.

FURTHER REASONS TO PREFER MY ACCOUNT

Not only is my account theoretically preferable to the mercy account, it also avoids some of the serious objections that mercy theorists have to deal with. Mercy is often seen as a 'soft' response that is in tension with the demands of justice.[36] The general argument put forward is that if mercy operates outside the domain of justice then exercising it will produce injustice. Within retributive theories, the seriousness of the offence is set by the harm caused and the offender's culpability. The offender is censured in relation to this offence in the context of dialogue that, I have argued, should be responsive to any relevant input from the offender. The sanction will then be in proportion to the deserved censure. Remorse, on my account, affects the overall censure deserved; crucially though, remorse does not do so on the mercy account.[37] Therefore, by operating to deviate from what is deserved, mercy appears to prevent retributive justice. On my account, mitigation on the grounds of remorse is required by responsive censure.

Further concerns over mercy arise when we consider its application. Whereas on my account mitigation would operate systematically (since it is required), allowing mercy to guide mitigation does not obviously produce this result. Murphy has argued that mercy, as a manifestation of an individual's sympathy, will be exercised randomly.[38] The judicial exercise of mercy is seen as the pursuit of 'some private, idiosyncratic, and not publicly accountable virtue of love or compassion'.[39] As a judge, I may be moved in some cases but not others, and other judges will surely differ from me in their propensities to be moved by remorse.[40] The general argument is that mitigation on the basis of individuals' varying sensibilities is likely to

---

[36] Murphy (n 8) 162–83.

[37] Tasioulas (n 4) 312: 'Mercy is a source of *pro tanto* reasons, defeasible in the context of an all-things-considered judgement, for punishing the offender less severely than they deserve. It is not a source of reasons showing that they deserve to be punished less severely'.

[38] Murphy (n 8) 183.

[39] ibid, 167–68.

[40] Indeed, such idiosyncratic exercise of mercy is enshrined in the sentencing practices of some jurisdictions. For example, the sentencing manual of Victoria, Australia, cites a Court of Appeal judgment as accepted precedent on the issue of merciful discretion: *Markovic* [2010] VSCA 105, a Full Bench of the Court of the Appeal stated at [1]: 'There must always be a place in sentencing for the exercise of mercy "where a judge's *sympathies are reasonably excited* by the circumstances of the case". This is a proposition of long standing and high authority, repeatedly affirmed in this Court', emphasis added.

produce unjustified discrepancies in sentencing. Mitigation based on a consistent principle, derived from a dialogical rationale for censure, however, should be applied across the board.

Why We Need a Principle Rather than Merciful Discretion

I have argued that remorse influences the censure an offender deserves, which is established prior to considering reasons to exercise mercy. So, in relation to repentance, mercy-based reasons are redundant (even if they might be otherwise justified—perhaps non communicative versions of retributivism might have recourse to mercy to justify remorse-based reductions). Even if mercy is justified in relation to other factors, such as terminal illness, a consistent principle will always be always preferable if available.

Ashworth speaks to this theoretical preference for articulating a principle if possible. He writes: 'The problem is that the judicial use of the concept of mercy suggests that the sentence reduction is discretionary [in a way that goes beyond the expected, fair operation of discretion]'.[41] Having cited a case in which the offender suffered from a serious medical condition that was difficult to treat in prison, he argues decisively that it is wrong to regard sentence reduction as a matter that should be left to the discretion of the court. Rather, he argues, that it

> must be decided whether, in principle, [a particular factor is one] that should or should not be allowed to affect sentence. If the answer is yes, it should then be for the court, as with other aggravating and mitigating factors, to assess its strength and to give appropriate effect to it. Referring to this as 'mercy' suggests a broad discretion, and that is only suitable for really extraordinary cases with unusual features, such as *Schumann*.[42]

My account has provided such a principle and so, for the sentencing factor of remorse, the exercise of merciful discretion is not needed.

Could Mercy Constitute a Principle?

It could be argued that there is an *obligation* for judges to exercise mercy when faced with a remorseful offender (even though the offender would not have a corresponding right to receive mercy). It could, as Tasioulas would

---

[41] A Ashworth, *Sentencing and Criminal Justice*, 5th edn (Cambridge, Cambridge University Press, 2010) 191.
[42] ibid. In this case a clinically depressed woman jumped from the Humber Bridge, carrying her young child with her. Although her intention was to kill them both, they survived and the mother kept her child from drowning. Despite pleading guilty to the attempted murder of her child, Lord Phillips CJ held that 'there are occasions where the court can put the guidelines and the authorities on one side and apply mercy instead'. The sentence of imprisonment was quashed and replaced with a community sentence with a supervision requirement [2007] 2 Cr App R (S) 465.

argue, be an obligation created by the virtuous nature of the charitable concern embodied in mercy; or perhaps simply in the humane concern to be less punitive whenever possible.[43] This would give merciful sentence reduction on the grounds of remorse the status of a principle in the sense that Ashworth requires: it should operate systematically and should not be variable from judge to judge. However, further reasons would then have to be given to justify why remorse generates an instance of this obligation. The reason could not be that remorse evokes charitable concern and compassion, as this simply bases the justification for the exercise of mercy on its antecedent feelings.

For Tasioulas, though, mercy is a source of reasons for leniency, reasons that exist for any judge irrespective of his sensibilities. On Tasioulas's account, compassion seems less of an emotion and more of a practice. Remorse provides reason for the practice of compassion. However, despite the potential universality of reasons, there may still be disagreement about whether remorse provides reasons for merciful compassion. Duff raises this concern:

> But the realm of practical reasons is, in this as in other contexts, a realm of rational conflict: the claims of mercy conflict irremediably with the demands of justice. That conflict is rational, in that it is a conflict between sets of reasons each of which have proper claims on us as agents; but it does not always admit of rational solutions that leave no moral remainder of legitimate but unsatisfied claims. Justice is not served by mercy; but sometimes it is properly defeated by mercy.[44]

The search for adequate reasons for systematic exercise might then lead to proposing a justice-friendly principle, such as that undergirding the practice of responsive censure. But, if this were the case, it is not clear what extra work mercy does, other than suggest that the already justified mitigation (justified by an account such as mine) might be accompanied by feelings and messages of compassion and concern which would then only serve at most to present the institution of criminal justice as less soulless (which may not be a bad thing).

CONCLUSION

My discussion in this chapter has examined the Merciful Compassion argument for the mitigating role of remorse at sentencing. In particular, I have attempted to show that, even if mercy were to justify lenient treatment of the remorseful offender, this justification is redundant due to the theoretical priority of establishing deserved censure, a claim that I have

---

[43] This is often referred to as the doctrine of 'penal parsimony'.
[44] RA Duff, 'The Intrusion of Mercy' (2006) 4 *Ohio State Journal of Criminal Law* 361, 387.

defended above. I have argued that censure is at its most legitimate when it is attentive to the offender and so should be sensitive to his communications about his offence. When it is remorse that is communicated—the response censure seeks—the quality of the censure must change in response. This is reflected in the sanction imposed to communicate the censure. Estimating the harshness of the censure deserved is prior to any considerations more external to retributive justice. Whilst merciful compassion may still have a role to play in exceptional cases, principled sentencing should be the rule, where possible. On the Responsive Censure account I have developed, the remorseful offender receives principled mitigation.

This chapter concludes the first part of the book. In the next part I examine the implications that my normative conclusions have for sentencing practice. Examining the practical implications of a normative argument serves to prompt reflection on its validity. I argue that implications of the Responsive Censure argument both reveal deficiencies in some aspects of sentencing guidance and render convincing the theoretical position itself.

Part II

Remorse and Sentencing Practice

7

From Murder to Marijuana

A Nuanced Approach to Remorse-based Mitigation

> [G]iven that immediately after the [fatal] attack you summoned the emergency services, I accept you had some remorse. However, the gravity of your offending is so serious that remorse can only play a very limited role in mitigation.[1]

> You're entitled to your opinion on cannabis, but you're not entitled to break the law because you don't agree with it.... We don't see much remorse. The impression you give is that you are somebody who is immature and lacking insight and lacking perspective.[2]

REMARKS SUCH AS those made by the sentencing judge in the first quotation above suggest that the mitigating role of remorse may be constrained in some cases. The implicit claim is that, when the offence is particularly serious, remorse can do little (if anything) to reduce the sentence that the offender receives. In this chapter, I am going to examine this particular claim and the broader possibility that remorse may not operate in the same way or to the same degree in all cases. In addition to examining how the nature and seriousness of the offence alters what remorse may do in mitigation, I also consider how the nature of the offender's response should be taken into account when considering whether and how much mitigation is justified. Indeed, for some offences, such as drug possession, it might actually be inappropriate to expect remorse. In developing a more nuanced account of the relationship between different offences, different moral responses and appropriate mitigation, I demonstrate that there are ways in which sentencing guidelines could benefit from attending to such nuance.

In many sentencing systems, remorse is treated as a mitigating factor of universal application across offences. The degree to which it actually reduces

---

[1] *R v Mehmet Ozen*, see www.judiciary.gov.uk/wp-content/uploads/JCO/Documents/Judgments/r-v-ozen-sentencing-remarks.pdf.

[2] www.independent.ie/regionals/fingalindependent/news/community-service-for-man-who-grew-cannabis-30081069.html.

severity is typically influenced by factors such as the perceived genuineness of the remorse, and possibly also its timing. These variables are independent of the nature of seriousness of the offence, although there may be some empirical relation between them. However, in addition to the influence of the sincerity and timing of remorse on receipt of mitigation, some have claimed that remorse is less relevant for certain forms of offending. Whilst this claim might be supported by intuition, if remorse is to be restricted as a mitigating factor for some offences, then this restriction ought to be based on a principle that is systematically applied. In the following section, I shall explore possible principles that could be used to justify variation in the degree of relevance of remorse to different offences, and consider whether certain offences are unique in warranting a more nuanced approach.

To begin this investigation, it is prudent to distinguish two features of offences that could be involved in an assessment of whether remorse for the offence in question could be a mitigating factor: offence *type* and offence *seriousness*. As a first approximation (which I shall develop below), we may say that offences will be of different types if they involve different sorts of conduct. For example, offences against the person, such as assaults, involve different sorts of conduct from that involved in property offences. In contrast, offences will differ in seriousness as a function of the *level* of harm caused and the culpability of the offender.

Distinctions will not always be easy to draw and can cut across conduct in different ways. Indeed, as I shall discuss below in the context of sexual offences, the nature of certain offence types is inherently tied to the specific *kind* of harm that the conduct causes. However, this does not mean that the two features that I distinguish above are co-extensive. To see why, it is important to acknowledge that although certain offence types may lead to particular *kinds* of harm, different instances of the same offence type can differ in the *level* of the same kind of harm that they cause. Accordingly, although the offence type may have an important effect on the seriousness of the offence (in so far as the offence type determines the kind of harm that the victim is caused), I believe that the clarity of the discussion will be best served by distinguishing the seriousness of the offence from the offence type, in so far as it is possible to cause different levels of the same kind of harm.

Furthermore, it should also be acknowledged that some offence types will generally cause kinds of harm that are more serious than the kinds of harm caused by other offence types (for example, it seems that murder will always be a more serious offence than assault). However, some offence types will overlap on the scale of seriousness: for instance, more serious thefts attract much harsher sentences than less serious assaults. Moreover, offences of different types can be thought to cause harms of roughly equivalent seriousness.

If, as the first judicial quotation at the beginning of this chapter suggests, offence type and/or offence seriousness influence the weight that should be assigned to remorse, this should be explicitly reflected in guidelines to ensure a principled approach. In the first section of this chapter I shall consider whether the offence type should influence the weight that should be assigned to remorse.

THE RELEVANCE OF OFFENCE TYPE

Why might the type—or, more specifically, the nature—of the offence make a difference to the importance or relevance of remorse? In the case to which the first quotation at the beginning of this chapter refers, the offender was convicted of spontaneously stabbing two people to death during an argument about rent money. The judge asserts that remorse cannot play much of a role in such a case. In relation to the type of the offence, there are two features of potential relevance to the scope for mitigation. There could either (1) be something specific about the *kind of harm* the victim suffers that precludes a role for remorse or (2) be something about the *state of mind of the offender* when committing the particular type of offence that affects the role remorse can play.

It might be argued that judges should place less weight on remorse when the offence has caused a harm of a certain kind to the victim. Offences such as murder and certain sexual offences cause harms that are qualitatively different from the harms that follow from being defrauded or burgled. The harms of these offences constitute a significant or devastating intrusion upon physical integrity and, in the case of sexual offences, are as humiliating and demeaning as an offence can be. The irreparable nature of the harm to the victim can also reverberate more widely, to family and friends. In the case introduced above, the judge highlights this aspect of the harm of murder:

> The psychological and emotional impact of the murder of these two young people on their parents and their siblings has been truly devastating. I have read the moving family impact statements of Charlotte's mother, father and sisters and of Darren's father. In a very real sense you have destroyed their lives as well.[3]

Harms of fraud or theft, on the other hand, are primarily intrusions on property and the harms associated with such intrusions are often qualitatively different. The frustration, inconvenience and (occasional) psychological harm that accompanies being a victim of property offences is nothing like the trauma of having one's body attacked, invaded and injured. Much of the harm of property offences can be adequately compensated, the harms of violent crimes mostly cannot; this is particularly clear in the case of murder.

Relatedly, but pertaining specifically to the offender's culpability, it could be argued that the violent nature of these offences distinguishes them from other types of offences, and that the violent nature of these offences might

---

[3] *R v Mehmet Ozen* (n 1).

render remorse irrelevant due to the particular reprehensibility of the conduct. In violent offences, the offender necessarily intends to cause physical harm to the victim and proceeds to do so in full awareness of the victim's suffering. The harm to the victim is the aim of the offence. This is in contrast to some non-violent offences, where harm to the victim will occur as a by-product of pursuing the aim of the offence (eg to acquire property) and is not an aim in itself. Indeed, the judge quoted at the outset of the chapter discussed aggravation and mitigation in relation to the 'the very nature of this savage and targeted attack'—the savageness and targeting being central to the offender's culpability.[4] Thus, the harms and culpability involved in these types of offence are connected (greater/worse harm is often born of worse intention) but distinguishable concepts.

The Sentencing Council's Consultation on Sexual Offences

In Chapter 9 I present an overview of the sentencing guidelines used in England and Wales, and explain the roles of the council that drafts them. For present purposes, it is sufficient to note that there are general and offence-specific guidelines that currently direct the sentencing decisions of judges in England and Wales. These guidelines are periodically reviewed and revised following consultation. A recent public consultation held by the Sentencing Council of England and Wales on the new definitive guideline for sexual offences suggests that there is public support for the view that the nature of certain offences can mean that remorse for such offences lacks mitigating force.[5] During the Council's consultation, the relevance of particular mitigating factors for sexual offences was reconsidered. Interestingly, simply by consulting the public on this matter, it seems that the Council are at least open to the possibility that some mitigating factors might not be relevant for all offences.[6] More importantly though, comments from the public suggested that they perceive a need to limit mitigation for sexual offences on the grounds of the nature of these offences relative to other types of offences. In their response to the consultation, the Council noted:

> There was general disquiet amongst some respondents at the consideration of any mitigation due to the nature of the harm caused by the offence and the very high culpability of any offender convicted of this offence.

---

[4] ibid.

[5] For the Council's report in response to the consultation, see www.sentencingcouncil.org.uk/wp-content/uploads/Final_Sexual_Offences_Response_to_Consultation_web1.pdf

[6] The mitigating factors addressed in the consultation were: No previous convictions or no relevant/recent convictions; Remorse; Previous good character and/or exemplary conduct; Determination and/or demonstration of steps taken to address sexual behaviour; Age and/or lack of maturity of the young offender; Mental disorder or learning disability, where linked to the commission of the offence.

The response below, from a member of the public, reflects a sentiment expressed by a number of people:

'The mitigating factors I do not agree with or support in any shape or form ... I cannot think of one mitigating factor which should warrant ... the defendant being treated less severely. The act of rape is brutal, life destroying and not only physical.'[7]

The remarks made here pertain to the particular nature of the harms of rape, and the necessarily high culpability of the offender. The brutal nature of the act and the enduring, perhaps irreparable nature of the psychological harm are thought to preclude any mitigation.

In response to these claims, the Council's considered decision was to retain all of the mitigating factors but place limits on some of them. Remorse and 'previous good character and/or exemplary conduct' received the most discussion. The Council recognised a particular difficulty in permitting a mitigating role for previous good character. As well as being a controversial mitigating factor in general due to its irrelevance to the offence, its application in sexual offences is even more problematic.[8] The reason it is so problematic is that it can be through maintaining the appearance of being trustworthy and benign that offenders gain access to their victims. In a sense, manipulating people into perceiving 'good character' is sometimes part of the grooming stage leading up to the offence.

In view of these difficulties, the Council considered a principled basis on which a caveat should apply to limit the mitigating role of previous good character. It decided that, given the breadth of sexual offending from rape through to exposure that the following caveat should be applied to all sexual offences:

Previous good character/exemplary conduct is different from having no previous convictions. The more serious the offence, the less the weight which should normally be attributed to this factor. Where previous good character/exemplary conduct has been used to facilitate the offence, this mitigation should not normally be allowed and such conduct may constitute an aggravating factor.[9]

Further, they decided that the following wording would be added to all sexual offences carrying a maximum of life or 14 years: 'In the context of this offence, good character/exemplary conduct should not normally

---

[7] Sentencing Council, 'Sexual Offences Response to Consultation' (Crown copyright, 2013) 17, http://sentencingcouncil.judiciary.gov.uk/docs/Final_Sexual_Offences_Response_to_Consultation_(web).pdf, 17.

[8] Previous good character was also seen not to mitigate in the case from which the introductory quotation was taken: 'Whilst it is true that you were essentially of previous good character, that can have little if any impact upon the severity of the sentence in view of the barbaric nature of these killings'.

[9] Sentencing Council (n 7) 19.

be given any significant weight and will not normally justify a substantial reduction in what would otherwise be the appropriate sentence'.[10]

However, although the Council noted that all mitigating factors will involve careful consideration by the judge, and should not just be automatically applied, remorse would not be limited in the way that previous good character would be. In the Council's view, the type of offence (and level of seriousness within this type) affects the relevance of previous good character as a mitigating factor. The nature of many sexual offences is such that previous good character becomes in some sense part of the offence, or at least is often crucial for its set up. It is, in fact, not good character but *seemingly* good character. Maintaining a benign persona for the purpose of gaining the trust of potential victims is deceitful and calculating in a way that is antithetical to good character in the sense intended in the guidelines. In many cases it is equivalent to planning and premeditation.

In contrast, the Council were of the view that the nature of sexual offences had no bearing on the relevance of remorse. Respondents expressed concern that offenders who were adept at deceitfully gaining trust will also be good at simulating remorse. However, this is a question of determining genuineness. In contrast with offenders who assume the guise of good character and exemplary conduct as a way to facilitate the offence—rendering it potentially aggravating rather than mitigating—the concern with genuineness of remorse is not based on the view that it is often necessary for, or even part of, sexual offending. It is a more simple concern about validation. Whereas calculated demonstrations of 'good' character are in some cases culpable, remorse is only problematic in so far as it is difficult to assess. In response to this the Council said:

> This factor appears in all Sentencing Council guidelines and is one that sentencers are adept at assessing. Sentencers sitting in courts on a daily basis are alive to the ease with which 'sorry' can be said but not meant. Evidence obtained during the course of interviews with judges confirmed the way in which judges carry out this assessment; often the judges used phrases in conversation with us such as 'genuinely remorseful', 'genuine remorse' and 'true remorse'. This confirms the Council's view that the consideration of remorse is nuanced, and all the circumstances of the case will be considered by the sentencer in deciding whether any expressed remorse is in fact genuine.[11]

The Council's view that remorse does justify mitigation for sexual offences was accompanied by a practical move to highlight the issues that emerged from the consultation with those responsible for judicial training. An issue of particular importance was noted to be 'that the fair consideration of the offender's remorse or character does not require the victim to feel like there has been an attack on their character by contrast with the offender's'.[12]

[10] ibid.
[11] ibid, 17.
[12] ibid, 19.

The position reached through this consultation process was that remorse-based mitigation is justified even for the most serious sexual offences. In contrast, this particular type of offence did not sustain the relevance of previous good character or exemplary conduct. However, as the first introductory quotation suggested, judges are often reluctant to place much weight on remorse for some types of offences, and the argument presented by the Council that remorse 'appears in all Sentencing Council guidelines' and that sentencers are 'adept at assessing' it is unlikely to convince those who believe that there can be no legitimate mitigation for offences such as rape and murder. Further, even if remorse is considered relevant, this still does not entail that it must carry substantial mitigatory weight. In the murder case cited, the mitigating role of remorse was considered by the judge to be very limited. I now turn to the possible arguments for the irrelevance or limited role of remorse to sentencing for some types of offence, drawing on the Responsive Censure and Merciful Compassion approaches.[13] I also consider potential consequentialist constraints, since my discussion takes place in the context of a sentencing system that requires sentencers to consider and balance multiple sentencing aims.

Offence Type and Responsive Censure

The idea that the appropriate punishment is attuned to the offender's expressions and displays of remorse focuses on the *censuring function* of punishment within a desert context. The offender deserves state censure that condemns the offence but does not ignore his or her anterior understanding and acceptance of this message. In line with this approach, it could be argued that, given the particularly violent and malicious nature of certain types of offence, we no longer want to address—to engage with—the offenders who commit them as moral agents.[14] Penal theorists such as von

---

[13] It is interesting to note that, were the mitigating role of remorse to be based on any of the Changed Person argument, the Reduced Harm argument or the Already Punished argument, the most harmful types of offences would typically justify a *greater* mitigating role for remorse. In the context of the Changed Person argument, the most profound changes would be seen in those who transform from thoroughly reprehensible to remorseful. On such arguments, the greater the transformation, the more the punishment should be reduced. In the context of the Reduced Harm argument, remorse can do much more work where there is considerable humiliation or degradation. Such harms attend the more serious violent offences and the greater this harm, the more it could be mitigated by remorse. (This, of course, could not be the case for murder, although remorse could reduce the harm for the victim's family.) In the context of the Already Punished argument, the greater the offender's remorseful suffering, the greater the pre-existing punishment. Since the most painful remorse will accompany the worst offences, the punishment will be most reduced in these cases.

[14] However, note Weismann who argues the compelling case that, from the perspective of society, an offender's remorse will maintain his membership in the moral community. According to his analysis, it is not the severity of the crime that means we do not want to engage with the worst offenders as moral agents but their remorselessness. R Weisman, *Showing Remorse: Law and the Social Control of Emotion* (Farnham, Ashgate Publishing, 2014).

Hirsch and Ashworth, who propose that censure is the primary function of punishment, emphasise that this censure addresses offenders as rational, moral agents who are capable of understanding and responding.[15] Perhaps it could be argued that offences of a certain nature are committed by people who are consequently 'beyond the pale'. As such, these offenders are not to be 'addressed' in way that acknowledges rational moral agency, thus precluding the more nuanced communication that remorse might occasion. However, if it were really the case that in committing an offence of a certain nature, the offender is no longer to be addressed by the state as a rational, moral agent, then we would have to give up on the project of censure all together in these cases. We would have to revert to what amounts to little more than what von Hirsch calls 'tiger control'.[16] It is inherent in censure that it appeals to reason and moral sensitivity.

There is a further problem with denying remorse-based mitigation for offenders convicted of certain types of offence. It is in the aftermath of offences causing the most physical and psychological damage to victims that remorse seems most appropriate. It would be strange to adopt an approach whereby offenders who have committed offences for which remorse is most appropriate—who are expected to respond the most comprehensively to the message of censure—are not addressed in a way that seeks this response. If this is the case, it might be that remorse is still very much relevant per se—*morally*—and that state censure persists in its appeal to the offender's reason and sensitivity, but that the censure for these most serious offences would somehow be overall insufficient if remorse were responded to with mitigation. Those proposing such an argument could draw on the dual purpose of censure to communicate state condemnation of the offence to the offender and to the general public. (Indeed, it was noted in Chapter 4 that Duff vacillates between emphasising one or the other of these purposes.) For offences of particular types, it could be that the communication to the public takes on an enhanced importance. Communication to the public does not, of course, seek a remorseful response from its recipient and no dialogue eventuates.

Offence Type and Merciful Compassion

If, in contrast to my position, the justification for remorse-based mitigation were instead to come from the idea of judicial *mercy*, how might the nature

---

[15] A von Hirsch and A Ashworth, *Proportionate Sentencing: Exploring the Principles* (Oxford, Oxford University Press, 2005).

[16] Von Hirsch argues that responding to predatory conduct with neutral sanctions that convey no disapproval is akin to treating people as tigers in a circus 'as beings that have to be restrained, intimidated or conditioned into compliance because they are incapable of understanding why biting people is wrong': A von Hirsch, *Censure and Sanctions* (Oxford, Clarendon Press, 1993) 11. Condemnatory sanctions, in contrast, treat offenders as sentient moral agents.

of the offence impose limits on its operation? Recall that the operation of judicial mercy is justified (by those who seek to do so) by invoking something like concern for the well-being of the offender. This merciful concern provides reasons for leniency which give rise to an obligation to mitigate. In relation to differences in the nature of different types of offence, a mercy theorist might argue that concern for the offender's well-being only extends so far, particularly when the offender has shown such a total lack of concern for the well-being of his victim. Lack of concern for the well-being of the victim is at its most flagrant in sexual and other violent offences. This is not to say that offenders committing property offences, for example, are not also displaying a lack of concern for the well-being of their victims; but these offences are often not intended to diminish the victim as the primary aim. In attempting a murder or inflicting grievous bodily harm with intent, the offender is confronted with the harm he or she causes to the victim as it is inflicted and, for assaults and attempts at murder (successful or not), devastating the victim's well-being is often the primary aim. When sentencing such offenders, the argument could go, mercy does not generate concern-for-well-being-based reasons for leniency, and so there is no judicial obligation to reduce the offender's punishment. Compassion does not extend this far.

Consequentialist Aims

Bearing in mind the multiple aims of sentencing, we must not forget that imposing a limit on the mitigating role of remorse might also, or instead, be justified on *consequentialist grounds*. Particularly when it comes to the most violent types of offences, sentencers will have the 'protection of the public'—one of the purposes the Criminal Justice Act 2003 sets out for sentencing—in mind. The public is protected when the incapacitation of the offender is guaranteed through his incarceration. Accordingly, this aim might 'trump' any mitigating influence remorse otherwise has in relation to offences of a violent nature. Notice that this argument for why remorse will not always mitigate operates differently to the above suggestions from censure and mercy perspectives. If convincing, these retributive arguments would *remove* the justification for remorse-based mitigation in particular cases. In comparison, the argument from consequentialist considerations does not render mitigating on the grounds of remorse unjustified per se, but suggests that the (persisting) justification to mitigate is *outweighed* by stronger reasons to protect the public.

THE RELEVANCE OF OFFENCE SERIOUSNESS

Having considered whether the type of offence might be the crucial factor limiting the mitigating role of remorse, I shall now consider whether in fact the concern is more to do with the seriousness of the offence; that is the *level* rather than the type of the harm caused. As I explained above, offence seriousness is related to offence type (some offence types are inherently more serious than others), but the principles that might justify restricting the influence of remorse based on seriousness would be somewhat different. If it were simply the seriousness of the offence that was the limiting feature, then the principles involved would extend to *all* offences of a particular level of seriousness or above, regardless of the type of these offences. If this was the principle in play, then the Sentencing Council would have to decide on a level of seriousness (perhaps represented by a particular length of time in custody proportionate to that level of seriousness) and note in the guidelines that, for offences attracting such sentences, remorse has a very limited role to play. As noted, if seriousness were the key factor then such a caveat would have to be added for all types of offences with sentencing ranges on or above this level.

At this point, it is important to note that, contrary to what my discussion in the previous section might be understood to imply, the argument that I am considering here involves an implicit assumption of the commensurability of seriousness across offence types. Commensurability requires that we can provide an estimation of the relative seriousness of, for example, a category one domestic burglary and a category two infliction of grievous bodily harm. The arguments for limiting the role of remorse on the grounds of seriousness would be similar to those that would seek to justify limitation on the grounds of offence type, but the application would be more general: more serious offences would attract censure that must be of a severity that incontrovertibly denounces the offence, and responding to remorse in these cases detracts from this message; any judicial obligation to mercifully consider the plight of the offender does not extend to those committing the most serious offences of any type because, regardless of their nature, they are serious enough to bring public condemnation to the fore and extinguish any compassion that steers towards lenient treatment. In the context of consequentialist sentencing aims, whilst public protection may justify restricting mitigation in the case of violent offence-types only, general and specific deterrence may justify restricting mitigation for all offences of and above a particular level of seriousness.

Although the concepts of type and seriousness overlap, determining whether it is the type of the offence or the seriousness of the offence matters because of the implications that the answer has for the extent of any limits imposed on the influence of remorse. If it is primarily the *type* of the offence that matters (due to its nature) then, for example, even the most serious drug, fraud and other non-violent offences will retain the potential to be mitigated by remorse. However, if it is primarily offence *seriousness* that matters, then all offences of equal or greater seriousness (above a determined threshold, assuming commensurability) will attract sentences that cannot be mitigated by offender remorse.

In my view, retributive arguments alone do not succeed in limiting the role of remorse based on offence type or offence seriousness: if the offender has fully understood the harm caused and repudiates his wrongdoing then less censure is deserved. However, it may be that even on a purely desert approach, the difference remorse can make is, in practice negligible due to the range of aggravating factors that often accompany serious offending: where the offence is especially serious, any effect that remorse has may be diluted to the point of being imperceptible. Further, if consequentialist aims are to be pursued alongside the aim of delivering deserved censure, the role of remorse might be limited by the need to protect the public or provide deterrence.

If limiting the role of remorse were justified on grounds of public protection, then this would seem more likely to operate in connection with *offence type*, rather than general estimations of seriousness. Protection of the public comes to the fore when an offender has committed a particularly violent offence. If we start from the position that remorse is generally relevant to reaching the appropriate sentence—to doing justice—then to restrict its relevance on consequentialist grounds would require strong justification in order to outweigh this presumption of relevance. As suggested above, there could be an argument that the need to protect the public from violent offenders (through the incapacitation that incarceration guarantees) trumps the otherwise-justified practice of mitigating on the grounds of remorse. If this were the case, then where and whether there should be limitation on the influence of remorse will depend principally on offence type, but perhaps also on offence seriousness *within* these types. Although general and specific deterrence may be thought to justify restricting mitigation for all offences of and above a particular *level of seriousness*, the consequentialist aims of deterrence are likely to be seen as less capable of comprehensively trumping the demands of justice. If the mitigating role of remorse is to be limited due to the operation of consequentialist aims, I suggest that this will be due to the particular value put on protection of the public and therefore that limits will be based on the (violent) *type of offence*.

In this section I have assessed the claim that some offence types cause kinds of harm that are too serious for remorse-based mitigation to be justi-fied. I now turn to the question of whether some offences are not serious enough for remorse, and where this leaves the possibility for mitigation on remorse-like grounds. I argue that a more nuanced approach to remorse would involve the court expecting different responses from the offender for crimes of different types and different levels of seriousness.

OFFENCE TYPE, SERIOUSNESS AND THE MORALLY SUFFICIENT RESPONSE

I suggest that there are some types of offence where an expectation for the offender to demonstrate remorse would be misplaced. If I am right, then this has important implications for any sentencing guidance that has a universal approach to remorse, and for what is expected from the offender. In some cases, judges would essentially be looking for too much from the offender, or even looking for the wrong thing. The case involving cannabis possession, quoted at the beginning of this chapter, might provide one such example. I here distinguish between offences for which a response of remorse would not at all be appropriate and offences for which a response of mild remorse or perhaps guilt would be more appropriate than archetypal remorse. The former offences will mostly be *mala prohibita* offences, but may also include some offences which only risked harm or do not have identifiable victims. The latter offences include less serious instances of offences where harm to the victim was not the aim.

So far, I have discussed whether some offences are so serious that they render remorse, even where wholly appropriate, of no relevance to determination of sentence. In contrast, the discussion in this section will show that what should be expected from offenders will differ depending on the type and seriousness of the offence. That is, for some offences, the response that justifies mitigation will not be full-blown remorse.

Mala Prohibita Offences and Civic Duty

A distinction is often drawn between offences that are *mala in se* and offences that are *mala prohibita*. Whilst the general idea behind this distinction is fairly straightforward, the task of determining on which side of the distinction some offences fall is much more difficult. In general, offences that are labelled *mala in se* are offences that are bad in themselves: these offences would be wrong regardless of whether there was a law against them. Clear examples of these sorts of offences would be violent offences, sexual offences and burglary. Offences that are labelled *mala prohibita* are offences that are not bad in themselves but are wrong because they are against the law. Offences in this category would include, for example, some driving offences and unlicensed possession of firearms. Very roughly, criminalisation of conduct such that it thereby becomes *malum prohibitum* serves social rather than moral ends. As Duff explains:

> [M]ala prohibita are, precisely, offences consisting in conduct that is not (or not determinately) pre-legally wrongful; conduct which is wrongful only because it is legally prohibited. Indeed, the conduct that constitutes a *malum prohibitum* might not even be possible in advance of the relevant legal regulation: it is not possible to fail to pay my taxes, or to fail to display a tax disc in my car, if there is no tax system with regulations defining who must pay what, and how, or a system of regulations for road vehicles that creates tax discs and the requirement that they

be displayed. What marks a *malum prohibitum* is that it consists in conduct that is not wrongful prior to or independently of a legal regulation that prohibits it.[17]

Although we may all agree on the status of many offences as wrong in themselves—murder, assault, theft, etc—things become more difficult at the boundaries. In itself, driving at 60 miles an hour is not morally different from driving at 20 miles an hour. However, in an area with many pedestrians, driving at 60 miles an hour would attract moral blame given that the difference between 20 and 60 miles an hour significantly affects stopping distances and the chance that a pedestrian would survive a collision. Although driving at 60 miles an hour is not wrong in itself—indeed, on the motorway it is not even wrong by law—it could be argued that, under the description 'driving at 60 miles an hour in a densely populated area' this act is wrongful prior to or independently of a legal regulation that prohibits it.

Given the difficulties involved in classifying acts as necessarily or contingently wrong, some have argued that the dichotomous approach to classifying crimes should be replaced with a scale taking into account a more fine-grained consideration of their relative levels of seriousness.[18] However, I am not here concerned with fine-tuning this distinction or recommending an alternative. Instead, I invoke the distinction because of its underlying point: some crimes do not seem to involve much, if any, moral wrong. Further, the offences that are more clearly morally wrong do not always involve tangible harm. For the remainder of the chapter, I shall use the term *mala prohibita* to designate offences that are not pre-legally wrongful, based on the assumption that there are such offences, even if not easily categorisable.

To illustrate the significance of *mala prohibita* for remorse-based mitigation I focus on the example of drug offences. These offences, especially at the lower end, are approached differently by different jurisdictions and over the course of time. Whilst public attitudes on the wrongfulness of private drug use diverge, many would suggest that it does not constitute a moral wrong.[19] Moreover, it is uncontroversial to claim that at least some private drug use causes no harm to others. Of course, it could be argued that some private drug use indirectly harms dependents if it impairs the user's ability to look after them, or that it harms society by perpetuating an activity that can cause health problems that cost the state public money. However, arguments like these do not succeed in supporting the claim that private drug

---

[17] RA Duff, 'Towards a Modest Legal Moralism' (2014) 8 *Criminal Law and Philosophy* 217, 219.
[18] MS Davis, 'Crimes mala in se: An equity-based definition' (2006) 17 *Criminal Justice Policy Review* 270.
[19] Whilst not making a moral argument, Husak has provided a compelling argument that there are no good reasons to criminalise drug use: DN Husak, *The Legalization of Drugs* (Cambridge, Cambridge University Press, 2005).

use is bad in itself. Only some drug users have dependents and those that do may be perfectly able to ensure that their drug use does not have a negative impact on their ability to look after dependents. Some private drug use may have knock-on effects for healthcare resources, but this does not make it immoral or even, on balance, necessarily undesirable. Many activities that are valued, such as sport and enjoyment of food and drink, lead to costs for the healthcare system.

Some of the aggravating factors presented in the English sentencing guideline for drug offences suggest alternative ways in which some instances of drug possession might be more harmful: 'presence of others, especially children and/or non-users'; 'possession of drug in a school or licensed premises'; 'established evidence of community impact'.[20] However, given that these are aggravating factors, to the extent that they do indicate harm of drug possession, this harm will only attend some instances.

Given that there is no clear harm of drug possession per se and certainly no victim, how should we expect the offender to respond to his behaviour? The English sentencing guideline for drug offences lists remorse as a mitigating factor for possession.[21] I suggest that this is not justifiable. Remorse is only appropriate where there has been significant harm to another person. Even a less victim-focused response like guilt might be too much for the court to expect. In a liberal society that allows, amongst other things, alcohol consumption and smoking it is not clear what the message of censure is supposed to convey other than that a law has been broken. To the extent that the criminalisation of drug use is supposed to be of benefit to society as a whole, the wrong that the offender has committed is to break a law designed to have the net effect of promoting the welfare of its citizens. The particular instance of drug possession is unlikely to have caused any harm, but collective adherence to drug laws is supposed to reduce harm overall.

It is the lack of clear wrongdoing that makes the second of the introductory quotations seem incoherent to me. On the one hand, the judge acknowledges that the offender is 'entitled to his opinion' about cannabis—it is not something undeniably wrong—yet, at the same time, the judge expects remorse. If the offender is indeed entitled not to believe he has done anything wrong (other than break the law) then the expectation of remorse appears misplaced. Whilst we might expect some contrition from the offender in response to his lawbreaking, the existence of a law does not alone entail that the proscribed conduct would itself be something from which one should abstain absent the existence of the law.

Perhaps the most that can reasonably be expected of the offender sentenced for drug possession or minor dealing is acknowledgement of what

---

[20] Sentencing Council, 'Drug Offences: Definitive Guideline' (Crown copyright, 2012) http://sentencingcouncil.judiciary.gov.uk/docs/Drug_Offences_Definitive_Guideline_final_(web).pdf.
[21] ibid.

Duff calls 'civic duty'. He discusses this duty in relation to *mala prohibita* offences. He claims that the state can

> justify the criminalization, as *mala prohibita*, of some breaches of legal regulations if it can be argued that such breaches are wrongful; and such breaches will be wrongful if the legal regulation in question is well designed to serve some aspect of the common good, and if the burden that obedience to it involves is one that citizens can properly be expected to accept as a matter of their civic duty.[22]

If the state is to punish its citizens for drug possession, the censure expressed by this punishment should communicate a message about the common good that the law is intended to serve and citizens' duties to accept the burdens thereby imposed. This would be much more appropriate than communicating a message of condemnation with the expectation that the offender comes to feel remorse.

If this is correct, then there are significant implications for guidelines. The acceptance of a civic duty is the sufficient response in such cases. The offender need not be sorry about engaging in the behaviour itself. Any feeling that one has done something wrong is contingent on the conduct having been proscribed by the state. It would be perfectly rational for the offender to fully accept and commit to her civic duty not to be in possession of controlled substances but, at the same time, know that she would resume private drug use were the laws to be withdrawn. This is not the same with remorse. Genuine remorse over wrongdoing is not consistent with the belief that one would commit the same act again if it were not to be penalised. This means that, for offences where wrongdoing is merely contingent, remorse should not be listed as a mitigating factor. The court is not justified in expecting the offender to repudiate the conduct itself. If the offender clearly demonstrates acceptance of civic duty and commitment to refrain from the proscribed conduct then this should be sufficient for mitigation. Such acceptance shows that the message communicated through the penalty—that citizens should exercise the restraint deemed necessary to promote the common good—has already been understood. This message can be sufficiently understood and accepted without the offender renouncing the act itself.

For all *mala prohibita* offences such as drug possession, it would follow from my arguments that the mitigating factor of remorse should be amended to something like 'genuine commitment to refrain'. If it remains as remorse, there is the possibility that deserved mitigation is not granted when the offender does not condemn the behaviour itself and show emotions consistent with a belief that one has done something deeply wrong. In such cases, the offender should not be expected to feel pained by his conduct.

However, there would be significant practical problems with trying to implement this suggestion. First, identifying the offences for which 'remorse'

---

[22] Duff (n 17) 219.

should be substituted with 'genuine commitment to refrain' would present a huge challenge. As noted above, it can be very difficult to draw a sharp line between offences that are wrong in themselves and those for which their wrongfulness is contingent on the existence of certain laws. Further, some instances of a particular offence may more clearly be said to involve wrongfulness than other instances of the same offence. As noted above, speeding is sometimes given as an example of a *malum prohibitum* offence. The speed limit is set at an arbitrary point—it varies on different roads and from country to country. However, as suggested, the context in which the speeding occurs can alter our perception of the degree to which it is morally blameworthy. Driving at fast speeds in circumstances that pose clear risk to others is something we are always likely to find blameworthy, even if there were to be no laws against speeding. The risk that the driver takes (with neither excuse nor justification) is large enough that the driving becomes culpably reckless.

A comparison can be drawn between Duff's approach to categorising the act of carrying a knife. He draws distinctions between possession that would constitute a wrong in itself and possession that would not:

> Of course, it is wrong to carry a knife with the intention of using it to attack persons or their property, or to carry it in a way that creates a clear and serious risk of harm; but merely carrying, let us suppose, is not a wrong, even when it is not a self-defensive measure.[23]

The mere act of driving at a certain speed is not a wrongdoing. Driving at a speed that, given the particular circumstances, creates a clear and serious risk of harm is wrong. This influence of context demonstrates that it will in some cases be difficult to sharply distinguish between offences that, as *mala prohibita*, do not justify judicial expectation of remorse and those that, in creating at least a clear and serious risk of harm, should occasion a species of moral response from the offender.

Finally, there are even some serious offences where the facts of the case would alter what we expect from the offender, and there may be significant disagreement. For example, Weisman's case of a father who killed his severely disabled daughter to end her suffering elicited diametrically opposed expectations from the public: those who saw the act as a murder expected the father to feel remorse, whereas those who believed the act to be a mercy killing expected no remorse: in their view, to show remorse would be to admit malicious intent.[24]

Cases occasioning such disagreement will be rare, and their possibility does not justify foregoing judicial consideration of remorse as the response usually expected of the individual who commits murder. I have suggested that basic *mala prohibita* offences should only be seen as occasion for

---

[23] RA Duff, 'Political Retributivism and Legal Moralism' (2013) 1 *Virginia Journal of Criminal Law* 179, 191.

[24] Weisman (n 14) chapter 4.

'genuine commitment to refrain' that amounts to recognition of the civic duty not to commit the offence. If it is considered impossible to identify offences that would qualify for this amendment, then it should instead be raised in judicial training: the judge reprimanding the offender in the quotation at the beginning of this chapter should indeed take note of his own claim: the offender is entitled to his opinion on cannabis because it is not pre-legally wrongful. However, as these offences acquire more aggravating features—such as drug use in the presence of children or speeding in densely residential areas—the offences become more blame-worthy and thus the message of censure increasingly seeks the offender's understanding of the wrongdoing and his condemnation of the act. In such cases, some sort of moral response on the part of the offender might be expected. Even so, as I will now argue, the response expected might not yet be remorse. The responses that courts should take into account are not limited to either neutral acceptance of civic duty or deep, painful remorse: offences that are at least somewhat wrong but have no clear victim or only risk or cause lesser harm may not be the appropriate objects of remorse.

'Victimless' Offences

There are many offences that do not have clear, identifiable victims. Thefts from large corporations, acting as an intermediary to transport controlled drugs, and tax evasion all lack a set of particular people who can be identi-fied as having been harmed. For the most part, these offences will not have a directly harmful impact on the living standard of any particular person, although downstream impacts and a more diffuse 'harm to society' might be invoked as consequences indicative of wrongdoing. Whilst we might expect offenders to acknowledge some level of wrongdoing for such offences, it would be incongruous to expect this acknowledgement to involve remorse. On most accounts of remorse, the wrongdoer is pained by the realisation of the harm and suffering he has caused to another.[25] Where there is no con-nection between the act and the suffering of any particular human being(s), remorse would be psychologically unlikely and normatively inappropriate. Instead, offenders might be expected to feel guilt or shame.[26]

---

[25] See Chapter 1.

[26] Attempts provide a further interesting case. Whilst there is no actual harm, in some cases there existed the intention to cause great harm. I suggest that for attempts at violent offences remorse may (and guilt certainly would) be appropriate in response to the harm one fully in-tended to cause to the person. For offences where harm to the victim is incidental to the offence (eg burglary) remorse would not be appropriate, but proportionate guilt would. This view contrasts with Fletcher who claims: 'Feelings of guilt and remorse are appropriate where harm is done, but if all is the same after as before the act, there would be nothing to be remorseful about, and the actor's feelings of guilt would make us wonder why he wanted to suffer inappro-priate anguish'. GP Fletcher, *A Crime of Self-Defense: Bernhard Goetz and the Law on Trial* (New York, NY, Free Press, 1988) 83.

Offences Causing Lesser Harm

Even where offences do cause clear harm to an identifiable victim, when this harm is minor, it might still be the case that remorse is not the appropriate moral response. Murphy illustrates this point though comparing the wrong of breaking a reasonably important promise and the wrong of blinding.[27] According to him, the fact that promise breaking does not cause irrecoverable harm renders any response of remorse from the promise breaker excessive and undermines its value as a moral response. He says:

> In such a case, some nontrivial guilt feelings would surely be expected of a morally serious person, but many would be reluctant to use the word 'remorse' to capture these feelings—preferring to reserve the word 'remorse' to capture those extremely powerful guilt feelings that are appropriately attached only to grave wrongs and harms. Indeed, for a person to feel and express remorse over wrongs or harms that are less than grave might well strike many not as a sign of moral seriousness, but simply as neurotic—nonneurotic remorse involving great and powerful guilt only in cases where this is proportional to what has been done.[28]

Murphy suggests that the difference between nontrivial guilt feelings and remorse is not just a matter of degree. Remorse is *qualitatively* different in involving a kind of hopelessness and inconsolability. The blinding or rape of another person is, according to Murphy, 'such a wanton assault on the very meaning of a person's human life, that one can in no sense ever make it right again—such a possibility being permanently lost'.[29]

I suggest that there are non-violent offences such as burglary that can (in some cases) leave irreparable psychological harm and, therefore, appropriately precipitate remorse. The knowledge that the victim will never fully relax in her own home again should occupy the mind of the offender who truly understands why the burglary was wrong. However, I agree with the broad picture Murphy paints. On his view, for example, a low-level theft would not be an appropriate precipitator of remorse, since all the harm caused can be made right through compensation. To illustrate: imagine that Fred impulsively steals a 20-pound note from a wallet sitting in front of a sleeping passenger on a train. Unlucky for him, Fred does not evade observation, and is hauled before a community support officer as he alights. We would hope that Fred would not appear defiant about his theft; we would hope he would offer a sincere apology and appear ashamed, but we would be surprised and perhaps confused if he were to break down, inconsolable, in tears on the floor, inflicting forceful blows to his own face and promising

---

[27] JG Murphy, *Punishment and the Moral Emotions: Essays in Law, Morality, and Religion* (New York, NY, Oxford University Press, 2014) 140.

[28] ibid.

[29] ibid.

to send a significant portion of his only modest income to the victim every month for the next 10 years as compensation and penance.

Whilst we would expect a mild response from Fred, this case demonstrates that expectations of remorse will vary depending on offence type and offence seriousness. Whilst burglary, even the less serious instances, might be an appropriate occasion for remorse given the pervasive nature of the harms, theft from a person (perhaps even more serious instances, not amounting to robbery) should not usually occasion remorse; instead, a more proportionate response of guilt would be morally appropriate. Such an extreme response from Fred would be disproportionate to the seriousness of the offence and its type. In fact, it would lead us to question Fred's grasp on the nature of what he had done: this nature being that it was wrong, but not downright terrible. What this shows is that it is not the case that more remorse is always better and that remorse should, in fact, not even be expected from all offenders.

For some offences, then, the appropriate moral response will fall short of remorse, even where there is a victim. To some degree, drawing a distinction between accepting responsibility, feeling guilty and suffering remorse is a matter of semantics and judges will have an intuitive notion of what sort of response they would expect in any particular case. However, the point remains that more remorse is not always morally superior to less remorse and that, for an offence likely to be classed as *mala prohibitum*, no renunciation by the offender of the act itself need occur for the message (that there is a civic duty to refrain) to be understood. Although there may be only theoretical value in drawing such fine-grained distinctions between different moral emotions, the current approach to remorse in the guidelines could be improved. I suggest how this might be achieved in the final section.

QUANTUM OF MITIGATION

A final consideration is the amount of mitigation that the remorseful offender should receive. Some commentators have argued that guidelines should specify weights for sentencing factors—including, presumably, remorse. Indeed, Ashworth says that

> [t]he least satisfactory aspect of aggravating and mitigating factors is that, in most instances, the English guidelines neither indicate the weight that they should bear (e.g. whether a particular factor can ever, or normally, take a case outside the intended range of sentences) nor how they should interact when there are both aggravating and mitigating factors in a case.[30]

---

[30] A Ashworth, *Sentencing and Criminal Justice*, 5th edn (Cambridge, Cambridge University Press, 2010) 193.

Specifying a precise weight that a factor should be given is probably unrealistic; it is impossible to specify a priori that a given factor should carry x weight or reduce severity by y per cent in all cases. The exception might be factors where the mitigating power reflects a single dimension on which all offenders may be fairly and objectively arrayed. For example, the quantum of mitigation associated with a guilty plea is partly determined by the facts relating to its timing: early pleas conserve resources more than late pleas; accordingly, the reductions offered may be directly tied to the timing of the plea (as they are in the definitive guideline). For most other factors, too many other variables supervene to permit such clear calibration. In the case of remorse, courts need the discretion to consider the genuineness of the remorse as well as a number of other dimensions such as its relationship to other factors including previous convictions (explored in the next chapter).

However, more guidance could be given, especially with regard to relative weights and interactions. One approach that might have intuitive appeal would be to set a 'ballpark' degree of mitigation and instruct judges to take the degree of the offender's remorse into account: the greater the remorse, the more mitigation can be granted. However, there is a problem with this approach. The most transformative moral response is expected of offenders who commit the most serious offences. If the level of mitigation were increased in response to the degree of remorse, we would end up with a paradoxical situation in which the worst offenders, if remorseful, receive greater mitigation precisely because their offence was more serious and they reacted in proportion to what they had done. The degree of remorse expected from someone convicted of murder would be much greater than that expected from someone convicted of assault, and a decision to respond with a greater proportion of mitigation to the murderer's remorse based on its relative intensity would be wrongheaded. It would therefore seem that the most rational approach would be to attach the most value to proportionate remorse, and the quantum (proportion) of mitigation this procures should be capped. 'Over-reaction' should neither be penalised nor 'rewarded', but a disproportionately weak or unconvincing display of remorse should fall below the threshold required for mitigation. Further, it should be emphasised that evidence of genuine commitment to refrain is sufficient to beget full mitigation where the offence is not inherently wrongful.

There is a strong case for providing more guidance for courts regarding the role of remorse at sentencing. One reason is that sentencers probably vary in the extent to which they accept remorse as a factor. Some judges may expect the offender to be remorseful—given the seriousness of the offence—and then allow him only a modest reduction in light of this expectation.[31] Others may regard the expectability of remorse as irrelevant, and

---

[31] See, eg, J Jacobson and M Hough, *Mitigation: The Role of Personal Mitigating Factors in Sentencing* (London, The Prison Reform Trust, 2007).

may accord consistent reductions across cases. Without guidance, judging remorse will be a highly subjective enterprise, and divergence in opinion about when it is relevant, and to what extent, will only increase the likelihood of inconsistency in approach.

CURRENT LEVELS OF GUIDANCE AND ADDING NUANCE

As noted, remorse is a mitigating factor of universal application in England and Wales, and many other jurisdictions. The current level of guidance is, for the most part, limited to simply asserting the relevance of remorse as a mitigating factor for all offences. Given the preceding discussion, I suggest that:

1. Judges should be directed—if not through guidelines then through training—that a genuine commitment to refrain is sufficient for mitigation when the inherent wrongfulness of the offence is disputable. Where this qualification is made, renunciation of the act itself should not be required for mitigation. This should apply, for example, to offences such as less serious drug offences, less serious driving offences, street prostitution and public order offences. This would be particularly attractive for the sentencing system of a liberal state. Where wrongfulness is reasonably disputable, censure should communicate the importance of civic duty, rather than condemnation. Of course, certain aggravating factors may change the degree to which the offence is clearly pre-legally wrongful.
2. For offences not involving great harm to a victim, judges should be directed—if not through guidelines then through training—that 'recognition of wrongdoing' is sufficient for mitigating. Where this qualification is made, renunciation of the act itself should be required for mitigation, but intense emotional suffering may not be required. This should apply, for example, to offences such as less serious property offences.
3. Remorse should remain as a mitigating factor for all offences causing great harm to others.
4. For all offences, the importance of the offender's prior acceptance of the message of censure should be at the fore. This prior acceptance is what justifies the mitigation. Remorse will be a necessary part of such acceptance for offences causing great harm to others but, in less serious cases, wrongdoing can be sufficiently renounced by the offender without such intense emotional suffering.
5. The quantum of mitigation the offender receives should be capped so that greater remorse should not continue to beget greater mitigation. This is because (a) the most intense remorse will be experienced for the gravest of offences and, conversely, (b) more proportionate responses will be more appropriate and just as deserving of mitigation for less serious offences.

6. If the mitigating role of remorse is to be limited for consequentialist reasons, this must done in a principled way. Public protection may justify restricting mitigation in the case of offences of a serious violent type. Less convincingly, general and specific deterrence may justify restricting mitigation for all offences of and above a particular level of seriousness. Guidelines should adopt an explicit, consistent position to ensure fairness.

CONCLUSION

The consequence of applying the Responsive Censure argument to sentencing practice is that it reveals what is of foremost value for remorse-based mitigation: the prior full acceptance and agreement with the message communicated by censure. This leads to considerations of what the message of censure amounts to for different types of offence and what the offender must demonstrate as sufficient acceptance of this message. I have argued that some offences should occasion more proportionate feelings of guilt, and that this would demonstrate sufficient prior acceptance of the message. Other offences need not occasion anything more than a genuine commitment to refrain from proscribed conduct. Of course, assessing the presence of less outward, emotional responses to conduct is more difficult, and this is why I suggest that here, judges should be inclined to require less in the way of evidence.

It is noteworthy that some of the other arguments considered throughout this book would recommend *more* mitigation for the remorseful offender who has committed a more serious offence. This is because more serious offences indicate the need and opportunity for greater character change, provide more opportunity for reducing some dimensions of harm and tend to inflict the most comprehensive emotional punishment. The Responsive Censure argument renders remorse-like responses consistently relevant and, considered in isolation, neither limits nor maximises their influence for the most serious offences. Merciful compassion *may* limit the role of remorse for serious offenders, but this is unclear.

Further, none of the arguments except Responsive Censure would support any remorse-based mitigation for less serious and *mala prohibita* offences. Small or no character change, no or little harm and no antecedent emotional punishment would all result in no mitigation. One would also wonder whether the judge should feel particularly compassionate towards the offender feeling moderate guilt and facing only a mild sentence. Responsive censure, however, requires judicial consideration of the offender's prior acceptance of the message, whatever the content of that message.

8

The Remorseful Recidivist

> He did on this occasion, as he had in the past, express remorse, but in the past
> he had continued to offend.[1]

> Thus, only criminal activity that suggests that the defendant's statements of
> remorse are untrue is relevant for purposes of assessing whether he has sincerely
> accepted responsibility. Guidry's continued criminal conduct prior to his arrest
> on federal charges was not inconsistent with his post-arrest acceptance of
> responsibility and therefore could not provide a basis for discounting the
> evidence that he had accepted responsibility.[2]

S O FAR, I have examined various potential justifications for remorse-based mitigation. In discussing the remorseful offender, one fact about the offender—his response to his wrongdoing—has been highlighted and isolated for analysis. But, in most cases that appear before the sentencing judge, there will be a whole raft of factors—relating to the offence and to the offender—that must be taken into consideration to determine the appropriate sentence. Whilst these factors will all be considered relevant independently, the sentencing judge will have to assess how they bear on the seriousness of the offence, and associated sentence, in combination. In this chapter I examine one particularly interesting potential interaction: the relationship between remorse and previous convictions. Through examining different justifications of the aggravating effect of previous convictions, I show that the mitigating factor of remorse and the aggravating factor of previous convictions should interact differently on each theory, with consequences for sentencing practice.

The English sentencing guidelines, which I will use to frame my discussion, list multiple factors for judges to take into account at different steps to determine the appropriate sentence. Some of these factors indicate greater harm or higher culpability whilst others indicate lesser harm or lower culpability; additional factors are to be taken into account in personal mitigation. The idea that aggravating factors should increase the severity of the offender's

---

[1] *R v Carl Anthony Swinburn* [2014] EWCA Crim 1373.
[2] 145 F.3d 1342: *United States of America, Plaintiff-appellee v Larry Patrick Guidry, Defendant-appellant.*

punishment and that mitigating factors do the opposite is straightforward. However, aside from the guilty plea discount,[3] there is no direction in the English guidelines (and few attempts in the sentencing literature) to suggest how factors should be weighted or how they may interact.[4] The only distinction in the guidelines is between factors taken into account at Step One (when determining the offence category) and factors considered at Step Two, which serve to modify the assessment of overall seriousness *within* the range of the offence category. In the new format guidelines, judges are instructed as follows:

> The table below contains a non-exhaustive list of additional factual elements providing the context of the offence and factors relating to the offender. Identify whether any combination of these, or other relevant factors, should result in an upward or downward adjustment from the starting point. In some cases, having considered these factors, it may be appropriate to move outside the identified category range.[5]

Whilst the aggravating or mitigating force of specific factors may be obvious, how different factors should interact is much less clear. For example, should aggravating and mitigating factors simply be weighed against each other, each aggravator cancelling out each mitigator? Or should mitigating factors have diminishing force as the number of aggravating factors increases? Or is there a more nuanced relationship between some particular factors, given what they imply about the offender or the offence?

Previous convictions appear in the new guideline format as a statutory aggravating factor at Step Two.[6] Remorse appears as a factor reflecting personal mitigation, also at Step Two. As a very rough indication of the effect of previous convictions on sentence outcome, the Crown Court Sentencing Survey reported that 'for offences of assault and public order, 77% of offenders with ten or more previous convictions taken into account were sentenced to immediate custody, compared to 34% of offenders with no previous convictions taken into account'.[7] The same report also

---

[3] Sentencing Guidelines Council, 'Reduction in Sentence for a Guilty Plea: Definitive Guideline' (Sentencing Guidelines Secretariat, 2007), http://sentencingcouncil.judiciary.gov.uk/docs/Reduction_in_Sentence_for_a_Guilty_Plea_-Revised_2007.pdf.

[4] See JV Roberts, 'Aggravating and Mitigating Factors at Sentencing: Towards Greater Consistency of Application' (2008) 4 *Criminal Law Review* 264, 264. Roberts describes the lack of guidance on sentencing factors as 'regrettable', saying 'Most guideline schemes around the world adopt a laissez-faire approach to the use of sentencing factors. Guidance regarding the application of these factors is usually quite limited, possibly reflecting the view that consideration of mitigation and aggravation is more properly left to the exercise of judicial discretion, with only minimal direction from the legislature, the guidelines authority, or the Court of Appeal'.

[5] See, for example: Sentencing Council, 'Assault: Definitive Guideline' (Crown copyright, 2011) http://sentencingcouncil.judiciary.gov.uk/docs/Assault_definitive_guideline_-_Crown_Court.pdf.

[6] It should be noted, however, that the old format, which is being superseded by the new, does not set out discrete stages.

[7] Sentencing Council, *Crown Court Sentencing Survey*, Annual Publication (Office of the Sentencing Council, 2012), http://sentencingcouncil.judiciary.gov.uk/docs/CCSS_Annual_2012.pdf, 21.

revealed that remorse was the mitigating factor most frequently taken into account for all offences other than sexual offences and robbery.[8] Both of these factors might influence the severity of an offender's sentence: previous convictions pulling in one direction and remorse pulling in the other.

However, the relationship between remorse and previous convictions could be more complex than the suggestion that they crudely pull against one another. An offender's previous convictions may *contextualise* her remorse: the nature of her response to her own crime is made clearer when we understand the history of this wrongdoing and, perhaps, her responses to earlier criminal convictions. This contextualising relationship is not present, for example, when we consider the aggravating factor of targeting a vulnerable victim and the mitigating factor of playing a subordinate role in a group or gang. The addition of either factor says nothing about the effect of the other: both seem to retain their intuitive pull when considered in combination. An increasing number of previous convictions, however, could be seen to put pressure on the mitigating force of remorse. The argument might be evidentiary—previous convictions make claims of remorse look dubious—or normative—that, notwithstanding the genuineness of an offender's remorse, her previous convictions preclude it from being relevant, or as relevant, to the sentence she receives.

To explore the relationship, I shall examine the prominent retributive justifications for the aggravating effect of previous convictions alongside the justification for remorse-based mitigation developed in this book. Previous convictions have received more attention than most other sentencing factors, and there are a number of competing models that have been put forward in defence of their aggravating effect.[9] I shall consider what these justifications entail for the interaction between recidivism and remorse. In particular, I contrast the Progressive Loss of Mitigation model with Enhanced Culpability models.

THE MITIGATING EFFECT OF REMORSE

In order to decide how remorse and previous convictions should interact in theory, we need accounts of why their independent effects are justified. Here, I shall briefly summarise the justification that I developed in Chapter 5 of this book for the mitigating role of remorse.

---

[8] ibid, 31.
[9] See: JV Roberts, *Punishing Persistent Offenders: Exploring Community and Offender Perspectives* (Oxford, Oxford University Press, 2008); JV Roberts and A von Hirsch, *Previous Convictions at Sentencing: Theoretical and Applied Perspectives* (Oxford, Hart Publishing, 2010); J Ryberg and C Tamburrini, *Recidivist Punishments: The Philosopher's View* (Lanham, MD, Lexington Books, 2012).

Modern desert theories emphasise the censuring function of punishment.[10] On such views, the offender does not deserve punishment per se, but rather censure—an expression of disapprobation from the state—communicated *through* punishment. I argued that the legitimacy of this state censure is maximised when a dialogical approach is taken, in which the message of censure *responds to* the offender's expressions of remorse. This is particularly attractive when considered in conjunction with von Hirsch and Ashworth's claim that penal censure has important moral functions that are not reducible to crime prevention. On their view, sentences are supposed to address offenders as moral agents who have the capacity to evaluate and respond to an official evaluation of their conduct.[11]

Within a Responsive Censure model, an expression of remorse is a significant, relevant contribution to the 'dialogue' about the offence: it is the offender's freely expressed condemnation of his own wrongdoing. As such, censure that ignored the offender's remorseful communication would fail to optimally appeal to the offender's reason and insight, because it would not address him in his present state of understanding. Instead, it would merely seek the response it should already have heard. Communication gains greater legitimacy and effectiveness when it is tailored to its recipient. If the state does not attend to would-be communications made by the offender, then its sentencing process becomes an asymmetric exercise in penal communication: the state broadcasts its censure and the offender passively absorbs the consequent punishment.[12]

So if, as von Hirsch and Ashworth argue, the offender's reflective process is important to the rationale underlying the censuring response, then an offender who independently engages with the reflective process should be censured in light of this. Adopting a limited dialogical model of censure achieves this by making room for input from the offender on the subject of his wrongdoing. Of course, this does not mean that censure is inappropriate in cases where the offender demonstrates remorse. The censure must still serve to reiterate and confirm the wrongfulness of the offence, but the offender's mind does not need to be drawn to the conclusion. Consequently, the magnitude of the censure required in response is altered. Failing to moderate the degree of censure would be to address the offender as if she lacked

---

[10] Particularly A von Hirsch, *Censure and Sanctions* (Oxford, Clarendon Press, 1993); A von Hirsch and A Ashworth, *Proportionate Sentencing: Exploring the Principles* (Oxford, Oxford University Press, 2005); see also A Duff, *Punishment, Communication and Community* (Oxford, Oxford University Press, 2001).

[11] See von Hirsch and Ashworth (n 10) 92.

[12] Further, whilst I have suggested that this argument has force on a minimally communicative account such as von Hirsch's, it has even greater force where *dialogue* between the state and offender is emphasised. For example, Duff argues that the offender should not be a 'passive recipient' but should actively participate in the dialogue. RA Duff, 'Penal Communications: Recent Work in the Philosophy of Punishment' (1996) 20 *Crime and Justice* 1.

any appreciation of the seriousness of the offence. To address her in this way would demonstrate deficient communication on the part of the state.

THE PENAL RELEVANCE OF PREVIOUS CONVICTIONS

Previous convictions have received considerable attention from sentencing theorists.[13] As with remorse, it should be noted that commentators are not always convinced of the relevance of previous convictions to desert-based sentencing. Theorists who argue that the offender's desert should be proportionate to the seriousness of the current offence and nothing else see no role for previous convictions. To take prior convictions into account, they argue, is to punish the offender for who he is, rather than what he has done, and results in double punishment.[14] However, as I will now discuss, other commentators disagree and propose arguments derived from retributive theory to support a principled approach to taking previous convictions into consideration.

I shall discuss four accounts. The first is the Lapse theory, which argues for a first-offender discount that is progressively lost. I then discuss the Enhanced Culpability model, which can be construed in different ways. Examining the model proposed by Julian Roberts, I show that the implications of his core tenets lead to a stronger conclusion than he himself reaches. I consider remorse in relation to this stronger conclusion—the Strong Culpability model—in relation to the model he seems to prefer—the Weak Culpability model—and finally in relation to a model he alludes to in his discussion of Duff—the Attuned Censure model. I do not intend to defend any of these accounts in particular; rather, my aim is to elucidate the way in which the mitigating factor of remorse might interact with the aggravating factor of previous convictions on each of these different theories. Finally, for the purpose of discussion I again assume that the remorseful recidivist is in fact remorseful. The tension only arises when the respective aggravating and mitigating factors are justified. The offender must be genuinely remorseful for this to be the case.

Progressive Loss of Mitigation and the Lapse Theory

The Progressive Loss of Mitigation model of the apparent aggravating effect of previous convictions has been defended by Andreas von Hirsch.[15]

---

[13] Roberts and von Hirsch (n 9).

[14] See, eg, M Bagaric, 'Double Punishment and Punishing Character: The Unfairness of Prior Convictions' (2000) 19 *Criminal Justice Ethics* 10; M Davis, 'Just Deserts for Recidivists' (1985) 4 *Criminal Justice Ethics* 29.

[15] von Hirsch (n 10); A von Hirsch, 'Commentary: Criminal Record Rides Again' (1991) 10 *Criminal Justice Ethics* 2; A von Hirsch, *Past or Future Crimes: Deservedness and Dangerousness in the Sentencing of Criminals* (Manchester, Manchester University Press, 1985).

The phrase 'progressive loss of mitigation' describes the manner by which an offender's sentence will become more severe each time he reoffends, until the 'full', unmitigated sentence is justified. The initial mitigation is not earned; it is an expression of tolerance which the state extends to those who may have lapsed into offending—a sort of 'benefit of the doubt', until the court becomes convinced of the offender's criminality. The following passage from Wasik and von Hirsch sets out the rationale underlying the Progressive Loss of Mitigation model:

> Our everyday moral judgments include the notion of a lapse. A transgression (even a fairly serious one) is judged somewhat less strictly when it occurs against a background of prior compliance. The idea is that even an ordinarily well-behaved person can have his or her inhibitions fail in a moment of wilfulness or weakness. Such a temporary breakdown of self-control is the kind of frailty for which some understanding should be shown. In sentencing, the relevant lapse is an infringement of criminal law, rather than a more commonplace moral failure, but the logic of the first offender discount remains the same—that of dealing with a lapse more tolerantly. A reason for so treating a lapse is respect for the process by which people attend to, and respond to, censure for their conduct. A first offender, after being confronted with censure or blame, is capable—as a reasoning human being presumed capable of ethical judgments—of reflecting on the morality of what he has done and of making an extra effort to show greater restraint. What we do, in granting the discount, is to show respect for this capacity—and thereby give the offender a so-called 'second chance'. With repetitions, however, the discount should diminish, and eventually disappear.[16]

The practical ramifications of this theory, according to those who propose it, are that previous convictions will remove a quantum of mitigation for the first two, three or four convictions, but then further convictions will have no additional, aggravating effect on the offender's sentence.[17]

Some theorists have questioned whether the progressive nature of the loss of mitigation is at odds with the core rationale of tolerating a lapse and giving an offender a 'second chance'.[18] Should the offender be given a third and fourth chance? Does the idea of a 'temporary breakdown of self-control' seem plausible once an offender has repeatedly broken the law? Thus, although those who expound the Lapse theory suggest that the loss of mitigation is progressive, others have suggested that the underlying notion of lapse points more coherently to a dichotomous effect, whereby offenders

---

[16] M Wasik and A von Hirsch, 'Section 29 Revised: Previous Convictions in Sentencing' (1994) *Criminal Law Review* 409, 410.

[17] Ashworth suggests the mitigation is lost after the second offence: A Ashworth, *Sentencing and Criminal Justice*, 5th edn (Cambridge, Cambridge University Press, 2010) 202; Wasik suggests that the mitigation may extend to the fifth conviction: M Wasik, 'Guidance, Guidelines and Criminal Record' in M Wasik and K Pease (eds), *Sentencing Reform: Guidance or Guidelines?* (Manchester, Manchester University Press, 1987) 101.

[18] Roberts (n 9) 58.

are given the benefit of the doubt the first time they offend, but thereafter should receive the proportionate sentence.[19] In contrast to the alternative theory discussed below, the mitigation afforded to first- (and second-) time offenders on the Lapse theory is not a direct function of desert; rather, it derives its justification from broader principles relating to anticipation of effective censure and the appropriate attitude the state should have to occasional weakness.

Remorse and Previous Convictions on the Lapse Theory

If the Lapse theory were to be the correct justification for the effect of previous convictions on the severity of the sentence, then how should the mitigating effect of remorse interact with the 'aggravating' factor of previous convictions? The Lapse theory essentially extends the benefit of the doubt to all first-time offenders, assuming that their offending was a temporary breakdown of self-control, and that they will be responsive to the reasons embodied in the censure to refrain from further offending. The censure is attenuated to reflect this assumption of understanding and future compliance. This is, then, very similar to attenuating censure to address the offender who already appears to have internalised its message, as evidenced by his remorse. On the Lapse theory, it is as if the mitigation afforded to the first-time offender treats him as if he were remorseful. Indeed, compare the phrases used by Wasik and von Hirsch above to justify first-offender mitigation with Tasiouslas's description of the immediately repentant offender. According to Tasioulas, we understand his offence as 'a lapse or aberration, a succumbing to temptation or the pressures of the moment, rather than the product of a settled determination to do wrong'.[20]

Interestingly, it would seem that a *lack* of remorse might be particularly relevant to sentencing when the offender has not yet exhausted the mitigation extended to him on the assumption that his offending constitutes a lapse. It is difficult to present the offender who does not denounce his behaviour as one who suffered a weakness of self-control, even if his offence occurred against a background of relative compliance: the Lapse theory extends the benefit of the doubt to the offender, but a lack of remorse may remove this doubt, convincing the court that the offender in fact embraces his criminal behaviour.

Does this mean a lack of remorse should result in the offender being denied a first-offender discount since it makes the idea of a lapse seem too far-fetched? The answer to this question is probably 'no'; if we accept the Lapse theory, there are still reasons to retain the mitigation even for the

---

[19] See, for example: J Adler, *The Urgings of Conscience: A Theory of Punishment* (Philadelphia, PA, Temple University Press, 1991).
[20] Tasioulas, 'Punishment and Repentance' (2006) 81 *Philosophy* 279, 308.

remorseless offender. First, an offender can consistently intend to make extra effort to show greater restraint without feeling remorse. He might intend to do so for prudential reasons rather than moral reasons: he might intend to stay out of trouble. Second, the language used by Wasik and von Hirsch is prospective:[21] even if an offender is not remorseful prior to sentencing, he should be considered capable of reflecting on the morality of what he has done *once he has been* confronted with censure or blame. Thus, the benefit of the doubt errs on the side of assuming that the first-time offender is or will become remorseful.

This still leaves an interesting interaction between the mitigating effect of remorse and the aggravating (or progressively less mitigating) effect of previous convictions on this account. If the message embodied in the reduced censure is one that treats the offender as if he does, or at least will, understand the wrongfulness of what he has done, then it would be duplication to further attenuate the censure on the grounds of remorse: it is essentially the same message. If the argument is that remorse changes the quality of the censure in response to the offender's ability to accept the message, then this is already the starting point for first offenders on the Lapse theory. First-time offenders are treated as if they do not need the full message: they get a benefit which we later only afford the remorseful offender.

The upshot of this is that remorse should have a reduced mitigating effect until the first-offender discount has been lost.[22] The first-offender discount is lost progressively so remorse-based mitigation will, correspondingly, be gained progressively. Since previous convictions do not aggravate the offender's sentence on this theory, remorse ceases to be in tension with them once the first-offender discount expires and the full sentence applies. Responding to remorse in fact has similarities to giving first offenders the benefit of the doubt that they do or will reflect sufficiently on the message embodied in the censure. Thus, if we accept the Lapse theory, lack of previous convictions mitigates until the offender has three or four convictions, but remorse does not mitigate until this same point (or at least until some of the quantum of lapse-based mitigation has been lost). After the full sentence is activated, previous convictions should not aggravate further and genuine remorse can mitigate sentence by any amount up to that granted to the first-time offender.

---

[21] Wasik and von Hirsch (n 16).

[22] It should be noted that there have be versions of this model that treat the first offender mitigation as an entitlement. On these accounts, the potential receptiveness or otherwise of the offender to the message of censure, or how realistic it was that the offence was a temporary lapse, would have no bearing on whether the mitigation should be granted. See JV Roberts, 'Re-Examining First Offender Discounts at Sentencing' in JV Roberts and A von Hirsch (eds), *The Role of Previous Convictions at Sentencing: Theoretical and Applied Perspectives* (Oxford, Hart Publishing, 2010).

The Enhanced Culpability Model

Julian Roberts has proposed a model of previous convictions according to which prior offending increases the culpability of the offender.[23] On such a model, the aggravating effect of previous convictions operates *within* the desert framework since the culpability of the offender, along with the harm caused, determines the seriousness of the offence. Roberts argues that previous convictions speak to the offender's state of mind prior to the commission of the offence, drawing a comparison between previous convictions and premeditation, which is also held to aggravate an offender's culpability.

Before presenting Roberts' model in more detail, a few notes on terminology will be helpful. Different penal theorists, and indeed legislators, use phrases such as level or harm, culpability, responsibility and offence seriousness in slightly different ways. In England and Wales, punishment must be proportionate to the seriousness of the offence, which is determined by the level of harm caused and the offender's culpability for it. Roberts deviates somewhat from this, using offence seriousness to refer principally to the offence type and the harm it causes, separating the offender's level of culpability as a 'second branch of proportionality'. Whether there is a 'best way' of organising and labelling the factors of interest to desert theorists is not a question for this chapter. However, it is important to be sensitive to the way the language is used by any particular writer to avoid confusion. The key thing to note is that, in denying that previous convictions are relevant to the seriousness of the offence, Roberts is not putting them outside the assessment of the offender's desert.

The core proposition of Roberts' Enhanced Culpability model is that previous convictions increase an offender's culpability because, like premeditation, they speak to the offender's state of mind at the time of the offence. The comparison is made as follows:

> Premeditation bespeaks a disregard for legality, and a commitment to offending that is not true of spontaneous offending. Having been charged, convicted and punished, repeat offenders also share a state of mind that renders them more blameworthy than first-time offenders. Both considerations speak to the relationship between the offender and the offence and constitute legitimate grounds for aggravating the severity of sentence.[24]

The offender's state of mind at the time of the offence is indisputably relevant to his culpability. It is the seat of *mens rea* and involves considerations of (some or all of) motive, intention, knowledge and belief that can make all the difference between murder and manslaughter, between GBH and GBH with intent and between negligence and recklessness. The state of mind of

---

[23] See Roberts (n 9).
[24] ibid, 85.

the offender can thus significantly affect the seriousness of the offence. In relation to the culpable mental aspect of premeditation, Ashworth explains that it demonstrates that the offender is 'more fully confirmed in his criminal motivation than someone who acts on impulse'.[25] Similarly, Roberts suggests 'when the act is premeditated we are more inclined, in the language of social psychology, to attribute the act to the actor rather than to his environment'.[26] The state of mind involved in premeditation is a conscious and persisting intention to perform the act that constitutes the offence: the offender makes a decision to do it, rather than 'finds himself' doing it, as may be the phenomenology of spontaneous offending.

The State of Mind of the Repeat Offender

If this is roughly the characterisation of the state of mind involved in premeditation, what then characterises the state of mind of the offender with previous convictions? For the Enhanced Culpability argument to work—for it really to be about the offender's *state of mind at the time of the offending*—we must be able to point to something blameworthy about the offender's offence-related motivations, intentions, beliefs or knowledge.

Before attempting to pinpoint the culpability-enhancing aspects of the offender's state of mind, it should be noted that Roberts does not think that prior convictions operate *exactly* like premeditation. Indeed, he is careful to explain that, in his view, premeditation, along with factors such as targeting vulnerable victims and using unnecessary force, fall into a primary category of sentencing factors, whilst previous convictions, along with, for example, the fact that the offence was committed whilst on probation are subordinate, secondary factors. The reason he gives for this is that primary factors are offence related, whereas secondary factors are offender related or contextual.[27]

Further, for previous convictions, but not premeditation, Roberts makes an additional argument deriving from the censuring function of punishment:

> Because the prescribed sanction is one which expresses blame, this conveys the message that the conduct is reprehensible, and should be eschewed. However re-offending is also reprehensible, particularly if the offender continually reoffends. The sentencing process should not refrain from communicating a message about repetitive criminal conduct—but without losing sight of the principal reason for censure—the current conviction.[28]

This is a supplementary argument. Censuring reoffending on the grounds that it is reprehensible is linked only very loosely to a consideration of the offender's state of mind at the time of the offence. Further, an argument

---

[25] Ashworth (n 17) 164.
[26] Roberts (n 9) 80.
[27] ibid, 89.
[28] ibid, 86.

that succeeded in showing that previous convictions enhance culpability on the basis of the offender having a certain state of mind—knowledge, beliefs etc—would justify aggravation on *any* retributive theory concerned with culpability, not just communicative theories.

Since Roberts' principal argument is about the offender's state of mind, let us examine the possible ways of elucidating it further. Having previous convictions (even those of a similar kind to the present offence) does not itself preclude spontaneous offending of the same or similar kind; previous convictions do not denote intention. A repeat offender might 'find himself' committing another assault or shoplifting again without having planned it. Previous convictions will also not determine the motivations involved in subsequent offences. An offender convicted of four alcohol-fuelled assaults might commit a fifth while completely sober to defend a vulnerable friend. To the extent that motivation is relevant to culpability at all, prior offending does not derive *its* relevance in this way.

Foresight and Culpability

I suggest, instead, that if previous convictions reflect anything relevant about the mental state of the offender, it is to do with the knowledge that he has. Here the concept of *foresight* is central. Having previous relevant convictions gives the offender foresight that the first offender does not have. This foresight pertains to two dimensions of the offence. First, the offender has *foresight of the harm* that acting in the particular proscribed way will cause. Having committed assault before, the offender is likely to have a fuller and more certain knowledge of the pain and distress his attack causes.[29] When he commits the offence again, he knows what will follow from his actions. This first-hand knowledge of the harmful consequences, particularly of those suffered by the victim, makes the offender more culpable when he repeats the acts that lead to them. This epistemic advantage acquired through prior offending precludes quasi-defences such as 'I didn't understand the gravity of what I was doing'; 'I didn't know I was that strong'; 'I didn't realise it would hurt so much'.

Second, the offender has *foresight of the factors that make him likely to reoffend*.[30] Through repeat offending, the offender will have come to know

---

[29] Whilst it could be claimed that repeat offending might lead to a degree of desensitisation to the harm caused, this does not alter the fact that the offender has considerable knowledge and experience of this harm. Even if he is less moved by it, what it consists in is clear.

[30] This second strand of the foresight argument has parallels with Y Lee, 'Recidivism as Omission: A Relational Account' (2008) 87 *Texas Law Review* 571. Lee argues that the recidivist's failure to steer clear of criminogenic triggers and contexts, if they do in fact lead to more reoffending, constitutes an omission, which increases the offender's culpability for the ensuing offence. Having been convicted and punished, the offender finds himself in a relationship with the state that confers on him the obligation to attempt to steer his life in a direction that reduces the likelihood that he will reoffend.

that certain types of environment, keeping certain company or perhaps taking certain substances increase the likelihood of his reoffending. His culpability is enhanced to the extent that he did not try to avoid them. If the offender knows that he is likely to become violent when he drinks, or have difficulty controlling his sexual urges around children, or knows that a particular group of associates put pressure on him to steal then he is, in a sense, *reckless* if he decides to remain in or return to these criminogenic situations, and thus more culpable if he does reoffend, even if the offence was not planned.[31]

In sum, the persistent offender's state of mind at the time of the offence involves knowledge of himself, his likely behaviour and of the harm that his actions will cause. Whilst the blameworthy mental features of premeditation are concerned with intention and resolve, the blameworthy mental feature of the repeat offender derives from the foresight his prior offending affords him: he knows first hand the harm that his actions will cause and he consciously disregards the likely influence of criminogenic triggers. Crucially, this rendering of Roberts' position is consistent with the cumulative approach. Foresight permits of degrees and the offender will become increasingly aware of the things he could do to reduce the likelihood of his offending and of the harm that his offending causes. After a number of offences, it might be expected that the offender has acquired full knowledge of harm and triggers, but awareness, of triggers in particular, would not be expected to be maximal until this point.

This conceptualisation of the Enhanced Culpability model also explains why previous convictions must be recent and relevant (ie of the same or similar kind as the instant offence): foresight will be offence specific and may be lost over time. The Lapse theory perhaps does less well in this regard: the idea that first offenders may have demonstrated a momentary weakness and thus should be given a chance to respond to censure suggests a more holistic approach to state tolerance and citizen law abidingness. To reconcile the Lapse theory with the view that previous convictions must be recent and relevant to count in aggravation, the Lapse theory would have to say that an offender's previous convictions for offences differing in kind from the instant offence are not relevant because the offender had not before shown *this* weakness. However, this would distort the idea that first offenders should be judged against a more general background of prior compliance. On the Lapse theory, it would seem, all prior law breaking

---

[31] See JWC Turner, 'The Mental Element in Crimes at Common Law' (1936) 6 *Cambridge Law Journal* 31; discussed in H Oberdiek, 'V.—Intention And Foresight In Criminal Law' (1972) 81 *Mind* 389. A classic definition of recklessness is as follows: 'Recklessness' denotes the state of mind of the man who acts (or omits to act when he should act) foreseeing the possible consequences of his conduct, but with no desire to bring them about. It may be that he does not care whether they happen, or do not happen, or it may be that he hopes that they will not happen. He persists in a course of conduct which he realises may produce those consequences.

is relevant to whether or not we should see the repeat offender as having experienced a temporary breakdown of self-control. In contrast, to say that an offender's previous convictions are not relevant because he lacked foresight of the harm of *this sort of* offending and of the factors that might lead him to offend *in this way* strikes me as more plausible.

This also makes comprehensible the particular cumulative outcome of Roberts' model, whereby 'the difference in culpability between a first offender and an individual with two priors is much greater than that which differentiates an offender with two from another with four priors'.[32] The first offence will be enough to give the offender knowledge of the harm he can cause. However, with more offences the offender acquires greater foresight. This will occur most prominently for his knowledge of personal and situational factors compounding his behaviour, which become clearer through repeated experience.

It may be, then, that previous convictions operate at the same point in the assessment of culpability as premeditation. The offender's knowledge and experience of the precise consequences of the offence, and his reckless-ness in sustaining the environments, associations and other activities that make him more likely to offend are relevant to the offender's culpability at the time of the offence. If this argument succeeds, the difference between premeditation and previous conviction may be less about the former being offence related and the latter offender related (as Roberts himself main-tains), and more simply a difference in the degree of blameworthiness that attaches to intention (central to premeditation) versus other components of *mens rea*, such as knowledge and recklessness.

Remorse and Previous Convictions on the Strong Culpability Model

If previous convictions enhance culpability because of what they imply about the offender's state of mind at the time of the offence, how should the mitigating factor of remorse interact with the aggravating factor of previous convictions? I have argued that the mitigating effect of remorse is justified on the grounds of the reduced censure that becomes appropriate in light of the offender's understanding and rejection of his wrongful conduct. In elaborating the Enhanced Culpability model, I have argued that previous convictions, whilst themselves being antecedent, tie the blameworthy ele-ment more closely to the time of the offence. This has similarities with plan-ning, which occurs prior to the actual act but is relevant to the offender's culpability at the time of its commission. The offender with previous con-victions is likely to commit the offence with greater knowledge of the harm he will cause and/or under the influence of factors he was reckless in failing to avoid. Remorse, on the other hand, has no bearing on the offender's state

---

[32] Roberts (n 9) 89.

of mind at the time of the offence. Remorse is therefore offender related, whilst the relevance of previous convictions might be offence related in the same way as premeditation, since they are relevant to the offender's culpability for the offence. This is important when considering the interaction between these factors, as it situates their influence at different points in the sentencing decision, rather than at the same point where they might appear more directly in tension.

Being remorseful does not change the offender's state of mind at the time of the offence. Thus, for the assessment of offence seriousness—an assessment that takes into account the culpability of the offender—previous convictions will have an aggravating effect to the extent that the previous convictions gave the offender greater knowledge of the harm the offence causes and of the factors that make him more likely to reoffend; he was reckless to the extent that he failed to avoid them. Remorse, having a role to play after the seriousness of the offence has been established, will justify attenuating the censure to address the offender in the context of his understanding of the wrongfulness of his conduct. Since, on this model, previous convictions affect the offender's culpability for the offence and are therefore arguably offence related, they should carry more weight than remorse, which is not part of the assessment of the seriousness of the offence. This will especially be the case where there are a number of previous convictions, which have cumulatively aggravated the offence and corresponding proportionate punishment.

However, even on this model, it could still be argued that there is some scope for remorse and previous convictions to interact; indeed, Roberts makes some claims that suggest this. Even though previous convictions and remorse theoretically operate at different points in the sentencing decision on this model (if previous convictions are of consequence for culpability), remorse may yet have an *evidentiary* role to play in indicating attempts at desistance. The criminogenic factors of which prior offending makes the offender aware are not always easy or even possible for the offender to avoid, and this should be taken into account when assessing the extent to which recklessly failing to avoid them enhances culpability. Roberts claims that 'consideration of the offender's previous convictions requires a more multidimensional approach, one which incorporates the individual's efforts to achieve desistance, even if these efforts are ultimately unsuccessful'.[33] The offender's response to his own wrongdoing may reveal frustration over his repeat offending, which he has attempted to stop. In this way, remorse may show that the state of mind of the persistent offender renders him only slightly more culpable. The reason for this is that attempts at desistance preclude or at least weaken the disregard implied by continued engagement with situations or activities that the offender knows lead to his offending.

---

[33] ibid, 89–90.

The relationship between remorse and previous convictions is somewhat complex according this model. Previous convictions alone have more weight than remorse alone due to previous convictions being tied to culpability for the offence. However, when previous convictions and remorse are present, it may be the case that remorse has an evidentiary role to play in indicating that the offender, whilst still possessing foresight relating to the harm that would be caused, is not as culpable for failing to avoid known criminogenic factors, but only where the remorse indicates that attempts to avoid them have been made. Where this is the case, the aggravating effect of previous convictions may be somewhat reduced. Since remorse is relevant to the communicative context of the censure, it will continue to have mitigating force that is independent from any evidence it provides to suggest a lesser aggravating role for previous convictions. To repeat, remorse does not dilute the aggravating effect of previous convictions on culpability, rather, in some cases, it reveals that the failure to avoid known criminogenic factors was not a direct result of reckless disregard: the offender was not unconcerned about putting himself in situations where he was likely to reoffend, and may have found avoiding them to be incredibly difficult.

Remorse and Previous Convictions on the Weak Culpability Model

It should be emphasised that in examining the relationship between remorse and previous convictions on the Enhanced Culpability model thus far, I have added elements to Roberts' account and even suggested that his account has implications that he denies. The most significant amendment was that previous convictions, if truly related to the offender's state of mind at the time of the offence, will be relevant to culpability in the same way as premeditation, but with less weight since they (alone) do not denote intention. In contrast, Roberts explicitly positions previous convictions as offender related and, although he argues that they enhance the culpability of the offender, he consequently does not see them as relevant to the assessment of the seriousness of the offence. If they are to aggravate the sentence outside of the central assessment of harm and culpability, then it might be that Roberts is committed to the idea he briefly intimates, wherein censure communicates a message about the reprehensibility of repetitive criminal conduct.[34] If this were to be the grounds for the aggravating effect of previous convictions, then the mitigating effects of remorse and the aggravating effect of previous convictions would potentially cancel each other out: the two countervailing communications would be in conflict. Any attenuation of sentence that remorse justifies may be outweighed by the communication of condemnation for repeat offending, especially as convictions become more numerous.

[34] See ibid, 86.

Remorse, Previous Convictions and Attuned Censure

There is one further potential approach to previous convictions that Roberts hints at in relation to Duff's penance account. Whereas Roberts claims that sentencing should condemn recidivism through harsher punishment, he suggests that an alternative approach would take previous convictions into account to '*assume a response [from the offender]* to the communication expressed by the court'.[35] The idea here is that, if sentencing comprises an attempt to communicate censure to the offender, then the offender's reactions to previous communications are relevant: previous convictions may demonstrate a failure to grasp, or even a deliberate disregard for, the penal communication. Subsequent censure is therefore adjusted in an attempt to make it more effective—to address the offender in the context of his demonstrable lack of understanding.

If this model were to be adopted, then the effects of remorse and previous convictions on censure would not simply weigh against each other. On this model the offender's previous convictions are used as a way of gauging how to pitch the censure, as it were. Where remorse is present, the court might attune the censure in light of the offender's likely (accepting) response to the censure. Indeed, such an approach to remorse has great similarities with my Responsive Censure account. In such cases, where genuine remorse demonstrates understanding of the wrongfulness of the conduct, previous convictions may have no role to play. Since remorse will be the most recent indicator of the offender's receptivity, it seems plausible that it should be given the most weight, but this will be a matter of case-by-case judgement. This is in contrast to the aggravating effect of previous convictions being 'cancelled out' by remorse, as it would be on a Weak Culpability model that explicitly advocated denunciation of repeat offending.

Summary of Consequences for Sentencing

Each of the models presented above gives a different outcome for the relationship between remorse and previous convictions. The following provides a summary:

The Lapse theory: the potential quantum of mitigation afforded by the recidivist's remorse will increase from zero for the first offence, up to its maximum once the number of previous convictions is such that the first-offender discount has completely expired. This is because the first-offender discount essentially treats the offender as if he will respond to the message of censure in the same way as the remorseful offender. After the full sentence has been reached, remorse will always mitigate the offender's

---

[35] ibid, 62, emphasis added.

sentence, regardless of how many previous convictions an offender has since they cease to have any effect on the severity of the sentence.

The Strong Culpability model—previous convictions increase culpability: remorse and previous convictions are relevant at different stages and so do not come into direct conflict. They should therefore both aggravate and mitigate independently, with remorse tending to have a smaller impact due to its less central relevance. However, remorse may provide evidence that the offender has made attempts to desist, which would speak against outright recklessness on his part in failing to avoid the social or behavioural factors that he has learnt make his offending more likely. (Remorse does not, however, have any consequences for foresight of harm.) Where this is the case, the aggravating effect of previous convictions will be lessened but not completely abated. Remorse continues to mitigate independently.

The Weak Culpability model—previous convictions denounced by censure: previous convictions and remorse both affect the penal communication. Previous convictions elicit explicit condemnation of repeat offending, and remorse elicits attenuated censure, responsive to the offender's communication of his repudiation of the wrongful conduct. These two elements of the communication weigh against each other and potentially cancel each other out.

The Attuned Censure model—previous convictions indicative of likely response to censure: previous convictions and remorse both provide an indication of the receptiveness of the offender to the message of censure. When both are present, the court must assess which is the more indicative and increase, reduce or maintain the sentence severity accordingly. Since remorse will be the most recent indicator, it seems plausible that it should be given the greatest consideration, but this will be a matter of case-by-case judgement.

REMORSE AND RECIDIVISM IN PRACTICE

Elsewhere, I have reported empirical analysis of the effects of remorse and previous convictions at sentencing.[36] The results showed that, for assault offences sentenced in England and Wales, remorse and previous convictions had independent effects on the likelihood of the offender receiving a custodial sentence. The overall effect of previous convictions was larger than that of remorse, but remorse continued to exert mitigating force even when previous convictions were numerous. Graphical representation of this relationship suggested that the aggravating effect of previous convictions plateaued at about six previous convictions.

---

[36] See H Maslen, 'Penitence and Persistence: How Should Sentencing Factors Interact?' in JV Roberts (ed), *Exploring Sentencing Practice in England and Wales* (Palgrave McMillan, in press).

These results are most compatible with the Strong Culpability model. The independent effects of remorse and previous convictions, and the larger effect of previous convictions support the idea that previous convictions have a more central role to play, and that previous convictions and remorse do not cancel each other out. Although the plateauing effect appears constant with a (very gradual) progressive loss of mitigation, it is not inconsistent with the Strong Culpability model. Although offenders will acquire clearer and clearer foresight as they commit more offences of a particular type, at some point this foresight will be as sharp as it can be. Further offences will not add anything to the offender's knowledge of likely harm and likely triggers. Thus, it is conceptually plausible that previous convictions enhance an offender's culpability for the first five or six offences but do not enhance it further beyond this point.

For the sake of discussion, this chapter has assumed that the remorse demonstrated by the recidivist is genuine. Of course, in practice it is likely that a judge will be suspicious of the remorse of an offender who keeps committing the same crime. In many cases, previous convictions may be used as an argument against the sincerity of the offender's remorse. This will involve a case-by-case assessment of any changes in the offender that suggest that he has indeed reached a turning point. It should be noted that genuine remorse and attempts at desistance are not incompatible with slipping back into some offending behaviour and therefore that previous convictions should not always be taken to discredit claims of remorse even where such claims have been made before.

Implications for Sentencing Guidelines

I have shown that the way in which previous convictions and remorse should (or should not) interact depends on the theoretical model adopted. Due to the underlying justifications, Lapse theory and the Attuned Censure model have more scope for interaction than the Strong and Weak Culpability models, although in many cases there will be room for both factors to play complicated evidentiary roles: remorse may make claims of attempted desistance more plausible; previous convictions may raise doubts about the genuineness of remorse, especially if it has been expressed at sentencing before.

On the Lapse theory it was argued that the mitigating effect of remorse should not take effect until the first-offender discount starts to be lost. The Attuned Censure model would require consideration of previous convictions and remorse together, to assess the offender's receptiveness to the message of censure. The two factors interact on these models as their individual effects change when they are both present.

On the Strong Culpability model, previous convictions increase culpability regardless of whether remorse is present, and remorse mitigates regardless of previous convictions. On the Weak Culpability model, previous convictions are condemned through an increase in censure regardless of whether the offender is remorseful. The extra message embodied in this enhanced censure is, *ex hypothesi*, part of what the genuinely remorseful offender will already accept. His censure is therefore moderated in response to his prior acceptance of the whole message embodied by censure.[37] On both these models, then, the factors do not interact, although both may have independent effects.

The data I analyse elsewhere shows that remorse and previous convictions do not interact in practice.[38] Given that this makes adherence to some models of previous convictions difficult, this finding will be of interest to those constructing sentencing guidelines. If the Sentencing Council considers the lack of interaction to be correct, then it may wish to officially endorse this practice. However, if the Council is of the opinion that there should be an interaction—for example, that recidivists should receive no remorse-based mitigation—then specific direction could be given in the guidance to correct the approach observed in current practice.

The new format guidelines in England and Wales (discussed in greater detail in the next chapter) cite previous convictions as an aggravating factor *and* lack of previous convictions as a mitigator. This conflates the Progressive Loss of Mitigation and Enhanced Culpability models, and indicates that the guidelines (at least in their presentation) are not committed to one over the other (or perhaps are committed to a hybrid account). Attempting to add theoretical precision to an approach that currently fails to adjudicate between the main competing models would thus be inadvisable, although a general statement could be made about whether there are limits to the mitigating effect of remorse.

I have demonstrated that a choice of model would have consequences for the shape of the interaction between previous convictions and remorse, such that weighing them against each other would proceed differently in both theory and practice depending on the preferred model. I have demonstrated the general patterns observable in current practice. This practice is either justifiable or not. In order for sentencing to be principled, penal theorists and those constructing guidance not only need to consider whether particular factors should affect sentence, but also whether the presence of other factors has consequence for the influence they should have.

---

[37] To the extent that remorse will always involve this acceptance, remorse-based mitigation remains unaffected by previous convictions.

[38] Maslen (n 36).

9

Remorse in the Sentencing Guidelines

T HUS FAR, I have focused mainly on desert theories to ask whether remorse can be justified as a mitigating factor and, if so, with what limitations. In practice, however, sentencing regimes tend not to be based solely on one theory of punishment. Although some jurisdictions' sentencing practices are shaped more by retributive considerations (such as proportionality) and others more by consequentialist goals (such as crime prevention), in most cases there will be a range of aims to which sentencers are to attend. This has the result that the relevance or irrelevance of some sentencing factors will be uncertain, and their potential impacts on sentence may even diverge depending on which aim is pursued. For example, from a desert perspective, if the offender suffered abuse as a child, this might serve to reduce his culpability if the court were to consider that the offence committed was linked to the earlier abuse. For example, in an Australian case, it was held that the offender's childhood abuse led to his failure to understand the proper boundaries of sexual conduct within a family.[1] Although this does not justify or excuse, it was held to demonstrate a diminished capacity to comply with the law, which is relevant to culpability. From a consequentialist perspective, however, if the lack of understanding wrought by the offender's abuse makes him likely to reoffend, then incapacitative punishment may be necessary to protect his family and perhaps wider society. The same factor would be mitigating on the former perspective and aggravating on the latter.

Thus, when desert and consequentialist aims operate concurrently, sentencers must decide which aims are of greater relevance in any particular case and assess the relevance of sentencing factors in light of the principal goals. The multiplicity of sentencing aims from differing penal theories generates a complicated background against which remorse-based mitigation can be seen to operate. In what follows, I show how remorse features and operates in the sentencing guidance of different jurisdictions against the backdrop of the underlying justifications supporting each system. I begin

---

[1] *Gallagher* 2/7/1997 CA Vic.

with a discussion of remorse in the sentencing guidelines of England and Wales. I then compare three other jurisdictions—Victoria (Australia), New Zealand and the United States—to demonstrate the range of approaches taken to remorse.

ENGLAND AND WALES

The sentencing system in England and Wales has an emphasis on proportionality, which derives from the desert tradition. The court is required to 'pass a sentence that is commensurate with the seriousness of the offence'.[2] The seriousness of an offence is determined by two main parameters: the culpability of the offender and the harm caused or risked by the offence. However, although the emphasis on proportionality influences the starting point for sentence severity, the final sentence must be arrived at via consideration of further sentencing purposes.

The court must have regard to the five purposes of sentencing contained in section 142(1) Criminal Justice Act 2003:

(a) the punishment of offenders,
(b) the reduction of crime (including its reduction by deterrence),
(c) the reform and rehabilitation of offenders,
(d) the protection of the public, and
(e) the making of reparation by offenders to persons affected by their offence.

The seriousness guideline explicitly states that the Act 'does not indicate that any one purpose should be more important than any other and in practice they may all be relevant to a greater or lesser degree in any individual case—the sentencer has the task of determining the manner in which they apply'.[3]

This mixture of purposes means it is not clear on what grounds remorse is to be justified as a mitigating factor, nor which aspects of an offender's remorse will be of most relevance to its mitigating role. For instance, if the justification for remorse-based mitigation is bound up with the purpose of reparation, the offender's reparative acts will be of greatest relevance. If it is to be justified on the grounds that it is of relevance to the purpose of deterrence, the likelihood that the remorse indicates desistance would be the principal consideration. Alternatively, remorse might be considered most relevant when it indicates that a rehabilitative approach should be

---

[2] Sentencing Guidelines Council, 'Overarching Principles: Seriousness: Guideline' (Sentencing Guidelines Secretariat, 2004) 3, http://sentencingcouncil.judiciary.gov.uk/docs/web_seriousness_guideline.pdf.
[3] ibid.

taken to deciding the sanction. The censure-based justification developed in Chapter 5 would be relevant to the quantum of punishment the offender deserves. Protecting the public might preclude a role for remorse.

Remorse in the Sentencing Guidelines of England and Wales

There are two sets of guidelines currently in effect in England and Wales. A number of guidelines, both offence specific and generic, were issued by the previous statutory authority (the Sentencing Guidelines Council—SGC). Until these guidelines are reissued in the new format by the Sentencing Council they remain in effect. The other guidelines are those issued by the Sentencing Council; these are also generic or offence specific and they reflect a revised format devised by the Council. There is a difference of emphasis across the different guidelines. The original guidelines adopt one of three main approaches: reiteration of generic guidance elsewhere; instruction limiting the influence of remorse; or instruction supporting a more extensive mitigating role for remorse. Finally, the revised format guidelines provide a further approach, raising questions about the effects this variability may have on sentencing practices.

Generic Guidelines: Offence Seriousness and Sentence Reductions for a Guilty Plea

The *Overarching Principles: Seriousness* guideline provides guidance on how judges should assess the seriousness of any offence.[4] The guideline also identifies aggravating and mitigating factors—both those that increase or decrease the seriousness of the offence, and those that have no impact on the seriousness of the offence, but which may still mitigate the punishment imposed. This latter class of mitigating factors is described in the guidelines as 'personal mitigation' and the factors are related to the offender rather than the offence. It is significant that remorse is the only personal mitigation factor explicitly identified in the seriousness guideline.

The relevance of remorse as a mitigating factor is also recognised in the guideline for sentence reductions to reflect a guilty plea. In *Reduction in Sentence for a Guilty Plea*, earlier guidance was revised to emphasise that 'remorse and material assistance provided to prosecuting authorities are separate issues from those to which the [Reduction in Sentence for a Guilty Plea] guideline applies'.[5] Remorse has value independent of a plea of guilty

---

[4] ibid.

[5] Sentencing Guidelines Council, 'Reduction in Sentence for a Guilty Plea: Definitive Guideline' (Sentencing Guidelines Secretariat, 2007), http://sentencingcouncil.judiciary.gov.uk/docs/Reduction_in_Sentence_for_a_Guilty_Plea_-Revised_2007.pdf, ii.

(which has pragmatic value in reducing court costs and sparing victims and witnesses from having to participate in a protracted trail). As these guidelines apply to all offences, it would seem that remorse should be considered by sentencers in all cases. However, the SGC's decision to flag the relevance of remorse for some offences but not others (rather than leave it to the general guideline) may lead to inconsistency of application.

Some of the SGC's offence-specific guidelines merely restate the paragraphs from the seriousness guideline.[6] These are serious crimes, and the presumption in the guidance therefore seems to be that remorse should have the potential to mitigate regardless of the seriousness of the offence. The remaining guidelines embody one of two broad approaches: either placing limits on the influence remorse can have, or supporting a more extensive, universal mitigating role for remorse, thereby highlighting its value.

Remorse is treated somewhat exceptionally in *Overarching Principles: Assaults on Children and Cruelty to a Child* where remorse features in mitigation of culpability.[7] It is widely agreed in the literature, however, that remorse cannot retrospectively alter the offender's state of mind at the time of the crime.[8] Since culpability is the primary indicator of offence seriousness, the positioning of remorse as a mitigator of culpability risks too much weight being attached to it.[9]

Guidelines Limiting the Influence of Remorse

The *Assaults on Children and Cruelty to a Child* guideline includes a statement about remorse that goes beyond the blanket assertion of relevance found in the overall seriousness guidelines. In this instance the advice is: 'the extent to which remorse should influence sentence will always have to be judged in the light of all the circumstances surrounding the case'.[10]

---

[6] This occurs in: Sentencing Guidelines Council, 'Attempted Murder: Definitive Guideline' (Sentencing Guidelines Council, Crown copyright, 2009) 10, http://sentencingcouncil.judiciary. gov.uk/docs/Attempted_Murder_-_Definitive_Guideline_(web)accessible.pdf; Sentencing Guidelines Council, 'Robbery: Definitive Guideline' (Sentencing Guidelines Secretariat, 2006) 7–8, http://sentencingcouncil.judiciary.gov.uk/docs/web_robbery-guidelines.pdf; Sentencing Guidelines Council, 'Overarching Principles: Domestic Violence: Definitive Guideline' (Sentencing Guidelines Secretariat, 2006) 10, http://sentencingcouncil.judiciary.gov.uk/docs/web_domestic_violence.pdf.

[7] Sentencing Guidelines Council, 'Overarching Principles: Assaults on Children and Cruelty to a Child: Definitive Guideline' (Sentencing Guidelines Secretariat, 2008) 9, http://sentencingcouncil.judiciary.gov.uk/docs/web_Overarching_principles_assaults_on_children_and_cruelty_to_a_child.pdf.

[8] A Ashworth, *Sentencing and Criminal Justice*, 5th edn (Cambridge, Cambridge University Press, 2010) 173.

[9] Sentencing Guidelines Council (n 2) 5: 'The culpability of the offender in the particular circumstances of an individual case should be the initial factor in determining the seriousness of an offence'.

[10] Sentencing Guidelines Council (n 7) 9.

In following this guidance, aspects of each particular case will determine the extent to which remorse should mitigate punishment for the particular offender. There is, however, no guidance on *how* the circumstances surrounding the case establish the extent to which remorse has influence. One reading is that a more serious crime, or the presence of particular aggravating factors, rules out any significant reduction.

Other offence-specific guidelines also endorse a model in which the impact of remorse varies within offence type. The *Fail to Surrender to Bail* guideline considers remorse within the section dealing with 'aggravating and mitigating factors':

> Prompt voluntary surrender might mitigate sentence where it saves police time in tracing and arresting an offender. It may also be an indication of remorse. This must be weighed against the degree of harm caused by the offence, which may still be significant.[11]

The phrase 'must be weighed against the degree of harm caused by the offence' suggests that, as the harm of the offence increases, remorse should have proportionately less influence. This implies that the mitigating influence is not equal across all offences of the same type. No further guidance is given regarding the way that remorse should be weighed against the degree of harm caused by the offence. The comment that the harm caused 'may still be significant' suggests perhaps that where the harm of the offence is ongoing, (for example, lasting physical injury) mitigating the offender's punishment for failing to surrender to bail may be less justified. The guidance here suggests that the mitigating impact of remorse depends on other aspects of the offence and/or offender.

The *Theft and Burglary in a Building other than a Dwelling* guideline might also appear to support a differential model by which remorse should operate.[12] The guidance on personal mitigation for this offence identifies the following mitigating factors: return of stolen property; the impact on sentence of offender's dependency; the fact that the offender was motivated by desperation or need.[13] Remorse is not mentioned, possibly because it is covered by the general 'seriousness' guidelines.

However, further guidance is given on the mitigating factors relating to particular forms of this offence, where 'factors to take into consideration' are

[11] Sentencing Guidelines Council, 'Fail to Surrender Bail: Definitive Guideline' (Sentencing Guidelines Secretariat, 2007) 6, http://sentencingcouncil.judiciary.gov.uk/docs/web_Fail_to_Surrender_to_Bail.pdf.

[12] This guideline is still in operation for the four forms of theft, but guidance in this document on 'burglary in a building other than a dwelling' are no longer effective; sentencing guidelines for this offence are now contained in 'Burglary offences' effective from 16 January 2012.

[13] Sentencing Guidelines Council, 'Theft and Burglary in a Building Other than a Dwelling: Definitive Guideline' (Sentencing Guidelines Council, Crown copyright, 2008) 4–5, http://sentencingcouncil.judiciary.gov.uk/docs/Theft_and_Burglary_of_a_building_other_than_a_dwelling.pdf.

detailed. Remorse does feature here, but for only one of these forms: 'theft in breach of trust'.[14] Under the subheading 'cessation of offending', we find stated:

> The fact that an offender voluntarily ceased offending before being discovered does not reduce the seriousness of the offence. However, if the claim to have stopped offending is genuine, it may constitute personal mitigation, particularly if it is evidence of remorse.[15]

Importantly, remorse is valued independently of its tendency to result in cessation of offending. Further, the word 'particularly' suggests either that the mitigating effect will be greater if evidence of remorse is present or that the presence of remorse makes certain the possibility that cessation of offending constitutes personal mitigation.

The guidelines discussed above reveal an implicit commitment to the principle that remorse should have a differential impact depending on the type of offence and also on the circumstances of the particular offence in question. Consequently, there should be between- and within-offence variation in the impact of remorse: remorse may be more relevant to some offences than others, and where it is relevant it can justify varying degrees of mitigation. But, as the discussion exposed, on what this variation depends is unclear. Little guidance is provided and it is ambiguous. The most detailed guidance instructed judges to weigh the remorse against the harm of the offence, but the offence of failing to surrender to bail is unusual as it is a secondary offence, making it unclear whether this particular instruction has application to sentencing more widely.

Guidelines Supporting a More Extensive Mitigating Role for Remorse

Whereas the above guidelines appear to place some limits on the relevance of remorse to the offender's sentence, others make more positive statements about the value of remorse and the influence it should have upon sentence. The most positive statement is found in the *Causing Death by Driving* guideline, which states:

> Whilst it can be expected that anyone who has caused death by driving would be expected to feel remorseful, this cannot undermine its importance for sentencing purposes. Remorse is identified as personal mitigation in the Council guideline and the Council can see no reason[16] for it to be treated differently for this group

---

[14] It is strange that remorse does not feature as a 'factor to be taken into consideration' for any of the other types of this offence ('theft in a dwelling' (ibid, 12), 'theft from the person' (ibid, 14), 'theft from a shop' (ibid, 16) and 'burglary in a building other than a dwelling' (ibid, 18)), particularly as it is not mentioned in the more general guidance on aggravation and mitigation. Why would remorse only be relevant when the theft is in breach of trust?

[15] ibid, 11.

[16] This language suggests that Council members specifically addressed this issue in meetings prior to issuing its guideline.

of offences. It is for the court to determine whether an expression of remorse is genuine; where it is, this should be taken into account as personal mitigation ... and genuine remorse may be taken into account as personal mitigation and may justify a reduction in sentence.[17]

The importance of remorse is therefore explicitly emphasised and the suggestion is that its value should be recognised even though there is an expectation of remorse, given the nature of the offence. Its value is not contingent on the degree to which it might reasonably be expected.[18] This is an example of explicit consideration of whether the general guidance on remorse in the seriousness guidelines is applicable to this offence. This guideline makes a clear claim that remorse should be taken into account as personal mitigation. The result is a categorical and uniform instruction to take remorse into account, with no suggestion that its influence depends on other factors.

The *Sentencing for Fraud—Statutory Offences* guideline also makes positive statements about remorse, and suggests mostly universal application:

> In some cases, particularly those where a fraud has been carried out over a significant period of time, offenders may stop offending (or claim to have stopped offending) before they are apprehended. Where there is objective evidence to support such a claim, particularly where it is accompanied by a genuine expression of remorse, this usually should be treated as offender mitigation.[19]

Remorse is again valued over and above the sorts of behaviours it tends to motivate. Genuine remorse serves to enhance the mitigating value of desistance. In addition to cessation of offending providing evidence of remorse, the guideline proceeds to add voluntary restitution as evidence, saying that 'the timing of the voluntary restitution may be an indicator of the degree to which it reflects genuine remorse...'.[20] However, the guidance also makes it clear that it is the intention of the offender to offer restitution and not only success at restitution that is important. It is recognised that an offender can be 'temporarily or permanently prevented by circumstances beyond his or her control from returning defrauded items'. What matters is the 'point in time at which, and the determination with which, the offender tried to

---

[17] Sentencing Guidelines Council, 'Causing Death by Driving: Definitive Guideline' (Sentencing Guidelines Council, Crown copyright, 2008) 6, http://sentencingcouncil.judiciary.gov.uk/docs/web_causing_death_by_driving_definitive_guideline.pdf.

[18] An example of judicial sensitivity to social expectations regarding remorse is found in the remarks of a judge hypothetically sentencing an offender for death by dangerous driving: J Jacobson and M Hough, *Mitigation: The Role of Personal Mitigating Factors in Sentencing*. The judge's dismissive response: 'it may sound harsh, but *I'd expect her* to feel intense remorse' 24, emphasis added.

[19] Sentencing Guidelines Council, 'Sentencing for Fraud—Statutory Offences: Definitive Guideline' (Sentencing Guidelines Council, Crown copyright, 2009) 10, http://sentencingcouncil.judiciary.gov.uk/docs/web_sentencing_for_fraud_statutory_offences.pdf.

[20] ibid, 11.

return the items'.[21] Therefore, not only does the guidance here provide advice on how to assess the genuineness of remorse, it also emphasises that the value is not found only in the reparative behaviours but in the offender's expressed intentions.

The relevance of remorse is also indicated in the *Manslaughter by Reason of Provocation* guideline where sentencers are told: 'The behaviour of the offender after the killing can be relevant to sentence: immediate and genuine remorse may be demonstrated by the summoning of medical assistance, remaining at the scene, and co-operation with the authorities'.[22]

The Sentencing Council Guidelines

In 2011 the Sentencing Council issued a new format of guideline, which is being adopted as a model for many of the new offence-specific guidelines. The first such guideline pertained to assault offences and became effective in June 2011. Since this time, guidelines have been produced for burglary offences, dangerous dog offences, drug offences, environmental offences and sexual offences.[23]

The new format creates two separate steps for a court to determine the seriousness of the offence. Step One determines the appropriate category of seriousness and contains an exhaustive list of factors for courts to consider. Once a category has been selected, Step Two provides a second, non-exhaustive list of sentencing factors relating to seriousness, culpability or personal mitigation.

The Step One factors are the most important ones; factors identified at Step Two have less impact on sentence severity and serve to 'tweak' the sentence within the range determined at Step One. Remorse is identified within the list contained in Step Two as one of a number of factors 'reducing seriousness or reflecting personal mitigation' and which might therefore merit downward adjustment from the starting point of the particular offence category. The format classifies remorse under the heading

---

[21] ibid.

[22] Sentencing Guidelines Council, 'Manslaughter by Reason of Provocation: Guideline' (Sentencing Guidelines Secretariat, 2005) 6, http://sentencingcouncil.judiciary.gov.uk/docs/Manslaughter_by_Reason_of_Provocation.pdf.

[23] Sentencing Council, 'Burglary Offences: Definitive Guideline' (Crown copyright, 2011) http://sentencingcouncil.judiciary.gov.uk/docs/Burglary_Definitive_Guideline_web_final.pdf; Sentencing Council, 'Dangerous Dog Offences: Definitive Guideline' (Crown copyright, 2012) http://sentencingcouncil.judiciary.gov.uk/docs/Dangerous_Dog_Offences_Definitive_Guideline_9web_final.pdf; Sentencing Council, 'Drug Offences: Definitive Guideline'; Sentencing Council, 'Environmental Offences: Definitive Guideline' (Crown copyright, 2014) http://sentencingcouncil.judiciary.gov.uk/docs/Final_Environmental_Offences_Definitive_Guideline_(web).pdf; Sentencing Council, 'Sexual Offences: Definitive Guideline' (Crown copyright, 2013) http://sentencingcouncil.judiciary.gov.uk/docs/Final_Sexual_Offences_Definitive_Guideline_content_(web).pdf.

'personal mitigation', and the influence of this factor is therefore restricted to affecting the sentence *within* the category range. No guidance is provided with respect to the weight that should be assigned to remorse (or any factors in the guidelines);[24] this reflects the view of the Council that determining the relevance and effect of remorse is properly left for judicial discretion to resolve.

One reading of the new format is that remorse may play a greater role than in the past. In many of the older guidelines, remorse is listed as a possible mitigating factor in a generic list with the caveat that the factors apply to a wide range of offences and not all will be relevant to the particular offence covered in the guideline. Indeed, this was the case in the previous assault guideline issued by the SGC in 2008. Remorse was not identified as a factor in relation to any of the particular forms of the offence of assault, and only appeared in the generic list with the caveat 'not all [factors] will be relevant to assault and other offences against the person'.

Under the new Sentencing Council definitive guideline, however, remorse is explicitly identified as one of eight factors listed at Step Two which reflect personal mitigation.[25] This explicit reference to remorse may encourage advocates to consider the issue in their submissions, and may strengthen claims for mitigation. Since the introduction of the *Definitive Guideline for Assault Offences*, the other guidelines following the new format all include remorse as a factor in personal mitigation at Step Two, reinforcing its role as a universally relevant sentencing factor.

Remorse in Sentencing Practice in England and Wales

In 2012 the Sentencing Council released the first annual wave of data from the Crown Court Sentencing Survey.[26] The results from the Survey confirm the importance of remorse as a sentencing factor. Although the number and nature of mitigating factors varies significantly across offences, one feature is consistent: in 2011, for eight of the 10 offence categories, remorse was the most frequently cited mitigating factor, and was the second most frequent factor for the remaining two offence categories (robbery and sexual offences). Table 9.1 summarises the proportion of cases in which remorse was cited by the court as a mitigating factor. The category where remorse

---

[24] Except the guideline on Sentence Reductions for a Guilty Plea.

[25] Three additional factors (assault involved a single blow; assault was an isolated incident; and there has been a lapse of time since the offence) reduce seriousness and accompany the eight personal mitigators.

[26] Sentencing Council, *Crown Court Sentencing Survey*, Annual Publication (Office of the Sentencing Council, 2012), http://sentencingcouncil.judiciary.gov.uk/docs/CCSS_Annual_2012.pdf.

appeared most frequently—cited by the court in 39 per cent of sentences imposed—was for offences causing death.

Table 9.1: Percentage of cases where remorse was cited, 2011

Offence Category	Percentage of all cases in which remorse was cited
Offences causing death	39%
Assault (old form)	37%
Arson and criminal damage	36%
Driving offences	34%
Robbery	32%
Assault (new form)	31%
Drugs (old form)	28%
Sexual offences (old form)	28%
Other offences	28%
Theft	27%

Source: Sentencing Council, *Crown Court Sentencing Survey*, Annual Publication (Office of the Sentencing Council, 2012), http://sentencingcouncil.judiciary.gov.uk/docs/CCSS_Annual_2012.pdf.

In time, analysis of the Survey will be able to answer other questions about the relative weights that courts ascribe to different factors. For example, it will be possible to estimate the amount of variance accounted for by various mitigating factors, including remorse. My exploratory quantitative analysis elsewhere examined the relationship between remorse and likelihood of custody, controlling for offence seriousness, and other aggravating and mitigating factors.[27] The results of this analysis suggested that remorse has a significant effect on the likelihood of custody for assault offences, although its effect decreased as offence seriousness increased, presumably because the most serious assaults almost always attract custodial sentences.

More complex analytic procedures will help explain why remorse is a more frequent source of mitigation for certain categories of offending. For the present, we can only speculate why remorse is more frequently cited for some crimes than others. One possibility is that fewer of the offenders who came before the court to be sentenced for robbery or a sexual offence demonstrated genuine remorse. A more institutional explanation might be that the guidelines for robbery and sexual offences may not emphasise

---

[27] H Maslen, 'Penitence and Persistence: How Should Sentencing Factors Interact?' in JV Roberts (ed), *Exploring Sentencing Practice in England and Wales* (Palgrave McMillan, in press).

remorse as a mitigating factor as much as for other offences. (The old sexual offences guidelines did not explicitly indicate remorse as a mitigating factor.) Finally, judges may have used their discretion to decide that offenders' remorse is not as relevant, or should not have as great an impact, when sentencing for robbery and sexual offences.

REMORSE IN OTHER JURISDICTIONS

It is beyond the scope of this book to offer a systematic analysis of how (if at all) remorse features in the sentencing legislation and guidance governing every jurisdiction. What I will do here is present and discuss some interesting examples of contrasting approaches. The three jurisdictions I discuss all consider remorse in detail and, in combination, offer a diverse range of reasons for its inclusion. The *Victorian Sentencing Manual* of the state of Victoria, Australia uses case law to support the practice of granting the remorseful offender a 'substantial reduction' in sentence. The justifications given allude to consequentialist aims, mercy and desert. Promoting elements of restorative justice, the New Zealand Sentencing Act (2002) puts particular emphasis on taking into account the offender's 'offer, agreement, response, or measure to make amends'. However, remorse itself appears secondary: it is the reparative acts and victim consolation that are at the fore. The *United States Sentencing Guidelines Manual* subsumes remorse under 'acceptance of responsibility'. Emphasising the societal benefits of allowing a reduction in sentence, remorse and the guilty plea discount are somewhat intertwined.

The Victorian Sentencing Manual

The most comprehensive treatment of the issue of remorse is found in the *Victorian Sentencing Manual* (VSM), published by the Judicial College of Victoria. The explicit aim of the manual is 'to promote consistency of approach by sentencers in the exercise of their discretion'.[28] Whilst it is not a piece of legislation, the manual 'provides ready access to the law for sentencers whilst in court, and gives guidance in interpreting and assessing the weight of the matters of fact significant to the instant case'.[29] Within its section on 'circumstances of the offender',[30] the manual includes a subsection

---

[28] *Victorian Sentencing Manual*, Part A; Section 1 http://www.judicialcollege.vic.edu.au/eManuals/VSM/index.htm#13879.htm.
[29] ibid.
[30] ibid, Part B; Section 10 http://www.judicialcollege.vic.edu.au/eManuals/VSM/index.htm#19425.htm.

devoted to remorse, addressing the legal basis for considering remorse, the nature of remorse, the significance of remorse, finding remorse, evidence of genuine remorse and conduct of proceedings. Through drawing on statutes and case law, the manual provides sentencers not only with direction, but also with the underlying justification for considering remorse at sentencing.

According to the VSM, proportionality is a fundamental sentencing principle (along with parsimony, the totality principle, avoidance of double punishment, avoidance of crushing sentences and parity between co-offenders). In this sentencing regime, proportionality is a *limiting*, rather than absolute, principle: 'The fundamental operation of the principle of proportionality is to act as a limiting principle, that is, to place an upper limit on the sentence that may be imposed'.[31]

However, despite this emphasis on proportionality, the VSM acknowledges that the purposes for which sentences may be imposed are diverse. An *exhaustive* list is set out in the Victorian Sentencing Act 1991, s 5(1):

(a) To punish the offender to an extent and in a manner which is just in all of the circumstances OR

(b) To deter the offender or other persons from committing offences of the same or a similar character OR

(c) To establish conditions within which it is considered by the court that the rehabilitation of the offender may be facilitated OR

(d) To manifest the denunciation by the court of the type of conduct in which the offender engaged OR

(e) To protect the community from the offender OR

(f) A combination of two or more of those purposes.[32]

Despite these additional purposes, conflict with the fundamental principle of proportionality is mostly to be resolved in the direction of maintaining proportionality. For example, the VSM states that a sentencer 'may not impose a sentence longer than that which is deserved in order to cure or rehabilitate an offender'.[33] Further, a fundamental operation of the principle of proportionality 'is as a bar to preventative detention'.[34] However, the High Court held that 'this does not in turn create a bar to application of the principle of community protection'.[35] The trumping of proportionality by the purpose of community protection is evident in the modified

---

[31] ibid, Part B; Section 6.2.1 http://www.judicialcollege.vic.edu.au/eManuals/VSM/index. htm#14939.htm.

[32] See ibid, Part B; Section 7.1 http://www.judicialcollege.vic.edu.au/eManuals/VSM/index. htm#15298.htm.

[33] ibid, Part B; Section 6.2.4.2 http://www.judicialcollege.vic.edu.au/eManuals/VSM/index. htm#14949.htm.

[34] ibid, Part B; Section 6.2.4.1 http://www.judicialcollege.vic.edu.au/eManuals/VSM/index. htm#14948.htm.

[35] ibid.

sentencing purposes for 'serious violent offenders' such as those who have committed murder or some species of sexual offence. In sentencing serious violent offenders,

> the court must *inter alia* regard the protection of the community as the principal purpose for which the sentence is imposed. The court has discretion, in order to achieve this purpose, to impose a sentence longer than that which is proportionate to the gravity of the offence considered in light of its objective circumstances.[36]

It is against this background that it explains the relevance of different aggravating and mitigating factors, although in some cases precedent is the only explicit justification given.

The Nature of Remorse

The VSM makes it clear the only genuine remorse will be relevant to sentence. It contrasts genuine remorse with feigned remorse, self-pity or depression at having been caught. It also directs judges to take into account the time at which remorse was first exhibited and the degree of insight that it reflects. Of note is the judicial remark: 'It is perhaps rare to encounter convincing evidence of genuine remorse, but, where it is found, it deserves to be reflected in the sentence imposed'.[37] This suggests that sentencers should be wary of over-finding remorse but that it should always be given weight in cases where they are convinced of its presence.

The justification for remorse leading to 'some, perhaps considerable, reduction of the normal sentence' is given through reference to case law.[38] I quote the manual at length to demonstrate the range of arguments involved in the justification:

> In *Phillips* [2012] VSCA 140, Harper JA noted: If there is evidence of remorse, and if that remorse is genuine, it is a very important element in the exercise of the sentencing discretion. Remorse of this kind *indicates realistic prospects of rehabilitation and a reduced need for specific deterrence*. An offender who pleads guilty because he or she has an accurate appreciation of the wrongfulness of his or her offending, and of its impact upon its victim or victims, and who desires to do what reasonably can be done to repair the damage and to clear his or her conscience, is *someone to whom mercy*—in the form of a very substantial reduction in what would otherwise be an appropriate sentence—*is very likely due.*

---

[36]   ibid, Part E; Section 26.4.4 and Part E; Section 31.4.5 http://www.judicialcollege.vic.edu.au/eManuals/VSM/index.htm#17841.htm; http://www.judicialcollege.vic.edu.au/eManuals/VSM/index.htm#8763.htm.

[37]   ibid, Part B; 10.13.2 http://www.judicialcollege.vic.edu.au/eManuals/VSM/index.htm#6229.htm.

[38]   ibid, Part B; Section 10.13.3 http://www.judicialcollege.vic.edu.au/eManuals/VSM/index.htm#6231.htm.

It has been noted that offenders who appreciate the wrongfulness of their offending and its impact on its victims, and express a desire to repair the damage and clear their conscience *deserve to receive a material reduction* in what would otherwise be an appropriate sentence (*Barbaro; Zirilli* [2012] VSCA 288 at [39]).[39]

Within this excerpt, reference is made to consequentialist justifications, based on optimism regarding rehabilitation and desistance. We also find the suggestion that there is an onus on the sentencer to show mercy to the offender with a heavy conscience who wants to put things right. Finally, the offender's appreciation of his wrongdoing and its impact is said to affect the quantum of punishment an offender deserves. The manual therefore gives a range of justifications—consequentialist, mercy and desert—in support of the practice of mitigating the sentence of the remorseful offender.

Rehabilitation and deterrence are amongst the sentencing purposes identified by the VSM: if an offender's remorse indeed indicates that less deterrence or rehabilitative effort is required then a reduction in sentence would be justified on consequentialist grounds. The reference to mercy is more difficult to reconcile with the identified purposes. The VSM includes a section on merciful discretion. It states that whilst there is no judicial pre-rogative of mercy, it is 'inherent in the concept of judicial discretion'.[40] This idea is supported by the claim that sentencers can show mercy by adopting the more favourable option open to them and, in so doing, treat offenders in a 'humanitarian fashion'. However, the VSM notes that whilst there is a strict duty upon a sentencer to do justice, there is no corresponding duty to also show mercy. The exercise of mercy is dependent upon the individual sentencer's assessment of the case, firmly based on the evidence presented. In *Kane*, the Court stated at 766: '[M]ercy must be exercised upon consid-erations which are supported by the evidence and which make an appeal not only to sympathy but also to well-balanced judgment'.[41]

This suggests that any merciful reduction in sentence should not be based solely on the sentencer's emotional response to all manner of facts about the offender. Indeed, the VSM emphasises that 'if a court permits sympathy to preclude it from attaching due weight to the other recognised elements of punishment, it has failed to discharge its duty'.[42] The approach taken to mercy is thus to direct sentencers to avoid overly emotional responses to the circumstances of the offender and to remain balanced in their assess-ment of all the facts. Whether the reference to the 'humanitarian aspects of the case' is intended or possible to extend to the offender's remorse is unclear.

---

[39] ibid, emphasis added.
[40] ibid, Part A; Section 3.1.1.5 http://www.judicialcollege.vic.edu.au/eManuals/VSM/index.htm#14227.htm.
[41] ibid.
[42] ibid, Section 3.1.1.5.

The final part of the VSM's justification for the mitigating effect of remorse refers to the reduced desert of the offender who has insight into the wrongfulness of his conduct and the harm it caused. Given that, according to the VSM, there is no judicial duty to show mercy, this appeal to desert coupled with the significance attached to remorse suggests a more principled justification for mitigation. The importance of remorse is further emphasised by the decoupling of the significance of remorse from that associated with the guilty plea, good character and making restitution.

Standard of Proof for Remorse

The VSM offers specific guidance on the standard of proof that the evidence of genuine remorse should satisfy.[43] Remorse is to be taken into account as a mitigating factor where it has been established on the balance of probabilities. In relation to this, the onus is on the offender to demonstrate his remorse by calling satisfactory evidence. Crucially:

> Such evidence must demonstrate much more than mere regret at being caught. It must also demonstrate that the offender understands the wrongfulness of their actions, genuinely regrets those actions and is determined to right the wrong and avoid repeating it.[44]

In the absence of direct evidence, sentencers are entitled to diminish the weight given to this factor, and even to find it unproven. The prosecution will ordinarily need to lead admissible evidence in order to disprove a claim of remorse. This standard is applicable to establishing the offender's remorse regardless of the type or seriousness of offence.

Stage at Which Remorse is Shown

Interestingly, the VSM adopts an approach to remorse similar to that adopted in the English guidelines to guilty plea discount. It sets out three discrete stages at which remorse might be shown and directs sentencers to amend the quantum of mitigation depending on the stage.[45] Different weights may be given where the offender indicates remorse:

— before discovery of the crime and/or the identity of the offender— *Cornwell* 27/7/1979 CCA Vic; *Lomax* [1998] 1 VR 551 at 560

---

[43] ibid, Part B; Section 10.13.4 http://www.judicialcollege.vic.edu.au/eManuals/VSM/index.htm#6232.htm.

[44] ibid.

[45] ibid, Part B; Section 10.13.5.5 http://www.judicialcollege.vic.edu.au/eManuals/VSM/index.htm#47098.htm.

— before arrest—*Kevich* 25/11/1977 CCA Vic
— before arraignment, by indication of an intention to plead guilty—
  Collier 8/12/1988 CCA Vic.[46]

Serious Violent Offences

Within the specific guidance on murder and sexual offences, the VSM explicitly includes remorse as a mitigating factor. However, given the modified sentencing purposes outlined above, it is likely that in practice the mitigating effect of remorse will be limited or outweighed. Such an approach would align with the suggestion made in Chapter 7 that, in sentencing regimes with multiple aims, the aim of protecting the public might trump the mitigatory effect of remorse for offences of a serious violent type.

New Zealand Sentencing Act

In 2007 a Sentencing Council was established in New Zealand to draft sentencing guidelines. However, although substantial work was undertaken, the succeeding government, elected in 2008, decided not to proceed with enacting guidelines.[47] The current situation, therefore, is that judges are directed by the New Zealand Sentencing Act 2002 and guideline judgments from New Zealand's Court of Appeal. The Act states that one of the purposes for which a court may sentence is to 'provide for the interests of the victim of the offence' and another is 'to provide reparation for harm done by the offending'.[48] Although the Act lists eight potential purposes, restorative justice goals are considered as being as important as the others. This is supported by the direction to take into account any outcomes of restorative justice processes that have occurred, or that the court is satisfied are likely to occur, in relation to the particular case.[49] Listed amongst the mitigating factors that the court must take into account is 'any remorse shown by the offender, or anything as described in section 10'.[50] Section 10 stipulates that the 'court must take into account offer, agreement, response, or measure to make amends'.[51] It sets out various offers or acts that are to be recognised. These include the offender offering to make amends to the victim through money or work,

---

[46] ibid.
[47] See W Young and A King, 'Sentencing Practice and Guidance in New Zealand' (2009) 22 *Federal Sentencing Reporter* 254.
[48] New Zealand Sentencing Act 2002, Part 1; section 7(1) www.legislation.govt.nz/act/public/2002/0009/latest/DLM135545.html.
[49] ibid, Part 1; section 8.
[50] ibid, Part 1; section 9(2).
[51] ibid, Part 1; section 10.

agreement between the offender and victim about how the offender will ensure desistance, the response of the offender or his family[52] to his offending, any measures taken by the offender or his family to apologise, and any other remedial action proposed.

Of note is the inclusion of acts and attitudes of the offender's family as relevant to the offender's sentencing. This is in stark contrast to sentencing regimes that consider the actions of anyone other than the offender as irrelevant to what the offender deserves. The idea that the harm of the offence might be reduced through apology and reparation already stretches the boundaries of how the offence for which the offender must be punished is individuated. Whilst reparative action on the part of the offender's family has the potential to benefit the victim, it cannot be understood to reduce the harm of the offence committed by the offender.

The offers and acts to be taken into account are suggestive of remorse but most do not require it.[53] The offender's response to his offending and measures taken to apologise are the most suggestive, but compensation and other comparative acts are not dependent on the offender's remorse. Further, any response or apology emanating from the offender's family, whilst perhaps suggestive of an appropriate level of third-party denunciation, are also not dependent on the remorse of the offender himself.

In relation to the list of relevant offers and acts, the Act states that, in deciding whether and to what extent any particular one of these matters should be taken into account, the court must take consider (a) whether or not it was 'genuine and capable of fulfilment'; and (b) whether or not it has been 'accepted by the victim as expiating or mitigating the wrong'.[54] In relation to the former consideration, the context suggests that the word 'genuine' is intended to pertain to the intention to carry out the offer rather than to the moral quality of the intention. An offer may be genuine without being capable of fulfilment (in the case of mistaken beliefs about what can be fulfilled) and capable of fulfilment without being genuine (in the case of an intention not to carry through the proposed act).

The reliance on the victim's acceptance of the reparative sufficiency of the proposed act presents a departure from the common view that, if reparation is to be taken into account, its mitigating force will apply regardless of whether the victim accepts it as sufficient. In most cases, it would be for the judge to decide the weight (if any) to be given to offers or acts of

---

[52] In relation to both the offender and the victim, the Act refers not just to their family but instead to their 'family, whanau, or family group'. Since any points I make are unaffected by this extension, I abbreviate to their 'family'.

[53] It should be remembered that the list of mitigating factors included remorse *or* anything listed as a relevant offer, agreement, response, or measure to make amends. This disjunction at least suggests that the latter set of mitigators are not dependent on the presence of remorse for their relevance.

[54] New Zealand Sentencing Act 2002, Part 1; section 10.

reparation. Further, in the English guidelines, attempts at reparation are to be considered in mitigation even if they are unsuccessful (thus having no tangible impact on the victim at all).[55] Perhaps the requirement to consider whether the offer or act has been accepted by the victim as expiating or mitigating the wrong is motivated by the belief that the victim is best placed to assess the gravity of the wrong since it was done to and experienced by them. However, whilst this will to some extent be true—and, indeed, motivates much of the practice of restorative justice—making the mitigating impact of apology and reparation at sentencing contingent on victim acceptance opens the door to great inconsistency. As argued in Chapter 3, for any sentencing regime concerned with parity and proportionality, making the significance of remorse (or apology or reparation) dependent on certain effects on the victim may be unfair and certainly limits the scope for remorse-based mitigation.

The New Zealand Sentencing Act ties remorse with offers and acts of reparation, including those emanating from the offender's family. This extension, combined with the requirement to consider the victim's acceptance of these acts as sufficient, suggests that the justification for mitigation will not be based on the moral quality of the remorse. Instead, mitigation appears to derive legitimacy from any harm-reducing effects of reparation, and the wider societal value of inter-group civility.

United States Sentencing Manual

The United States Sentencing Commission *Guidelines Manual* (USSM) includes an explicit discussion of the rationale behind its guidance.[56] It explains that because of the difficulty of deciding on one penal philosophy over another—just deserts or consequentialism—it would neither seek to decide on one theory nor to reconcile them, although the USSM states that 'most observers of the criminal law agree that the ultimate aim of the law itself, and of punishment in particular, is the control of crime', suggesting a consequentialist core.[57] To develop its guidelines, the Commission sought to solve the problems of developing a coherent sentencing system by taking an empirical approach, essentially codifying precedent rather than trying to work from a single underlying philosophy. The approach used data estimating pre-guidelines sentencing practice as a starting point. It analysed data

---

[55] See, for example, Sentencing Guidelines Council, 'Sentencing for Fraud—Statutory Offences: Definitive Guideline', 11: 'If an offender has been temporarily or permanently prevented by circumstances beyond his or her control from returning defrauded items, the degree of mitigation should depend on the point in time at which, and the determination with which, the offender tried to return the items'.

[56] United States Sentencing Commission, *Guidelines Manual* 2013, §1 A1.3.

[57] ibid.

drawn from 10,000 pre-sentence investigations, the differing elements of various crimes as distinguished in substantive criminal statutes, the United States Parole Commission's guidelines and statistics, and data from other relevant sources in order to determine which distinctions were important in pre-guidelines practice. After consideration, the Commission accepted, modified or rationalised these distinctions.

The philosophical dilemma was, according to the Commission, helpfully resolved by this empirical approach:

> Those who adhere to a just deserts philosophy may concede that the lack of consensus might make it difficult to say exactly what punishment is deserved for a particular crime. Likewise, those who subscribe to a philosophy of crime control may acknowledge that the lack of sufficient data might make it difficult to determine exactly the punishment that will best prevent that crime. Both groups might therefore recognize the wisdom of looking to those distinctions that judges and legislators have, in fact, made over the course of time. These established distinctions are ones that the community believes, or has found over time, to be important from either a just deserts or crime control perspective.[58]

Given the inherent difficulties in following either approach, established precedent, which draws on both desert theory and consequentialist considerations, is to be preferred as a solution to the impossibility of perfectly implementing either penal theory. The US Code states that the purposes of sentencing are:

(A) to reflect the seriousness of the offense, to promote respect for the law, and to provide just punishment for the offense;
(B) to afford adequate deterrence to criminal conduct;
(C) to protect the public from further crimes of the defendant; and
(D) to provide the defendant with needed educational or vocational training, medical care, or other correctional treatment in the most effective manner.[59]

Although the ostensibly theory-neutral approach and mixture of sentencing aims suggest equal concern for just deserts and consequentialism, the structure of the sentencing decision is such that consequentialist aims are given a particularly prominent weight. This is due to the role that previous convictions play in determining the severity of the punishment for federal sentencing. Sentencers work from a grid that has two axes. The vertical axis represents increasing offence seriousness—the 'offence level'—whilst the horizontal axis represents the extent of the offender's criminal history— determined by the number of 'criminal history points'. Each 'square' on the grid provides sentencers with a range of months of imprisonment, within

---

[58] ibid.
[59] See 18 US Code §3553—Imposition of a sentence, www.law.cornell.edu/uscode/text/ 18/3553.

which they are to determine the appropriate sentence by following the guidelines on different factors covered in the guideline. Chapter 3 of the USSM provides instructions for adjustments. It is here that remorse features under the broader heading of 'acceptance of responsibility'.

Acceptance of Responsibility

In the USSM remorse is subsumed under 'acceptance of responsibility'.[60] Acceptance of responsibility is broader than remorse and may not even require it. Its significance appears to be in part bound up with the administrative benefits that accrue when responsibility is accepted early. This differs from the weight given to remorse in the other guidelines discussed, which separate remorse from the guilty plea discount. The manual directs the sentencer as follows:

(a) If the defendant clearly demonstrates acceptance of responsibility for his offense, decrease the offense level by 2 levels.

(b) If the defendant qualifies for a decrease under subsection (a), the offense level determined prior to the operation of subsection (a) is level 16 or greater, and upon motion of the government stating that the defendant has assisted authorities in the investigation or prosecution of his own misconduct by timely notifying authorities of his intention to enter a plea of guilty, thereby permitting the government to avoid preparing for trial and permitting the government and the court to allocate their resources efficiently, decrease the offense level by 1 additional level.[61]

From this it can be seen that acceptance of responsibility in itself will reduce the offender's sentencing by two levels. The administrative benefits of an early guilty plea will reduce the offender's sentence by one additional level, but only if the offence is above a particular level of seriousness and the court has received an official statement demonstrating the administrative benefits. These limitations on the mitigating effect of a timely guilty plea are in contrast to the approach taken in England and Wales, which does not require the offence to be above a certain level and allows the judge to mitigate the offender's sentence by up to a third. This discount is larger than the migratory weight that would ordinarily be put on remorse.

It might appear therefore that the United States puts a greater weight on remorse than on the guilty plea discount. However, on closer inspection, it would be artificial to separate out the independent effects of remorse and guilty plea: it appears they are both a part of what it means to accept responsibility and that some of the benefits arising from a guilty plea are taken into account in the two-level reduction. Further mitigation is afforded where this has demonstrably aided the criminal justice process.

---

[60] United States Sentencing Commission, *Guidelines Manual*, §3 E1.1.
[61] ibid.

The manual's explicit justification for reducing the sentence of the offender who has accepted responsibility does not tease apart justifications for remorse on the one hand and for guilty plea discount on the other. It is unlikely that instruction (a) pertains only to remorse. The manual provides an overarching justification as follows:

> The reduction of offense level provided by this section recognizes legitimate societal interests. For several reasons, a defendant who clearly demonstrates acceptance of responsibility for his offense by taking, in a timely fashion, the actions listed above (or some equivalent action) is appropriately given a lower offense level than a defendant who has not demonstrated acceptance of responsibility.[62]

The actions listed include: 'truthfully admitting the conduct comprising the offence(s) of conviction', 'voluntary termination or withdrawal from criminal conduct or associations', 'voluntary payment of restitution prior to adjudication of guilt', 'voluntary surrender to authorities promptly after commission of the offense', 'voluntary assistance to authorities in the recovery of the fruits and instrumentalities of the offense', 'voluntary resignation from the office or position held during the commission of the offense', 'post-offense rehabilitative efforts (e.g., counseling or drug treatment)' and 'the timeliness of the defendant's conduct in manifesting the acceptance of responsibility'.[63]

Whilst many of these would be expected of the remorseful offender, they could also be undertaken for other reasons. There does not seem to be much, if any, emphasis on the depth or even genuineness of the offender's remorse. All of the actions listed imply that the offender has accepted responsibility for the offence, but all are compatible with doing so in a neutral or even cynical manner. Acceptance of *responsibility* is more neutral than remorse. It is not necessarily acceptance of *blame*. This contrasts with the approach taken in the VSM, which is at pains to distinguish between genuine remorse, feigned remorse and other forms of emotional suffering, and states that genuine remorse is a rare phenomenon.[64]

The most telling part of the acceptance of responsibility section—indicating that acceptance of responsibility is less demanding than remorse—states that whilst a plea of guilty alone does not generate a right to the reduction afforded under subsection (a), a guilty plea and admission of the offence (not undermined by countervailing conduct) is sufficient to demonstrate acceptance of responsibility:

> Entry of a plea of guilty prior to the commencement of trial combined with truthfully admitting the conduct comprising the offense of conviction, and truthfully admitting or not falsely denying any additional relevant conduct for which he is

---

[62] ibid.
[63] ibid.
[64] See *Victorian Sentencing Manual*, Part B; Section 10.13.2.

accountable ... will constitute significant evidence of acceptance of responsibility for the purposes of subsection (a). However, this evidence may be outweighed by conduct of the defendant that is inconsistent with such acceptance of responsibility. A defendant who enters a guilty plea is not entitled to an adjustment under this section as a matter of right.[65]

The approach taken here appears to require somewhat less of the offender in terms of emotional display. All of the actions listed as demonstrating acceptance of responsibility could coherently be carried out without the offender renouncing the conduct as wrongful. The appropriate reading of acceptance of responsibility is further illuminated by remarks intended to contrast 'assistance to authorities' (which attracts further, independent mitigation) with acceptance of responsibility.[66] The USSM states that substantial assistance is 'directed to the investigation and prosecution of criminal activities by persons other than the defendant', while acceptance of responsibility is 'directed to the defendant's affirmative recognition of responsibility for his own conduct'.[67] Affirmative recognition of responsibility appears to be a holding up of hands, but does not in itself imply self-criticism. Whilst therefore not capturing the central features of remorse, this approach—if in fact adopted as set out here—would justify the claim that *mala prohibita* offenders might have to mitigation (insofar as truthfully admitting the conduct comprising the offence and voluntary termination or withdrawal from criminal conduct or associations were sufficient for acceptance of responsibility).

Specific direction on quantum of mitigation is provided by the USSM. When an offender accepts responsibly the penalty range is reduced to that which is associated with an offence two levels of seriousness below. This means that as the offence becomes more serious, the proportion of mitigation reduces. However, after a certain level, additional mitigation can be granted where the offender assisted authorities in the investigation or prosecution of his own misconduct—essentially a guilty plea discount. This suggests that acceptance of responsibility (as a combination of remorse-like behaviours and early guilty plea) is not given significantly diminished importance in the case of the most serious offences, although the proportion of mitigation will become somewhat smaller again as the additional, one-level sentence reduction is diluted at the highest sentence ranges.

It is also clear that, in this jurisdiction, previous convictions and acceptance of responsibility do not interact, but each maintains its independent effect on the offender's sentence regardless of whether the other is also present. In line with the approach of fusing just deserts and consequentialism, the relevance of previous convictions is justified both with reference

[65] United States Sentencing Commission, *Guidelines Manual*, §3 E1.1.
[66] ibid, §5K 1.1.
[67] ibid.

to enhanced culpability and to general deterrence and protection of the public.[68] Even so, sentencers are directed to adjust the offence level where acceptance of responsibility applies, even when the standard grid is supplanted with a table of harsher penalties for so-called 'career criminals'.[69]

CONCLUSION

Different jurisdictions place different emphasis on what is important about remorse and offer different justifications for mitigation on its basis. The reparative actions motivated by remorse that are of great importance in New Zealand bear little resemblance to the societal benefits that are reaped when an offender accepts responsibility for his offence in the United States. Victoria places great weight on the 'rare phenomenon' of genuine remorse, which demonstrates reform and permits the extension of mercy. Of course, the extent to which practice operates as the guidelines direct is a matter for empirical research. The introduction of the UK Crown Court Sentencing Survey makes quantitative analysis possible in England and Wales. This resource will offer new opportunities for sentencing research, which has until now mostly been conducted through the qualitative analysis of sentencing remarks.

The inclusion of remorse in all these guidelines, and the lack of a unified reason for doing so (even within each jurisdiction) demonstrates that remorse most likely came to have a role to play because it was intuitively thought relevant. Since different justifications have different implications for practice, those constructing sentencing guidelines around the world may benefit their respective systems by reconsidering the principal justification (if any) underlying their remorse-related practice. Spontaneous judicial practice may have coalesced towards a certain approach, but practice is likely to be more consistent when principles are made explicit through carefully constructed guidance.

---

[68] See ibid, §4A 1.
[69] ibid, §4B 1.1.

10

Implications for Penal Theory and Sentencing

I HAVE ARGUED that, on communicative accounts of deserved punishment, the remorseful offender's punishment should be mitigated because censure that is responsive to the offender has greater moral and communicative legitimacy. I have shown how adoption of the Responsive Censure justification for remorse-based mitigation has implications for arguments about sentencing practice, regarding whether there are limits to the role of remorse, what the morally sufficient response from the offender involves and how other sentencing factors might influence or be influenced by the presence of an offender's remorse.

Crucially, the Responsive Censure argument is not just a new label for current practice: it suggests revisions and, importantly, does so in ways that the other potential justifications would not. Responsive Censure permits the widest application of remorse-based mitigation. Although remorse is the central phenomenon, the argument I developed demonstrates the relevance of other responses to censure, which become more or less appropriate depending on the type and seriousness of the offence. Acceptance of the message of censure is at the fore, even if remorse is often integral to this. The other arguments considered could only ever succeed to justify mitigation in the face of intense experiences of remorse: persons are only considered 'changed' when there is a dramatic shift in their beliefs, desires and behaviour; only the most comprehensive displays of self-condemnation will serve to reduce a victim's persisting psychological harm; for remorse to be considered at all punishing, it must be significantly aversive; merciful compassion is inspired by the most moving hardship of the offender. Responsive Censure, however, makes sense of the mitigation afforded to the petty thief who feels proportionately ashamed and the cannabis user who commits to refrain despite retaining a positive attitude towards drug taking.

None of this is to say that offenders do not have to demonstrate all the suffering inherent in remorse in order to receive mitigation for the worst offences. Indeed, such suffering is part of what it is to understand the gravity and reality of what one has done. If the offender has already taken on board the message that censure seeks to communicate about the most serious offences, then she will behave in a way that clearly demonstrates this. If there is much doubt, then it is unlikely that the remorse is genuine nor that the message is entirely pre-empted. In such cases, the full censure would be warranted.

So, although my account does not dilute what is expected of the offender in the face of serious wrongdoing, it has the advantage that it can also explain what is expected in the face of less serious offending and why these less intense responses still justify mitigation. Since such responses will be less immediate to the observer, even when optimal, judges should be inclined to require less in the way of evidence. Responsive Censure, therefore, justifies mitigation all the way down, whilst other justifications would only secure mitigation for the transformed, the wretched, the self-flagellant and the pitied.

As well as justifying mitigation from murder to marijuana possession, the Responsive Censure account makes mitigation less a matter of degree based on the offender's response. Changes to character, reductions of harm, punishing emotions and merciful compassion all permit of degrees. Correspondingly, the quantum of mitigation afforded to the offender would depend on the degree of change, reduced harm, emotional punishment and compassion. In contrast, responding to the offender's appreciation of the wrongfulness of his conduct is only appropriate where the content of the communication has, in fact, already been accepted. An agent who partially understands a message does not have his rational agency undermined if the message is presented as if he does not understand. Thus, the offender has either fully understood or has not; and mitigation does not permit of degrees. Whilst partial understanding permits of degrees, it does not affect the appropriate censure.

Penal theorists interested in remorse have tended to focus only on the most intense experiences of remorse and considered the relevance of these for sentencing. This is entirely understandable, as intense remorse represents the core instance of the moral response to wrongdoing and I, too, have been no exception in focusing principally on remorse. However, the argument that I developed revealed that what is central to the justification of mitigation is not the intense emotion per se, but the offender's proportionate response to his wrongdoing and pre-emptive acceptance of the message of censure. In many cases this will involve intense remorse, but not always.

Those who argue that remorse is not relevant to sentencing may see the broader implications of Responsive Censure as counting against it: if it has such wide-reaching implications then there must be something wrong with the argument. However, I do not think I have provided a *reductio*. The implications are not more absurd than those that attend the other arguments for remorse-based mitigation and, I believe, make better sense of many of the intuitions we have about the relevance of different moral responses to different types of offending.

Nonetheless, I am sure many will remain unconvinced. However, for those open to the possibility that remorse-based mitigation might find justification in retributive theory, I hope I have demonstrated that Responsive Censure is both supported by the tenets of communicative theories and is superior to the alternative justifications. At the very least, I have offered new avenues of argument to the widening debate on the relevance of remorse within penal theory and demonstrated that any conclusions one reaches about how remorse is justified in theory have significant implications for sentencing practice.

Index

Lightning Source UK Ltd.
Milton Keynes UK
UKHW020040210521
384105UK00004B/146